The English Setter

POPULAR DOGS' BREED SERIES

BASSET HOUND	*George Johnston*
BEAGLE	*Thelma Gray*
BOXER	*Elizabeth Somerfield*
CAIRN TERRIER	*J.W.H. Beynon, Alex Fisher, Peggy Wilson and Doreen Proudlock*
CAVALIER KING CHARLES SPANIEL	*Mary Forwood*
CHIHUAHUA	*Thelma Gray*
COCKER SPANIEL	*Veronica Lucas-Lucas and Joyce Caddy*
COLLIE	*Margaret Osborne and Aileen Speding*
DACHSHUND	*E. Fitch Daglish, Amyas Biss and Jeff Crawford*
DALMATIAN	*Eleanor Frankling, Betty Clay and Marjorie Cooper*
DOBERMANN	*Fred Curnow and Jean Faulks*
FOX TERRIER	*Elsie Williams*
GERMAN SHEPHERD DOG	*J. Schwabacher, Thelma Gray and Madeleine Pickup*
GOLDEN RETRIEVER	*Joan Tudor*
GREAT DANE	*Jean Lanning*
IRISH SETTER	*Janice Roberts*
LABRADOR RETRIEVER	*Lorna, Countess Howe and Geoffrey Waring*
MONGREL	*Angela Patmore*
OLD ENGLISH SHEEPDOG	*Ann Davis*
POODLE	*Clara Bowring, Alida Monro and Shirley Walne*
PUG	*Susan Graham Weall*
ROTTWEILER	*Judy and Larry Elsden*
SCOTTISH TERRIER	*Dorothy Caspersz and Elizabeth Meyer*
SHETLAND SHEEPDOG	*Margaret Osborne*
SHIH TZU	*Audrey Dadds*
SPRINGER SPANIEL	*Dorothy Moorland Hooper and Ian B. Hampton*
STAFFORDSHIRE BULL TERRIER	*John F. Gordon*
WELSH CORGI	*Charles Lister-Kaye and Dickie Albin*
WEST HIGHLAND WHITE TERRIER	*D. Mary Dennis and Catherine Owen*
YORKSHIRE TERRIER	*Ethel and Vera Munday*

THE
ENGLISH SETTER

LESLEY ALLAN-SCOTT

POPULAR DOGS
London Sydney Auckland Johannesburg

Popular Dogs Publishing Co. Ltd

An imprint of Century Hutchinson Ltd
Brookmount House, 62–65 Chandos Place,
Covent Garden, London WC2N 4NW

Century Hutchinson Australia (Pty) Ltd
20 Alfred Stree, Milsons Point, Sydney 2061

Century Hutchinson New Zealand Limited
191 Archers Road, PO Box 40–086, Glenfield, Auckland 10

Century Hutchinson South Africa (Pty) Ltd
PO Box 337, Bergvlei 2012, South Africa

First published 1989
Copyright © Lesley Allan-Scott 1989
The Breed Standard Copyright © The Kennel Club, 1986

All rights reserved

Printed and bound in Great Britain by Mackays of Chatham PLC

Set in Baskerville by Selectmove Ltd, London

British Library Cataloguing in Publication Data
Allan-Scott, Lesley
The English setter.
1. English setters
I. Title
636.7'52

ISBN 0 09 173892 X

CONTENTS

	List of Illustrations	7
	Acknowledgements	11
	Introduction	13
1	The Origins and History of the Breed	15
2	The Breed Post-War	25
3	Character and Conformation	36
4	Choosing a Puppy, Feeding and Training	50
5	Care and Accommodation	62
6	Establishing a Line	73
7	Breeding	81
8	Shows and Showing	98
9	Gun-Training and Field Trials	108
10	English Setters Overseas	112
11	Leading Kennels	157
12	Ailments	174

APPENDICES

A	Glossary of Dog Terminology	191
B	Specialist Breed Clubs in Great Britain	196

C	Crufts Challenge Certificate Winners 1958 to 1988	198
D	Post-War Registration Figures	201
E	Pedigrees of Key Dogs	202
F	Post-War Champions and Show Champions	212
G	Post-War Field Trial Champions	241
H	Bibliography	249
	Index	251

ILLUSTRATIONS

Between pages 80 and 81

Countess – the first dual champion
Bred and owned by Edward Laverack

Ch. Maesydd Mustard
Bred by Mr D. Steadman. Owned by Mrs M. Bilton (formerly Mrs M. Eadington)

Ch. Ernford Evening Flight
Bred by Mr A. V. Webb. Owned by Mrs A. Broadhead

Ch. Shiplake Sincerity
Bred by Miss A. B. Jones. Owned by Mrs J. English

Sh. Ch. Rombalds Templar
Bred and owned by Mrs M. Crowther

Ch. Shiplake Dean of Crombie
Bred by Mr G. Crawford. Owned by Mrs J. English

Ch. Shiplake Dean of Crombie – working
Bred by Mr G. Crawford. Owned by Mrs J. English

Sh. Ch. Shiplake Swift
Bred by Mr D. Paterson. Owned by Mrs J. English

Iroquois Ernford Irresistible – foundation bitch of the Iroquois English Setters
Bred by Mrs A. Broadhead. Owned by Mrs Lesley Allan-Scott

Between pages 112 and 113

Sh. Ch. Silbury Soames of Madavale
Bred by Mr and Mrs P. Gardiner-Swann. Owned by Mrs A. Williams

Sh. Ch. Iroquois Casanova
Bred by Mr and Mrs I. Allan. Owned by Mrs Lesley Allan-Scott

Sh. Ch. Iroquois Stormcloud
Bred by Mrs Wilson and Mrs Wilkinson. Owned by Mrs Lesley Allan-Scott

Sh. Ch. Bournehouse Enchantress
Bred by Mr G. Williams. Owned by Mr and Mrs H. Wheeler

Sh. Ch. Bournehouse Dancing Master
Bred and owned by Mr G. Williams

Sh. Ch. Hurwyn Wigeon
Bred by Mrs S. Wilkinson. Owned by Mr D. C. Mulholland

Sh. Ch. Iroquois Rainbow
Bred by Mrs C. Allan. Owned by Mrs D. Bowen

Sh. Ch. Iroquois Whiteseal Silvermorn
Bred by Mrs V. Neill. Owned by Mrs Lesley Allan-Scott

Sh. Ch. Snowstorm of Upperwood
Bred by Mr and Mrs P. Castle. Owned by Mrs D. Goutorbe

Between pages 144 and 145

N.Z. Ch. Chilworth April Love
Bred and owned by Mr and Mrs Colverwell

Sh. Ch. Hurwyn Cupie Doll
Bred and owned by Mrs S. Wilkinson

Sh. Ch. Tragus Night Breeze
Bred by Mr and Mrs P. Upton. Owned by Miss T. Watkins

Sh. Ch. Northgate Blue Brocade
Bred and owned by Mr and Mrs W. L. Fuller

Sh. Ch. Northgate Grenadier
Bred and owned by Mr and Mrs W. L. Fuller

Sh. Ch. Suntop Starling
Bred by Mr and Mrs Harris. Owned by Miss M. Barnes

Illustrations

Sh. Ch. Iroquois Concerto and Sh. Ch. Iroquois Sansovino of Sundeala
Concerto bred and owned by Mrs Lesley Allan-Scott
Sansovino bred by Mrs Lesley Allan-Scott. Owned by Mrs B. Davies

Am. Ch. Guys 'n' Dolls Annie O'Brien
Bred by Neal Weinstein. Owned by Lloyd and Linda Talbot, and Lee and Francis Amster

Between pages 176 and 177

Sh. Ch. Starlite Express of Valsett
Bred by Mrs A. Wick. Owned by Mr and Mrs J. Watkin

Sh. Ch. Elswood Vagabond King
Bred by Mrs V. Foss and Miss M. Gilchrist.
Owned by Mrs V. Foss and Mrs P. Wadsworth

Puppies feeding

Puppies
Bred and owned by Mr and Mrs M. Winch

Sh. Ch. Iroquois Regalia
Bred and owned by Mrs Lesley Allan-Scott

Sh. Ch. Iroquois Crescendo
Bred and owned by Mrs Lesley Allan-Scott

Sh. Ch. Iroquois Concerto
Bred and owned by Mrs Lesley Allan-Scott

Sh. Ch. Iroquois Concerto
Bred and owned by Mrs Lesley Allan-Scott

Sh. Ch. Iroquois Concerto with one of his puppies
Bred and owned by Mrs Lesley Allan-Scott

In the text

Figure

1. Points of the English Setter   40
2. a) A poor head–note lack of stop and wedge-shaped appearance
   b) A good head   40

3	Dentition and bite	43
4	Forequarters from the side	43
5	Forequarters from the front	45
6	Hindquarters from the side	45
7	Hindquarters from the rear	46
8	Feet	46
9	Life cycle of the flea	65
10	Cutting a nail	68
11	Gestation table showing when a bitch is due to whelp	87
12	Whelping bed	88

ACKNOWLEDGEMENTS

I would like to express my grateful thanks to everyone who has been kind enough to help with the writing of this book by providing me with information.

I would especially like to thank Mrs Kaye Bliss whose help with the preparation of the list of champions and show champions was invaluable, Mrs Joan Tudor for her help with Chapter 9, Gun-Training and Field Trials, a subject in which she is very much more knowledgeable than I, and also to thank her for her assistance in checking and correcting the manuscript. I would like to thank Mr Jack Bowen for his assistance in procuring numerous items of information, which involved him in delving into the archives at the Kennel Club Library. I send special thanks to Mrs Valerie Foss, who as always has been a 'mine' of information and has provided me with some lovely photographs, and indeed to everyone who has sent me such beautiful photographs of their dogs. I only wish it were possible to publish them all!

I would also like to thank all the people overseas who have so kindly sent me information about English Setters in their countries, especially Mr R. McGinnis and Mrs S. Shuman (USA), Miss W. Fulton (Canada), Mrs B. Swift (South Africa), Mrs P. Johnson (Australia), Mrs E. Culverwell (New Zealand), Miss G. Fels (Germany), Miss S. Chapman (Sweden), Mrs I. Schoneville (Eire), Mr J. Requena (Spain), and Mr P. Halstead for his in-depth research (Holland and Belgium).

My sincere thanks also to my daughter, Mrs 'Sandy' Bolton, and to Mrs Jean Hurt for their joint efforts in typing out the manuscript, and to Mr A. Hurt and Mr M. Winch for their untiring efforts in taking photographs.

INTRODUCTION

The English Setter is truly a dog of matchless beauty, well-balanced and built on graceful lines, complemented by his white silky coat flecked with blue or orange. From his well-chiselled head, and dark eyes with soft benign expression, through his proudly arched neck, to his ever wagging tail with the feather hanging in soft pendant flakes, he looks every inch an aristocrat!

His looks can be matched only by his gentle, loving nature, and although he will require regular grooming, trimming and bathing to keep him looking his best, he is certainly worth all the trouble one takes, as this will be repaid a hundredfold by the love received in return.

I have owned and bred this lovely breed for nearly fifty years (which makes me feel very old indeed!) and I can honestly say that I have never wanted to own any other breed.

I first saw a photograph of an English Setter in a copy of *Dog World Annual*, and thought it the most beautiful thing I had ever seen. From that day I dreamed of owning one. I cannot say that my parents were very 'doggy'; although my mother always kept a few Cairns and bred the occasional litter, she never showed them.

When I left school I was given some money as a birthday present to buy a dog of my own, and of course it had to be an English Setter (much to everyone's astonishment, as I don't think any of my family even knew what an English Setter looked like). As it was now wartime I had great difficulty in obtaining a puppy. I wrote to everyone who advertised in the aforementioned *Dog World Annual* and received but one reply from Miss 'Archdale' Rumball, who said she had two bitch puppies. So clutching my money I set off by train and bus to Warlingham, Surrey. On arrival Miss Rumball informed me that one puppy had died and she had decided to keep the other one. I think I must have looked so crestfallen that she offered me a 15-month-old bitch on breeding terms (I hadn't enough money to buy her outright). Of course I brought her home, much to the family's surprise as they were expecting a cuddly little puppy!

I had a couple of litters from her, and kept one of her daughters, but even then I did not think of showing, until a friend of mine who bred Boxers asked me to take her to a show, and suggested I enter my bitch. I entered her in three classes and she won all of them, the judge being the late Mr Fred Cross. I sailed home on a pink cloud, well and truly hooked on showing.

I attended the first English Setter Association Championship Show in 1954 and there saw Ch. Ernford Evening Flight, and to me she was the personification of everything an English Setter should be. I purchased a daughter of hers, and this bitch became the foundation of the Iroquois strain – everything I have ever bred since goes back to this bitch – and over all these years I have never regretted my choice. I have never had any bad temperament, and in addition to producing twenty show champions and the winners of over 100 Challenge Certificates, my dogs have provided me with so much love and companionship that life would indeed have been empty without my English Setters!

1
The Origins and History of the Breed

The ancestry of the English Setter, as of all the varieties of setters, can be traced back hundreds of years to the spaniels first mentioned in literature in 1387 by a Frenchman, one Gaston de Foix, in his book *Livre de Chasse*.

The earliest reference to Setters written in English appeared in what is believed to be the first book devoted entirely to dogs, entitled *Of Englishe Dogges*, by Abraham Flemming published in 1576. This was in fact a translation of a book written in Latin by Dr Johannes Caius six years earlier. Setters are described as dogs which make no noise either with foot or tongue, who should approach their quarry with great stealth, creeping forward on their bellies. When they reach the point where the game is located they should stay very still in a crouched position, lifting one front leg and so 'pointing' out the position of the birds. Nets were laid and the dogs then given the order to rise, thus driving the birds into the nets.

Over the next two or three hundred years, there were numerous references to Setters, Setting Dogs or Setting Spaniels, and the English Setter of today has certainly evolved from these breeds. By the nineteenth century the different varieties were beginning to emerge; there were the English, Irish, Scottish and Welsh Setters. These were further subdivided into various strains, named either after the locality in which it was to be found, or after the laird or squire who owned that particular strain.

In England one of the principal strains appears to have been the Ossulton Setter, which was an all black dog and hailed from Northumberland. This strain was named

The English Setter

after Lord Ossulton, who was later to become the Earl of Tankerville. The other principal strain appears to have been the Lort Setter, named after William Lort, who was a well-known dog judge of the time. The Lort Setter was black and white or lemon and white and was to be found in the Midlands.

The Irish Setter was originally the red and white variety, now enjoying a great revival and becoming very popular in this country. The Irish Red Setter was evolved from crossing the red and white with some other strain, probably one of the black varieties.

The best known of the Scottish Setters were the Lovat Setters, who as their name implies were bred by Lord Lovat and who worked on his estate around Inverness. This dog was black, white and tan in colour. The Southesk Setter was a large powerful dog of the same colouring as the Lovat, bred by the Earl of Southesk in Forfarshire. The Seafield Setter, named after the Earl of Seafield, was finer built, but was known for its excellent coat and feathering. This strain was also mainly black, white and tan in colour, though there is mention of some being lemon and white or orange and white. The above three strains, with the possible infusion of other strains, were no doubt the forerunners of the modern-day Gordon Setters.

In Wales could be found the Welsh Black, a handsome jet-black dog, and the Welsh or Llanidloes White, the latter being very unusual, having a curly coat and no feathering, rather similar to the Curly Coated Retriever, but described as chalk-white in colour. Lastly we come to the two strains, the Laverack and the Llewellin, named after their breeders who were eventually to mould the English Setter into a standardized breed; it is generally admitted that these two did more than any other Setter breeders to develop the English Setter into the dog we know today.

Edward Laverack, born at Keswick in Westmorland in 1798, was as a boy a shoemaker's apprentice. However, he was lucky enough to inherit a legacy from a distant relative which provided him with sufficient income to live the life of a country gentleman and follow his hobbies of shooting and breeding dogs. In 1825 he purchased his first pair of

The Origins and History of the Breed

English Setters from the Rev. A. Harrison of Carlisle. These were the dog Ponto and the bitch Old Moll, both blue beltons, and from these two Laverack founded his strain. Laverack considered Old Moll the most perfect specimen he had ever seen. In his book, *The Setter*, published in 1872, Laverack purports that his strain was the result of around fifty years' breeding with no outcrosses, but as Ponto and Old Moll were the result of similar inbreeding for about thirty years prior to this, it seems unlikely that some outcrosses were not introduced, especially since prior to 1873, when the Kennel Club opened a register, there were few records or pedigrees that could be relied on.

It might be interesting to note here Laverack's description of the breed: 'Head long and light, not snake-headed or deep flewed, but a sufficiency of lip, remarkable for being very strong in the forequarters, chest deep, wide, and the ribs well-sprung behind the shoulders, carrying the breadth of the back to where the tail is set on, immensely strong across the loins. Shoulders very slanting or oblique, particularly short from the shoulders to where the hindquarters meet. A Setter should not rise or be too upright in the shoulder, but level and broad, tail well set on in line with the back, rather drooping, scimitar-shaped and with plenty of flag. Legs remarkably short, and very short from hock to foot, and from knee to foot, feet close and compact, thighs particularly well-bent or crooked, well-placed and close under the body of the animal, not wide or straggling. Colour, black, or blue and white ticked, coat long, soft and silky in texture, eyes soft, mild and intelligent, of a dark hazel colour, ears low set on and close to the head, giving a round development to the skull.' When one considers this was written over a hundred years ago, it compares very favourably with our modern standard.

By the time the first dog shows were held Laverack was in his sixties; even so, he was able to make up two of his strain into champions and many of his dogs were bought and bred from by other leading fanciers of the day. The first of all the gundog breeds to produce a dual champion (both show and field) was Laverack's Countess whose pedigree is reproduced opposite. It will be noted that there are gaps in Countess's pedigree which probably indicate where fresh blood was introduced. Laverack in fact states in his book: 'There are several secrets connected with my system of inter-crossing that I do not think advisable to give to the public at the present time'. Laverack died in 1877 at his home in Whitchurch, Shropshire.

Purcell Llewellin, born in 1840, was the son of a well-known Welsh sportsman. He began breeding with Gordon Setters and some of the local strains of English Setters, his main aim being to produce field trial winners. This, however, did not prove very successful, so he outcrossed by introducing Irish red and white, but again he was not wholly satisfied with the results. Success came when he introduced Laveracks into his strain. It should be noted that unlike Laverack, Llewellin did not appear to mind what his dogs looked like. His main aim was to produce an excellent field trial dog and in this respect he eventually succeeded. His stock were in great demand among the shooting fraternity.

Over the years the difference in type widened, and so today we look upon the Laverack as the show type and the Llewellin as the field trial type. Llewellin stock was very much sought after both in this country and overseas, especially in the United States, where they were bred so successfully that many were imported back to this country by Llewellin himself and others. Llewellin died in 1925, and like Laverack is buried in a village in Shropshire. This county seems to have played a big part in the history of the Llewellin Setter, as following on Llewellin himself there came William Humphrey, who bred his dogs and entered them in competitions, bearing the Bondhu affix with great success.

Early Field Trials

The first Field Trial recorded took place in 1865. It was open to pointers and setters, and it appears all the setters were Gordons. However, in 1866 the second Field Trial was held and this time both the dog and bitch winners

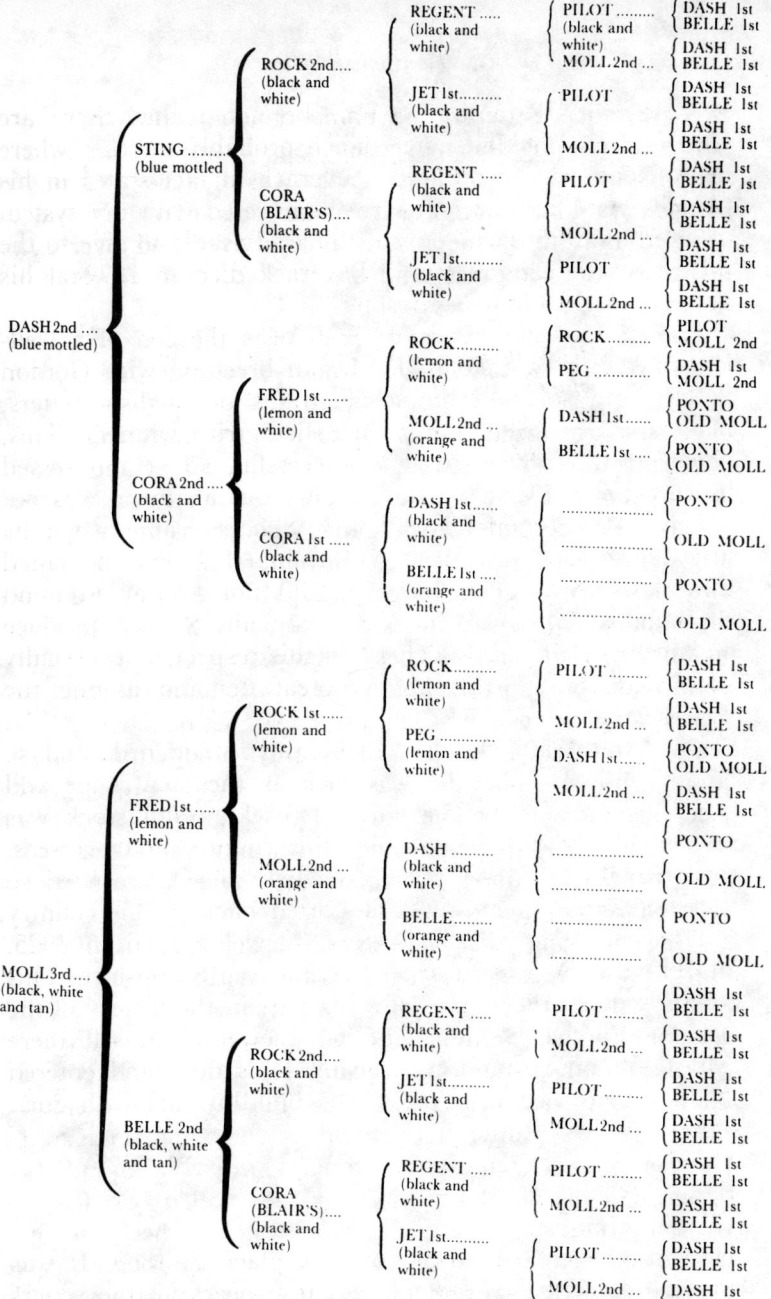

The pedigree of Dual Ch. Countess and her field trial winning sister Nellie.

were English Setters. The names given were Mr Vernon Darbishire's dog Bang, whose pedigree was unknown, and Mr J. Spode's bitch Flash, who was by the Marquis of Anglesey's Flash out of Mr Wilkinson's Flash. It will be noticed that the same names appear over and over again on these old pedigrees, and are probably not very reliable (see pedigree of Countess).

Early Dog Shows

The first organized dog show took place in Newcastle-on-Tyne in 1859. There were classes for pointers and setters, but as far as I can ascertain there were no English Setters placed. The second British show, which took place later in the same year, was held at Birmingham. The winner of the class for English Setters was Mr Frederick Burdett's Brougham, who was in fact a Gordon Setter! In 1860, again in Birmingham, was held what was designated 'The First Exhibition of Sporting and Other Dogs'. In the class for Setters the winner was, in dogs, Mr J. Bayley's Bob, a lemon and white English. The only other thing known about him was that he was bred by Major Irving, who also happened to be the judge. He was, however, quite a successful show dog following this win with several other successes. The winner in bitches at the exhibition was a Gordon Setter.

The following year the second Exhibition of Sporting and Other Dogs was staged again at Birmingham, and at this show there were for the first time specific classes for English Setters. The winners in dogs were first Mr T. Woolf's Sanko and second Mr J. Bayley's Bob. In bitches first was Rev. T. Pearce's Regent and second the same owner's Ruby. These two bitches appeared to be Gordon Setters, but at this time, if any Black and Tan Setters (as the Gordon Setter was then called) carried any white markings, as many did on the head, chest and feet, it was likely to be shown as an English Setter. As I have previously stated, pedigrees as such were most unreliable and in many case non-existent, and this is probably the answer to this apparent absurdity.

The Origins and History of the Breed

By the turn of the century, dog shows were well-established, and so were the individual setter breeds, the English setter breed being divided into the two distinct types that we have today, the Laverack (show type) and the Llewellin (field trial type).

In 1890 the English Setter Club was formed by a number of fanciers, the object being the improvement of the English Setter, not only in perfection of looks, but in its use in the field. The club held its first field trial in 1892 with Purcell Llewellin acting as one of the judges. The Setter and Pointer Club was founded in 1924 by Professor Turton-Price, and this club also fostered interest in both the show and working Setter as it still does today.

Between 1861 and 1892 eleven champions were of 100 per cent pure Laverack breeding, and out of the 25 champions during this period only three had no Laverack breeding. Many people continued to breed with Laverack stock, and some famous names emerged, foremost certainly must be Mr Thomas Steadman and his son Mr David Steadman, whose affixes Mallwyd and Maesydd respectively were to become world famous. Ch. Mallwyd Albert was a beautiful-headed dog and just one of the many great dogs to emerge from this kennel. The three litter-brothers, Mallwyd Ned, Mallwyd Rock and Mallwyd Mumm, caused a minor sensation when Mr Steadman brought them out, and between them they swept the boards. Ned was sold to Mr Holgate; Mr George Roper bought Rock, and Mumm, remaining with his breeder, went on to win his title. Ch. Mallwyd Sarah was a beautiful bitch; I believe she was virtually unbeaten when she was exported to the United States.

Both the Mallwyd and Maesydd kennels contributed much to Mr J. Cockerton's Furness breeding. This kennel was founded around 1850 and ten years later Mr Cockerton bought the bitch Sprig from Edward Laverack. In 1930 Mr Cockerton's son Mr Miles Birket (who had changed his name from Cockerton by deed poll) bought from Mr David Steadman the bitch Missing Link (by Maesydd Mariner ex Maesydd Countess). This bitch, mated to Int. Ch. Bayldone Buccaneer, produced Auld Times who was the dam of Gorse of Haverbrack. Mr Tom

The English Setter

Steadman bred 17 English Setters who became champions or show champions around the turn of the century. Mr David Steadman followed on after the First World War and continued up to the outbreak of the Second World War, during which time he produced 11 champions, all home-bred.

Mention must be made of Maesydd Minnie, who not only won two C.C.s but produced seven litters by seven different dogs. Two of these became Champions Maesydd Mustard and Bayldone Buccaneer, the latter becoming an American champion who sired two show champions in this country. Buccaneer was the maternal grandsire of Gorse of Haverbrack, whose son, Archdale of Corncrake of Haverbrack, and daughter, Celandine of Haverbrack, produced respectively Sh. Ch. Ripleygae Mallory and Ernford Easter Parade, two of our greatest post-war sires.

Ch. Maesydd Mustard was indeed a model for the breed, a great show dog and an even greater sire. He produced five show champions and had a tremendous influence on the breed. In fact he was the model for the Royal Doulton china English Setter. He was owned by Mrs Marjorie Eadington, later to become Mrs Bilton, whose Withinlee affix was to become almost as famous as Ch. Maesydd Mustard.

Another great kennel of this era was the Crombie Kennel of Professor Turton-Price. The winners coming from this kennel were legion, the first being Ch. O'by Jingo, another dog who had a great influence on the breed. On Professor Turton-Price's death the kennel and the Crombie affix passed on to Mr George Crawford, who continued to produce many champions over the years, some of the most famous being Irish Ch. Banner of Crombie, Ch. Marilyn of Crombie, winner of 15 Challenge Certificates, and the litter brother and sister Ch. Shiplake Dean of Crombie and Ch. Shiplake Daystar of Crombie. These last two were both owned by Mrs Jocelyn English, whose Shiplake dogs were well-nigh unbeatable during the 1950s and early '60s, though of course she did produce many champions pre-war. In 1938 she entered for Crufts 'not for competition' three champions, namely Ch. Shiplake

Surprise, Ch. Shiplake Silver Lining and Ch. Shiplake Sybil. Surprise was bred by Mr David Steadman and Silver Lining by Mrs A. W. Rhodes; Sybil was home-bred.

Another outstanding dog was Mr G. Atkinson's Ch. Crossfell, who was born in 1920 and was to win 16 Challenge Certificates during the next eight years. Other influential kennels of the post-war era were Mr and Mrs Alec Rhodes's Bayldone, which produced numerous beautiful specimens, amongst them Bayldone Baronet, Int. Ch. Bayldone Buccaneer and Bayldone Breeze. Mrs A. C. Crowther's Rombalds had tremendous success with such dogs as Rombalds Ranger, (Sh. Ch.) Rombalds Tempest, Rombalds Flack, Rombalds Fan and (Sh. Ch.) Rombalds Templar. The Archdale Kennel of Miss E. Rumball produced many winners; two lovely bitches were (Sh. Ch.) Archdale Sapphire and Archdale Merry, whilst her Archdale Corncrake of Haverbrack proved to be a wonderful sire. Mr Arthur Eggleston's Pennine Pointers and Setters often won in both the show ring and the field, as did the English Setters bearing the Fermanar affix belonging to Miss K. Lewis. Another famous name that must be mentioned here is the Boisdale affix of Mrs Mary Darling whose kennel of English and Irish Setters produced champions in both breeds both before and after the war. Originally situated at Englefield Green in Surrey, she later moved to Devon and has in later years resided at Bethlehem, a lovely old farmhouse set in beautiful woodland country outside Honiton. Mrs Darling's first English Setter was Longworth Lavinia, born in 1934 by Ch. Withinlee Whisper ex Longworth Marvella. From this bitch she bred Ch. Longworth Lyric. Her granddaughter was Ch. Boisdale Buttercup, born in 1954, who was sired by Boisdale Bellman out of Shiplake Snow White. Mrs Darling gun-trained and ran her show dogs in field trials, thus enabling them to qualify for their titles. One of her best dogs was undoubtedly Ch. Boisdale Puffin, a handsome tricolour dog by Boisdale Kestor ex Boisdale Butterpuff.

It should be noted that prior to 1958 there was no such title as Show Champion. No matter how many Challenge Certificates a dog had won the only title was Champion (a dog who has won three or more Challenge Certificates under three different judges, and at least a Certificate of Merit at a recognized field trial). For field trial champion and dual champion dogs that won three or more Challenge Certificates prior to 1958, I have therefore put the Show Champion title in brackets thus (Sh. Ch.).

2
The Breed Post-War

Breeding was naturally severely curtailed during the years 1939–45, but with the cessation of hostilities, life in the dog world slowly returned to normal. The first championship show to be held after the war was run by the Setter and Pointer Club and was held on 20 November 1946 at the Winter Gardens, Blackpool. The C.C. winners were, in dogs, and Mr and Mrs W. Foss's Rombalds Revel, who was sired by Rombalds Tempest ex Rombalds Rovigo, bred by Mrs A. Crowther, and, in bitches and chosen Best of Breed, Mrs J. English's Ch. Shiplake Shining Light, by Rombalds Punchinello ex Diana of Canfield, bred by W.R. Bennetts.

Bill and Elsie Foss were very successful during the next few years with (Sh. Ch.) Pamina of Ketree, (Sh. Ch.) Elswood Blue Lady and her son by (Sh. Ch.) Gorsebrook Berry, (Sh. Ch.) Elswood Dotterel, winner of six C.C.s and seven Reserve C.C.s. Following the sad death of Elsie Foss, the Elswoods dropped out of the picture for several years to emerge again in the early '60s with even greater successes, which I will chronicle later. Chapter 11 is devoted to the top breeders and exhibitors currently active in the breed.

Mrs Rae Furness, better known for her most successful Raycroft Kennel of Irish Setters and in more recent years for her Clumber Spaniels, had some beautiful English Setters, one of the best being (Sh. Ch.) Raycroft Jewel, whilst Raycroft Orange Boy, later sold to Mr T. Watkinson, was an influential sire. Tommy Watkinson, whose father bred and showed Shire horses, kept a large kennel at his home in St Helen's, Lancashire. His Mawdsley prefix was prominent amongst the winners for many years, some of his top winners being Ch. Mawdsley Lisette of Langlea, a lovely dark-blue bitch, born in 1952, bred by Miss Kirkland, by (Sh. Ch.) Ripleygae Mallory ex Crombie Sally of Sharvogue. Sh. Ch. Mawdsley Ladybird of Barningham, another dark-blue bitch, bred in 1957 by Capt. Kendall, by Ernford Kingfisher out of Ch. Suntop Carnival Queen, was litter sister to the immortal Suntop Songbird. Capt Kendall also bred Sh. Ch. Jewel of Thrumall, born in 1962 and owned by Mr H. Scofield. Jewel of Thrumall was by Mawdsley Thrumall Talent ex Mawdsley Bella. Sh. Ch. Hepton Mawdsley Aloysius was by Mawdsley Nickodemus ex Mawdsley Harvest Moon and owned by Mr J. Taylor. Sh. Ch. Suntop Royal Mark of Etherwood, winner of six C.C.s was by Sh. Ch. Suntop Royalbird ex Mawdsley Magnolia Blossom and owned by Mr S. Crane.

Mrs F. Webster will always be remembered as the first secretary of the English Setter Association, founded in 1951. She and her husband worked tremendously hard to establish the association, to such effect that a mere three years later, in 1954, they were to hold their first championship show. Mrs Webster ran a large gundog kennels at Fillongley near Coventry which housed both English and Irish Setters as well as Cocker Spaniels. She had several C.C. and Reserve C.C. winners.

A superb dog, born in 1946, was (Sh. Ch.) Ripleygae Mallory, winner of 16 C.C.s and owned by Miss Mary Jarry. He was by Archdale Corncrake of Haverbrack out of Heatherdrake Diane bred by Miss E.M. Clarke. As well as being a most successful show dog, Mallory became a great sire. He sired no less than six show champions and numerous other C.C. winners and was no doubt at that time the most influential sire. Miss E. Rumball's (Sh. Ch.) Archdale Sapphire was his litter sister. Miss Jarry was one of the nicest people one could possibly meet, always willing to help a novice and I shall always be grateful for the advice and help she gave me. Following Mallory, she continued her success with his son (Sh. Ch.) Ripleygae Topnote who was Reserve Best in Show at Crufts in 1952; she later made up Topnote's full brother (Sh. Ch.) Ripleygae Fanfare. These two dogs were out of Ripleygae Music. It is interesting to note that whilst both Mallory and Music

The Breed Post-War

were tricolours, Topnote was a very light-blue belton and Fanfare a deep orange.

Miss Millicent Allen had a lovely kennel of English Setters and Cocker Spaniels situated at Albourne in the heart of the beautiful Sussex countryside. She bred the long-time C.C. record-holder in Cockers. Sh. Ch. Colinwood Silverlariot was owned and campaigned by Mr Alf Collins, whose daughter Mrs Phyllis Wolfe is one of our most respected gundog judges. Of the English Setters one remembers the litter brothers Snowdrift of Truslers and Ch. Shiplake Stonechat of Truslers, the latter owned by Mrs J. English. They were both by Archdale Corncrake of Haverbrack ex Truslers Gaygirl. Pride of her kennel was the beautiful orange bitch (Sh. Ch.) Willow Wren of Truslers. Homebred, she was by Rothina Galahad of Emeraldisle ex Snowbunting of Truslers. Her son, (Sh. Ch.) Wiseman of Truslers by Ch. Shiplake Dean of Crombie and owned by Miss P. Barlass, also gained his title.

Mrs A.C. Crowther, who produced so many winners from her Rombalds Kennel before the war, continued with more successes. In 1945 Rombalds Rhythm had two litters, the first, by Rombalds Furious, produced the lemon belton (Sh. Ch.) Rombalds Flack and the second, by Gorse of Haverbrack, the tricolour (Sh. Ch.) Rombalds Sentinel. She also made up (Sh. Ch.) Rombalds Foxup Flamingo sired by Rombalds Faust, but the greatest was surely (Sh. Ch.) Rombalds Templar (Rombalds Tempest ex Rombalds Fan), whose 20 C.C.s was a record for some years until his son, (Sh. Ch.) Shiplake Swift, took the record with 21 C.C.s.

Mrs B. Enright bred many good English Setters at her Kirket Kennels at Rotherham in Yorkshire, including severfal show champions, one of the best being the delightful lemon belton bitch, (Sh. Ch.) Kirket Koola, sired by Ernford Easter Parade out of (Sh. Ch.) Kirket Marinette (Kirket Mariner of Haverbrack ex Shiplake Sunrise). Mrs Enright also bred (Sh. Ch.) Kirket Karen, owned by Mrs Perkins, whose son Neville is a well-known figure in gundog circles and an all-round gundog judge. Mrs Perkin's dogs were always handled by Mr Bernard Child, who is also a championship show judge these days. Karen was by (Sh. Ch.) Ripleygae Mallory ex Kirket Karmina.

Ernford Easter Parade, the leading sire of this time along with (Sh. Ch.) Ripleygae Mallory was owned by Mrs Angela Broadhead and was out of Celandine of Haverbrack, litter sister to Mallory's sire, Archdale Corncrake of Haverbrack. Easter Parade produced no fewer than six bitches who attained their titles, amongst whom was the great Ch. Ernford Evening Flight, whom I considered to be one of the best bitches I had ever seen. I was so impressed with her that I decided to found my line on this strain and my foundation bitch, purchased from Mrs Broadhead, was in fact a result of a father to daughter mating, i.e. Ernford Easter Parade and Ch. Ernford Evening Flight. This bitch, Iroquois Ernford Irresistible, mated to Sh. Ch. Prince Charming of Ketree, produced in her first litter Int. Sh. Champion Iroquois Casanova and Continental Ch. Iroquois Cinderella. A repeat mating produced another pair of show champions in Sh. Ch. Iroquois Courtesan and Sh. Ch. Pride of Noyna. Born in 1959, Courtesan was undoubtedly one of the best bitches of her generation, winning seven C.C.s before she tragically died at three years of age. Ch. Ernford Evening Flight, also mated to Sh. Ch. Prince Charming of Ketree, produced Sh. Ch. Ernford Rosy Dawn, who in turn was the dam of Sh. Ch. Ernford Chaffinch, sired by Int. Sh. Ch. Suntop Royal Sunglint, thus making three generations of orange belton bitches to attain their titles.

Mrs Broadhead's Ernford Kennels, situated in acres of farmland in Thetford, Norfolk, was one of the all-conquering kennels of the '50s and '60s and she, like Mrs Darling, worked her show dogs and several gained their qualifier. One that kept the Ernford flag flying was Int. Sh. Ch. Ernford Highflier, who was exported to the USA after winning his English crown to gain his international title. He was sired by Ernford Apollo ex Teal of Yaresyde, the dam of Evening Flight, as was Sh. Ch. Shiplake Ernford Cowslip by Easter Parade. Another great stud force was Ernford Kingfisher, a son of Ch. Ernford Evening Flight. He was by Kirket Kerryboy. Ch. Ernford

The Breed Post-War

Cilldara Felicity bred by Miss P. Kelly was another bitch to gain her full title. She was by Grouse of Capard ex Minx of Medehamstead and, mated to Kingfisher, produced American Ch. Ernford Oriole, a very dark-blue belton dog who did well to gain his American title as preference leans very heavily towards the orange beltons in the USA. Mrs Broadhead gave up showing in 1965 to enable her to devote more time to her other interests of breeding Welsh mountain ponies and silver pheasants. She did, however, breed one more litter in 1966 which produced the outstanding orange belton brothers, Sh. Ch. Monksriding Ernford Flamingo, owned by Mr and Mrs H. Pearson and Sh. Ch. Ernford Falcon, owed by Mr and Mrs R. Burns. Flamingo won 15 C.C.s (I gave him his first) and was twice Best in Show at the English Setter Association Show in 1969 and 1971. He also won the gundog group at Leicester in 1970. He later became a highly successful sire, one of the most famous of his progeny being the immortal Sh. Ch. Bournehouse Dancing Master. Flamingo and Falcon were by Sh. Ch. Oldholbans Pirate out of Sh. Ch. Ernford Chaffinch.

Mrs Jocelyn English continued her winning ways with her powerful Shiplake Kennel. In the early '50s, she had in her kennel at the same time Ch. Shiplake Shining Light, Ch. Shiplake Stonechat of Truslers and Ch. Shiplake Symphony of Swo, as well as the Show Champions Shiplake Shining Chance (a daughter of Shining Light) and Shiplake Sheila of Sharvogue. There followed what was possibly her greatest star, Ch. Shiplake Dean of Crombie, whelped in 1952; bred by Mr George Crawford, he was by (Sh. Ch.) Ripleygae Mallory ex Crombie Sally of Sharvogue. Dean won 13 C.C.s and was Reserve Best in Show at Crufts in 1957, thus emulating the feat of another Mallory son (Sh. Ch.) Ripleygae Topnote. Dean's litter sister Ch. Shiplake Daystar of Crombie also attained her full title; another litter sister was Sh. Ch. Dawn of Crombie, who was shown by their breeder and later sold to Mrs A. Broadhead. Other title holders to emerge from this top kennel were (Sh. Ch.) Shiplake Shot Silk (Ch. Shiplake Stonechat of Truslers ex Sh. Ch. Shiplake Sheila of Sharvogue), Sh. Ch. Shiplake

Silverflash bred by Mrs Guarella by Sh. Ch. Shiplake Swift ex Randa of Lake, Sh. Ch. Shiplake Sweet-briar (Ch. Shiplake Dean of Crombie ex (Sh. Ch.) Shiplake Shot Silk). Winner of 11 C.C.s and later exported to the USA to become an American champion was the beautiful blue bitch Sh. Ch. Shiplake Skyblue. (Home-bred, she was by Sh. Ch. Shiplake Swift ex Shiplake Simone.) Last but by no means least, was Sh. Ch. Shiplake Swift himself. Bred by Mr Douglas Paterson, he was by (Sh. Ch.) Rombalds Templar ex Truslers Freckles of Frejendor. With 21 C.C.s, Swift held the record for the number of C.C.s won, until that record was broken in 1964 by Sh. Ch. Silbury Soames of Madavale. Mrs English retired from the show ring in 1962, her last C.C. being won by Sh. Ch. Shiplake Skyblue at WELKS, the judge being Miss Margaret Barnes. The kennel was then disbanded, some of the dogs going abroad and some to exhibitors in this country. All the Shiplake dogs were housed and cared for (and always most beautifully presented) by Mrs Ethel Ely at her lovely kennels at Kingwood Common in Oxfordshire, and I will always remember the wonderful sight of 20 or 30 English Setters galloping about in her large beautifully mown grass paddocks.

Mrs D. Borrowdale produced many winners from her Frejendor Kennel at Burton-on-Trent; the most famous was undoubtedly (Sh. Ch.) Typhoon of Frejendor. Home-bred, he was by Ch. Hurricane of Craiglands out of Emeraldisle Frolic of Chastleton. He was also a great success at stud. Other inmates of this kennel worth a mention were Sultan of Frejendor by Cumbrian Sheik out of the same bitch as Typhoon, his home-bred son Sheik of Frejendor, Highflight of Frejendor and his son Evening Flight of Frejendor, who won 2 C.C.s for Mr Gordon Williams and sired, amongst others, the show champion litter sisters Sh. Ch. Bournehouse Ballerina and Sh. Ch. Bournehouse Meadowfern, these bitches being out of Iroquois Jasmine, who was the foundation bitch of the now famous Bournehouse Kennels.

Mr and Mrs C. Upton produced numerous winners from their Gorsebrook Kennel, the pride of place necessarily going to the litter brother and sister Sh. Ch. Gorsebrook

Berry and Sh. Ch. Ripleygae Gorsebrook Bramble. Sired by Irish Ch. Banner of Crombie, ex Gorsebrook Cherry, Bramble was owned and campaigned by Miss Jarry. Mr D. Paterson, who bred the then C.C. record holder Sh. Ch. Shiplake Swift, also bred and owned Ch. Scardale Avocet, who was by Mrs Pears' Ch. Breeze of Bowbridge, a son of (Sh. Ch.) Rombalds Templar, out of Kestrel of Scardale. Avocet in turn, mated to Sh. Ch. Senglish Early Mist, produced Ch. Scardale Teal.

Mrs C. Ercalani indulged in some unusual breeding with her Neighbours English; using the Canadian import Shiplake Skidby's Guy Fawkes to her Silbury Satin of Neighbours, she produced Sh. Ch. Yankee of Neighbours, whose daughter Neighbours Sybilla she mated back to Guy Fawkes to produce the C.C.-winning bitch Neighbours Pearly Queen. She then mated Sybilla to Field Trial Champion Sharnberry Glenahroo, which produced F.T. Ch. Neighbours Noblesse, whom Mrs Heather Alkin owned, trained and ran with great success to achieve the unique distinction of making a show-bred (on his dam's side) English Setter into a field trial champion.

Mr and Mrs W. A. Jackson owned a lovely dog in Sh. Ch. Tuppence of Whiteseal whom they bred in their very first litter. A dark tricolour dog by (Sh. Ch.) Ripleygae Mallory ex Ripleygae Penelope, he won Best in Show at the English Setter Association Championship Show in 1958; they repeated this feat the following year, this time with Tuppence's son Sh. Ch. Whiteseal Ononis, a flashy light-tricolour ex Whiteseal Sunset. Ononis was a terrific showman and went on to win 14 C.C.s.

The Hepton affix of Mr John Taylor was always well to the fore in the early '60s, his biggest winners being the two orange bitches Sh. Ch. Hepton Saucy Sue, winner of 13 C.C.s (Hepton Jaffa ex Mawdsley Misty Maiden), and Sh. Ch. Hepton Jaffa's Girl, also sired by Hepton Jaffa, this bitch being out of Oldholbans Black Princess. The Hepton and Oldholbans breeding were combined quite frequently, one of the most successful outcomes being Mrs Gill Bond's Sh. Ch. Oldholbans Dill, winner of 5 C.C.s; he was by Hepton Orangeman ex Oldholbans

The English Setter

Patience (Shiplake Skidby's Guy Fawkes ex Oldholbans Queen Isabel).

Mrs Ann Findlay's first C.C. winner was bred, like that of Mr and Mrs Jackson, in her first litter. This was Sh. Ch. Oldholbans Pirate who later became a leading stud dog. Pirate was all Hurwyn breeding, being by Hurwyn Hurricane ex Hurwyn Sunset.

The Noyna Kennel of Mr and Mrs K. Bradshaw from Colne in Lancashire took the breed rather by storm during the 1960s, producing no fewer than five show champions, starting with their foundation bitch Sh. Ch. Pride of Noyna who was litter sister to Sh. Ch. Iroquois Courtesan. Pride mated to Fencefoot Farmers Lad produced Sh. Ch. Sea Fairy of Noyna and mated to Sh. Ch. Suntop Royal Sunglint produced the lovely orange winner of six C.C.s, Sh. Ch. Noyna Gazelle. Sh. Ch. Sea Fairy of Noyna was the damn of Sh. Ch. Noyna Rockette by Suntop Songbird. She was later exported to Australia to become an Australian champion. Sh. Ch. Noyna Sunfairy (Noyna Suntop Royal Wizard ex Noyna Cassandra) was later owned and campaigned by Mrs Lucille Sawtell.

Another kennel, unfortunately now no longer breeding, that had a great influence on the breed during the '60s was the Trodgers kennel of Mrs Angela Tate. Situated at Mark Cross in Sussex, the English Setters were part of a large farm and estate, as Mr and Mrs Tate also bred and showed pedigree cattle and horses. Her Trodgers Red Clover was a wonderful brood bitch, producing many winners, including Sh. Ch. Trodgers Impala, winner of five C.C.s and owned by Mrs J. Furneaux, and the outstanding and unusual coloured Sh.Ch Trodgers Meadow Fescue. This beautiful dark-tricolour bitch was the winner of seven C.C.s. She was sired by Ch. Boisdale Puffin and mated to Sh. Ch. Iroquois Strathspey; she produced the outstanding litter brother and sister Sh. Ch. Trodgers Bluebell and Sh. Ch. Trodgers Scots Oat, who won the gundog group at Crufts in 1971. Also sired by Sh. Ch. Iroquois Strathspey ex Trodgers Goosegrass was Mrs Jean Noble's very successful Sh. Ch. Hayricks Ploughboy, winner of four C.C.s and Best in Show at WELKS 1973.

The Breed Post-War

Sh. Ch. Trodgers Hurwyn Heaven (Int. Sh. Ch. Iroquois Casanova ex Hurwyn Bluecloud) bred by Mrs Wilkinson and her mother, Mrs C. Wilson, was litter sister to Sh. Ch. Iroquois Stormcloud and was twice Best of Breed at Crufts; other notable winners to emerge from this kennel were Heaven's Son, the dual C.C.-winning Trodgers Oregon, Irish Champion Trodgers Yarrow (by Trodgers Wild Mint ex Faybe of Fermanar) and Australian Champion Trodgers Lucerne.

Mr Murray and Mrs Pearce bred numerous outstanding dogs bearing their Ketree affix. Their kennels were situated deep in Cornwall, and consequently Mr Murray and Mrs Pearce themselves did not show much, though I do remember them showing Paymaster of Ketree, a beautiful-coated blue dog, a feature in which the Ketree strain excelled. Mr Stan Christopher did extremely well with Sh. Ch. Postmaster of Ketree, winning 8 C.C.s and his daughter Sh. Ch. Postmistress of Ketree, who was out of Princess of Ketree as was Mr Brian McNally's Sh. Ch. Prince Charming of Ketree. Prince Charming of Ketree in 1956 won four classes and the C.C. at the English Setter Association Championship Show at the tender age of 13 months. He again won the C.C. at the ESA Championship Show in 1960, this time winning Best in Show when owned in partnership by Mr McNally and myself.

Secretary of the English Setter Association during the early '60s was Mr A. Jenkinson, who enjoyed great success during this period with his bitches bearing the Littlewoodcote affix. His first title holder was Sh. Ch. Regalia of Littlewoodcote, a striking light-blue belton bitch sired by Suntop Highlight ex Raytone Fantasy. There followed the litter sisters Sh. Ch. Littlewoodcote Trickster and Sh. Ch. Littlewoodcote Temptress, both tricolours and both sired by Regalia's litter brother Regent of Littlewoodcote ex Pandora of Whiteseal (Sh. Ch. Tuppence of Whiteseal ex Iroquois Sirota). Trickster's daughter Sh. Ch. Littlewoodcote Carousel by Int. Sh. Ch. Iroquois Casanova also gained her title, Carousel being litter sister to Iroquois Littlewoodcote Caprice, the dam of Sh. Ch. Iroquois Cointreau.

The English Setter

Mr and Mrs W. Parkinson, long associated with Pointers under the Blenmar (and later Davium) affix, had for many years bred a few English Setters but none achieved the fame that their American import did. This striking deep-orange, typically American type bitch, Sh. Ch. and Am. Ch. Clariho Whimsey of Valley Run won 10 C.C.s. She was by Am. Ch. Clariho Rough Rider ex Am. Ch. Pinny Page of Valley Run.

Although no longer exhibiting, Mr and Mrs S. Boulton still play an active part in English Setter affairs, serving on various committees and frequently acting as stewards. They won seven C.C.s with their home-bred Sh. Ch. Ednasid Wuster, by Sh. Ch. Suntop Royal Sunglint ex Ednasid Senglish Whisper, and a similar number with his son, Sh. Ch. Ednasid Blue Baron, bred by Mrs A. Kennedy out of Gorsebrook Blonden. Blue Baron proved to be a very successful sire producing many winners, amongst them Mr F. Vallender's Sh. Ch. Amber Starlight and Mrs Daphne Walker's Sh. Ch. Carofel Sunshine, bred by the owner out of Carofel Firefly. Sunshine was the winner of five C.C.s. Mrs Walker also made up with five C.C.s Sh. Ch. Carofel Whispering Romance. She was by Suntop Winterbird ex Carofel Gay Whisper.

A very influential sire and winner of four C.C.s, before an unfortunate accident in which he severed a tendon put an end to his show career, was Mrs Doreen Kay's glamorous light-tricolour Sh. Ch. Senglish Early Mist; bred by the owner, he was sired by Suntop Songbird out of Senglish Evening Star. Early Mist sired many winners, amongst whom was Mrs Maureen Brown's Sh. Ch. Lad of the Haar and his C.C.-winning full sister, Maid of the Haar, these two being out of Shadowlight of the Haar. She also made up the very lovely orange bitch Sh. Ch. Suntop Seamoss of the Haar, bred by Mrs Mary Sedgley. She was by Int. Sh. Ch. Suntop Seabird ex Sedgeford Bathsheba of Beclands, and this bitch mated to Sh. Ch. Senglish Early Mist produced the C.C. winner Misty Blue of Beclands, owned by Miss Susan Rippingale, whose father was a very well-known Fox Terrier man. As previously mentioned, Early Mist was also the sire of Mr Douglas Paterson's Ch. Scardale Teal,

The Breed Post-War

but undoubtedly his greatest son was Mr and Mrs W. Foss's Sh. Ch. Elswood Renmark Baronet, bred by Mrs M. Neave and Miss P. Neave out of Renmark Melody. These two also bred Baronet's son Sh. Ch. Renmark Nimrod ex Renmark Hostess.

Mrs Carol Duffield purchased her foundation bitch from me to start her select Ashpenda Kennel and what a foundation she turned out to be. By Suntop Songbird ex Sh. Ch. Iroquois Courtesan, Sh. Ch. Iroquois Bluemoon not only won nine C.C.s but also produced Sh. Ch. Elswood Renmark Baronet, Sh. Ch. Elswood Ashpenda Moonquest, winner of six C.C.s and Best in Show at Leicester in 1971. Moonquest's litter sister, Ashpenda Silvery Moon, mated to Sh. Ch. Ernford Falcon, produced Ashpenda Petite Etoile, who became a great brood bitch, being the dam of many winners including the litter brother and sister by Suntop Winterbird, Sh. Ch. Ashpenda Red Robin, winner of six C.C.s, and Sh. Ch. Ashpenda Kittiwake who, when Mrs Duffield gave up breeding and showing, became the property of Mrs V. Foss and, mated to Mr Gordon William's Sh. Ch. Bournehouse Dancing Master, produced the breed's current C.C. record-holder with 40 C.C.s, Sh. Ch. Elswood Vagabond King.

3
Character and Conformation

The English Setter is by nature one of the most, if not the most, gentle and loving of all breeds. He is not by nature a 'loner' and loves company, be it human, canine or feline. They are tolerant to the point of saintliness and ask for nothing more of life than to be with you and please you. They are wonderful with children and will never growl, even when an over-enthusiastic child pulls their tail. I always warn new owners to watch their children to make sure they do not tease their dog, as this tolerant attitude should not be abused. There is never any danger of an English Setter fighting; if anything, their fault is over-friendliness. They will cheerfully run up to any other dog, tail wagging and wanting to play, but remember, not all breeds are as friendly, and this trait can often land them in trouble. They are in no way guard dogs. Although some will bark if a stranger approaches the house, they are much more likely to jump up and make a fuss of the visitor than attempt to ward him off. This delightful temperament is to be fostered, as an English Setter (nor any other gundog for that matter) should never be aggressive, although, on the other hand, he should never be timid or nervous.

When selecting a pet, temperament is a much more important factor than construction: a slight fault, which may debar him from becoming a top show dog, in no way detracts from his qualities as a pet. A good temperament, kindliness, affection, devotion, intelligence and obedience are far more important than straight shoulders or a shortish neck.

English Setters on the whole are very sensitive to punishment and generally a stern reprimand is a sufficient deterrent; the mere fact that you sound displeased will usually be

Character and Conformation

punishment enough, as an English Setters wants nothing more than to please you, and you will reap far better results with praise and affection than with harsh treatment.

English Setters are not perhaps the easiest dogs in the world to train, and many people regard them as rather lovable goons, but although they may be somewhat slow to learn, and even obstinate, stupid they most definitely are not.

Conformation

The English Setter is truly an animal of matchless beauty. Ideally balanced, with graceful lines and a long white silky coat flecked with blue or orange, he will always attract attention wherever he goes. If one were asked to choose one word to describe an English Setter, I think the word would be 'elegant'.

The new revised Kennel Club standard is given in full. This is a guide to breeders, whose aim should be to produce a dog which conforms as nearly as possible to this standard. Of course everybody interprets the standard somewhat differently, so we will then analyse each point.

The Revised Kennel Club Standard

General Appearance: Of medium height, clean in outline, elegant in appearance and movement.

Characteristics: Very active with a keen game sense.

Temperament: Intensely friendly and good-natured.

Head and Skull: Head carried high, long and reasonably lean, with well-defined stop. Skull oval from ear to ear, showing plenty of brain room, with a well-defined occipital protuberance. Muzzle moderately deep and fairly square, from stop to point of nose should equal length of skull from occiput to eyes, nostrils wide and jaws of nearly equal length, flews not too pendulous; colour of nose, black or liver, according to colour of coat.

Eyes: Bright, mild and expressive. Colour ranging between

The English Setter

hazel and dark brown, the darker the better. In liver beltons only a lighter eye acceptable. Eyes oval and not protruding.

Ears: Moderate length, set on low, and hanging in neat folds close to cheek, tip velvety, upper part clothed in fine silky hair.

Mouth: Jaws strong, with a perfect, regular and complete scissor-bite, i.e. upper teeth closely overlapping the lower teeth and set square to the jaws. Full dentition desirable.

Neck: Rather long, muscular and lean, slightly arched at crest, and clean cut where it joins head, towards shoulder larger and very muscular, never throaty nor pendulous below throat, but elegant in appearance.

Forequarters: Shoulders well set back or oblique, chest deep in brisket, very good depth and width between shoulder blades, forearms straight and very muscular with rounded bone, elbows well let down close to body, pasterns short, strong, round and straight.

Body: Moderate length, back short and level with good round widely-sprung ribs and deep in back ribs, i.e. well ribbed up.

Hindquarters: Loins wide, slightly arched, strong and muscular, legs well-muscled including second thighs, stifles well-bent and thighs long from hip to hock, hock inclining neither in nor out and well let down.

Feet: Well padded, tight, with close, well-arched toes protected by hair between them.

Gait/Movement: Free and graceful action, suggesting speed and endurance. Free movement of the hock showing powerful drive from hindquarters. Viewed from rear, hip, stifle and hock joints in line. Head naturally high.

Tail: Set almost in line with back, medium length, not reaching below hock, neither curly nor ropy, slight curved or scimitar-shaped but with no tendency to turn upwards: flag or feathered hanging in long pendant flakes. Feather commencing slightly below the root, and increasing in length towards middle, then gradually tapering towards

Character and Conformation

end, hair long, bright, soft and silky, wavy but not curly. Lively and slashing in movement and carried in a plane not higher than level of back.

Coat: From back of head in line with ears slightly wavy, not curly, long and silky, as is coat generally, breeches and forelegs nearly down to feet, well feathered.

Colour: Black and white (blue belton), orange and white (orange belton), lemon and white (lemon belton), liver and white (liver belton) or tricolour, that is blue belton and tan or liver belton and tan, those without heavy patches of colour on body but flecked (belton) all over preferred.

Size: Dogs: 65–68 centimetres (25½–27 inches). Bitches: 61–65 centimetres (24–25½ inches).

Faults: Any departure from the foregoing points should be considered a fault and the seriousness with which the fault should be regarded should be in exact proportion to its degree.

NOTE: Male animals should have two apparently normal testicles fully descended into the scrotum.

General Appearance

The standard calls for a dog of medium height, clean in outline, elegant in appearance and movement. The word to be emphasized here is **elegant**. An English Setter needs to be ideally balanced and symmetrical, and one looks for that indefinable element 'quality', that look of a thoroughbred horse, which has been described as 'the look of Eagles'. He should be proud, with head held high, and should look every inch the aristocrat he undoubtedly is. However, let it be stressed that it is no good looking superb standing if he cannot move. If the construction is correct then the movement should be also, but a dog that looks wonderful standing (which may be due to extremely good handling) will often disappoint when moving, by a high front action, caused by straight shoulders, or a poor rear action due to weak hocks.

The English Setter

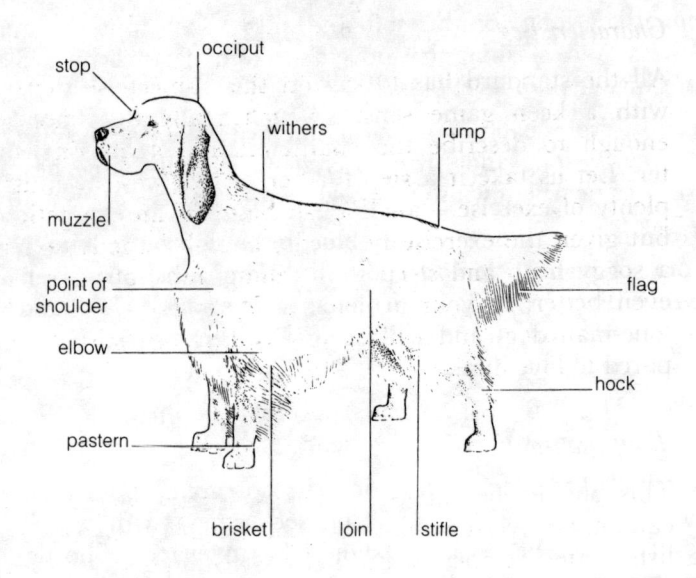

Figure 1 *Points of the English Setter*

Figure 2 *a) A poor head – note lack of stop and wedge-shaped appearance*
b) A good head

Character and Conformation

Characteristics

All the standard has to say on this subject is 'Very active with a keen game sense', which really does not go far enough to describe the characteristics of an English Setter. Let us take it a step further; active, yes, he must have plenty of exercise – an English Setter is an energetic dog – but given the exercise he needs, he will happily collapse in a soggy heap and sleep the evening away at your feet (or, even better, in your armchair). He is not on the whole a 'one-man dog' and will cheerfully love anyone who is prepared to love him.

Temperament

This should be intensely friendly and good-natured and cannot be over-emphasized. The *essential* trait of an English Setter temperament is his friendlinesss to everyone, including other dogs, and any form of aggressiveness is to be frowned upon. We must not let any bad temperament creep into the breed; this lovely nature is so much part of the English Setter we must not lose it. The keen game sense is obviously a part of his make up and it is not unusual to see a youngster setting birds without any prior training.

Head and Skull

The standard goes into this point very thoroughly; however, one should stress that there should be no sign of a 'dish face' (as in a Pointer) or a 'Roman nose' (as in a Bull Terrier). The head should be well-chiselled, with the cheek bones not too prominent. A weak or snipey foreface is very undesirable, giving the head a wedge-shaped appearance. The skull should not be too broad without any sign of coarseness, the whole head to be clean cut and completely balanced.

Eyes

The eyes should be dark brown, the darker the better.

The English Setter

Although any shade of brown from hazel to dark brown is permitted, it should be remembered that the lighter the eye colour, the more it detracts from the desirable soft expression. The shape of the eye can also enhance or detract from the expression; the eye should be oval and well-set, never round or protruding, which will give a hard, staring expression. The eye rims should be black (or on an orange belton, as dark brown as possible). The English Setter should have a nice, tight eye; any looseness in the rims will cause the haw (the red inner eyelid) to show, which is most undesirable, and again, detracts from the expression, which should be soft and kindly, bright and expressive. The only coat colour where a light-yellowish eye is permitted is the liver belton, seldom seen these days and not to be confused with a deep-orange belton. The liver coat colour always carries these light eyes, and as this detracts from the desired expression, this probably accounts for the fact they were never very popular.

Ears

The standard calls for ears of moderate length; they do vary somewhat in length, but a rough guide is, if the ears are pulled forward over the eyes, the tips should meet at the 'stop', i.e. the indenture between the eyes. They should be set on low and hang in neat folds close to the cheek. The ear is covered in fine silky hair, which is rather thicker towards the top and which tends to make the ear look high set; this hair should therefore be stripped off, as should the thick tufty hair which grows under the ear, so the ear has a smooth silky appearance.

Mouth

This really refers to the teeth, which should have a scissor-bite, in which the top teeth closely overlap the bottom teeth when the jaw is closed. Occasionally one will find a misplaced tooth; although not desirable, this should not be confused with an overshot or undershot jaw (see diagram opposite). It is preferable for a young puppy to be

Character and Conformation

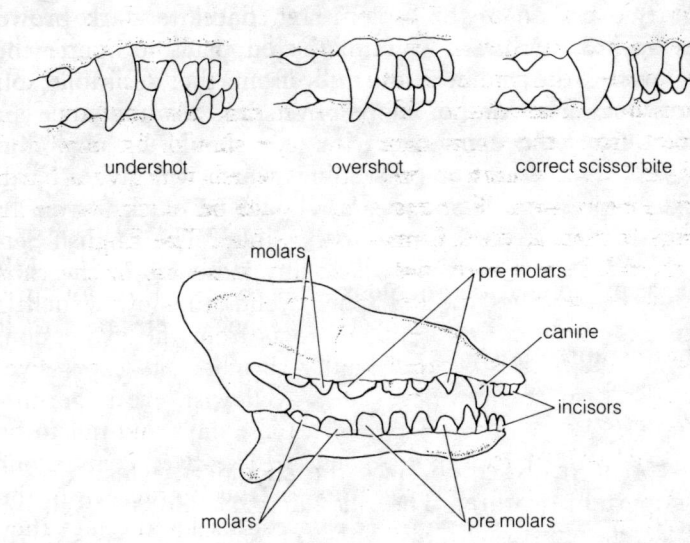

Figure 3 *Dentition and bite*

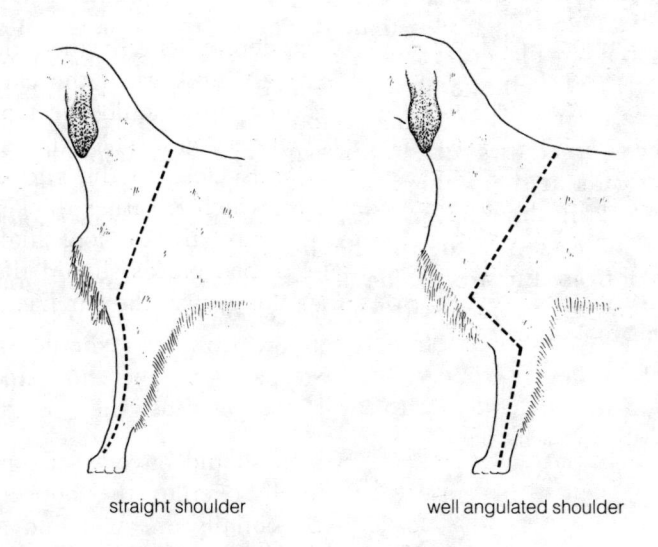

Figure 4 *Forequarters from the side*

43

The English Setter

slightly overshot, as the bottom jaw continues to grow after the top jaw, and if the bite of the puppy is too perfect, it may well end up undershot. Full dentition is desirable, but many dogs have one or more pre-molars missing; this is a disqualification in some countries.

Neck

The neck should be long, muscular and lean, arched to give a proud aristocratic look, the throat clean and free from dewlap, the whole effect to be one of elegance as in a thoroughbred horse.

Forequarters

This point really emphasizes the shoulders, which are an all-important feature. The shoulders should be well set back, referred to as 'lay back of shoulder'. A straight shoulder placement will result in a high or hackney action, which is most undesirable; an English Setter should cover the ground with a long, low, sweeping action. Faulty shoulders are a terrific problem in the breed today, and unless the shoulder placement is correct, the dog cannot move correctly. The elbows should be well let down and tucked in close to the brisket; there should be no perceptible gap between the elbows and the brisket. The blades should not be too wide at the withers; otherwise the dog will be heavy or loaded in shoulder. Alternatively, the shoulders should not be too close together or the dog will be narrow in front. Viewed from the front, the legs should be straight from the elbow to the foot with neither elbows nor feet turning out. The width of chest between the front legs should be roughly a hand's span. The pasterns should be short and strong with no tendency to lay back, nor must they be too upright, as in a Terrier.

Body

The body should be of moderate length but, above all, well-balanced. To be so, not only length but depth must also be in proportion. He should be short, coupled with well-

Character and Conformation

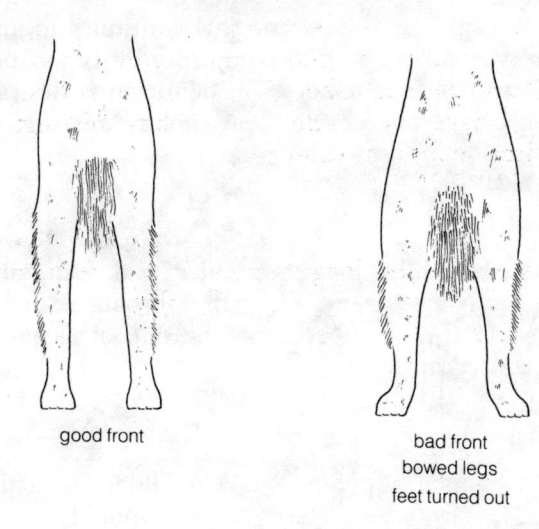

good front

bad front
bowed legs
feet turned out

Figure 5 *Forequarters from the front*

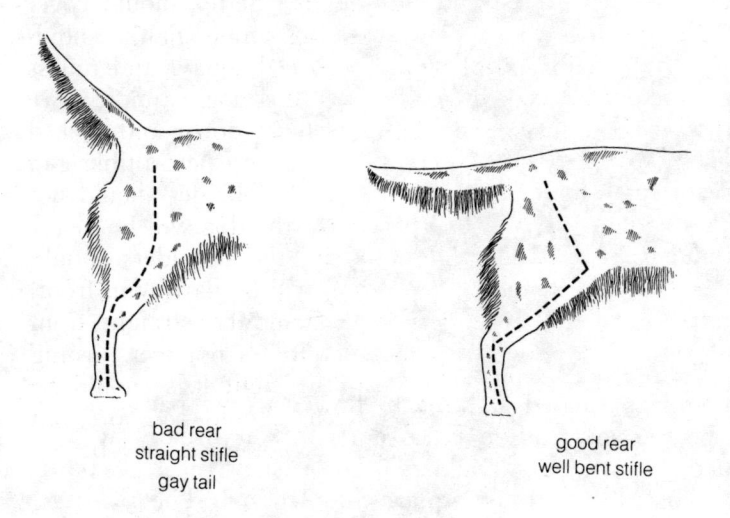

bad rear
straight stifle
gay tail

good rear
well bent stifle

Figure 6 *Hindquarters from the side*

The English Setter

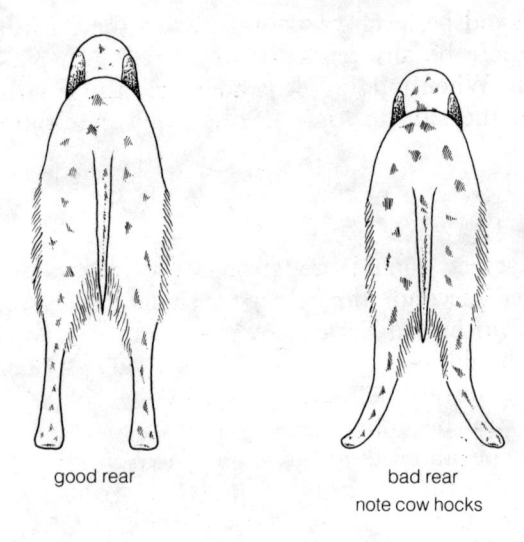

good rear

bad rear
note cow hocks

Figure 7 *Hindquarters from the rear*

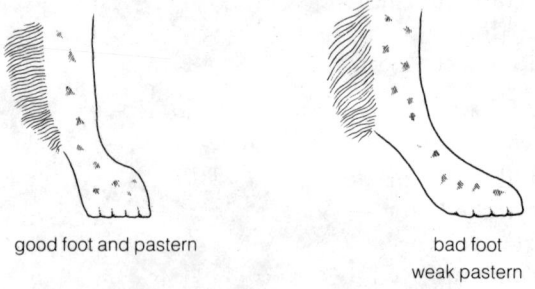

good foot and pastern

bad foot
weak pastern

Figure 8 *Feet*

sprung ribs carried well back; however, the back should not be too short as an ultra-short back is usually accompanied by straight shoulders and a short neck, making the whole dog look too square and 'cobby'. The rib cage should have depth in addition to spring, as if the dog is too shallow in body he will look 'shelly'. Many dogs look good in profile and even have the desired depth of brisket but lack spring of rib, i.e. are slab-sided, and this may only be seen by looking down on the dog from behind. The back

Character and Conformation

or topline should be level, not sloping as in the Irish Setter, nor should there be any tendency to dip behind the shoulders or roach. When judging, it is advisable to view the dog moving from the side to ascertain he holds his topline on the move.

Hindquarters

The hindquarters should be strong and muscular with well-developed second thighs, good bend of stifle, the thigh long from hip to hock, with the hock well let down. The hocks should not turn either in or out. A dog with hocks turning inward is said to be cow-hocked, a weakness which can be inherited or environmental (puppies should never be allowed to stand on their hindlegs). The hindquarters are the dog's propelling power, so to achieve the desired long, free stride it is essential to have good angulation, well-bent stifles (though one does not want over-angulation as in the German Shepherd) and good hard muscle. The croup should not slope towards the root of the tail but should continue level with the rest of the back; a dog with a sloping croup generally has weak quarters, often accompanied by straight stifles.

Feet

These should be rounded and cat-like, well-padded with close, well-arched toes. Long flat 'hare' feet, open or splayed feet are very undesirable. The last named can sometimes be improved by road walking, which of course also helps keep the nails short, but like most points good feet are in the breeding.

Movement

Referred to in the USA as *Gait*. This should be long and free striding with a graceful action, covering the ground with sweeping stride. Any tendency to a high 'hackney' action in the front should be frowned upon, as this undoubtedly results from straight shoulders, and although people may think this is a showy action, it is completely untypical. There should be powerful drive from the hocks; viewed from the rear the hip, stifle and hock joints should be perpendicular. The head should be carried high in moving, giving a proud and aristocratic appearance.

Tail

The tail should be set on in line with the back, medium length, not reaching below the hock, although an inch or so above the hock is quite permissible. It should never be curly, but hang in long silky flakes commencing slightly below the root, increasing in length towards the middle and tapering off towards the tip. The hair or feathering on the tail should be long, soft and silky; a slight wave is permitted. A lively slashing tail-action when the dog is moving is desirable; a slight curve or scimitar-shape is permissible, but the tail should never be carried higher than the level of the back. A 'gay' tail should be penalized.

Coat

Commencing from the back of the neck and over the entire body, the coat should be long, soft and silky, slightly wavy but never curly. The chest, brisket, forelegs and breeches to be well feathered.

Colour

The standard lays down all the variations of colour. However, one must realize that blue belton can be used to describe a dog who is virtually white with just a few bluish-grey spots on his muzzle and similar colour on his ears as well as to describe a dog that is so dark a steel grey all over that he shows very little white on his coat at all. Similarly the orange belton can vary from the very dark-orange 'roan' colour to the almost-white lemon belton, just showing a little colour on the ears and muzzle. Obviously the lighter colours are more eye-catching and glamorous but one should remember the old adage 'a good horse is never a bad colour'. The standard states flecked all over is preferred, and the flecking is very much more obvious

Character and Conformation

on the lighter coat colour. Heavy patches of colour other than over the eye or on the ear are not desirable, but one should stress that they should not be unduly penalized on an otherwise very nice dog.

Size

The height stipulated in the standard is 25½ to 27 inches for a dog and 24 to 25½ inches for a bitch. However, my opinion is that very few dogs or bitches these days measure up to these rather vast proportions. To illustrate this, five of my champion dogs all measured between 24¼ and 25¾ inches. The last measurement was considered to be that of a big dog; goodness knows what a dog measuring 27 inches would be like. A more realistic measure for bitches would be 23 to 24 inches. The revised standard has dropped any weight stipulation, but as this was nonsensical in the old standard, i.e. dogs 60 to 66 pounds, bitches 56 to 62 pounds, perhaps it is just as well. The same five dogs mentioned above weighed between 70 and 78 pounds; can one imagine what a dog measuring 27 inches and weighing 66 pounds would look like? Size can be deceptive. A short coupled compact dog will appear smaller than a long-bodied rangy one. The most important factor is for the dog to have everything in proportion and to be balanced.

Faults

We have covered most of the faults to look for in this summary under each separate heading. The revised standard really says nothing, but the old standard did list amongst faults the following: coarse or lumpy shoulders, short foreface, tapering nose, lack of stop, light or obliquely set eyes, high ear placement, flat ribs, too long loin, wide feet, weak pasterns, straight stifles, narrow quarters, gay flag, lightness of bone, mouth undershot or overshot, lacking freedom of action. Quite a formidable list. What we are really looking for is a sound, well-balanced dog that can move freely and soundly, has style and elegance and, above all, a good temperament.

4
Choosing a Puppy, Feeding and Training

Where to go to purchase your puppy? First you must think why you want the puppy – as a pet, as a show dog or as a foundation to a kennel. You should try to build up a mental picture of what a good English Setter should look like, and there is no better way of doing this than visiting one or two dog shows, preferably championship shows. At such shows you will not only have the opportunity of seeing a number of top-quality dogs but will also have the chance of meeting and chatting to the top breeders. You will probably find that one particular 'type' appeals to you more than another, and having decided which dogs you like, a visit to the owner's kennel can be arranged where further stock of theirs will be on view. By doing this, you can see not only their young stock but other fully grown dogs and bitches, and the chances are that the puppy you choose will grow up to be not unlike these, as most kennels or 'lines' breed true to type.

Having considered all these factors and having satisfied yourself that you have seen sufficient dogs and located a breeder of repute, the question of colour arises. Let it be stressed that conformation and temperament are far more important factors than colour, but if you have decided that you like the very light-blue belton, or perhaps an orange, it would be foolish to go to a kennel that breeds predominantly very dark blues. Be honest with the breeder about your requirements; it is false economy, as well as dishonest, to try to obtain a puppy on the pretence that it is just for a pet when you really plan to show the puppy, although I hasten to add that many a successful

Choosing a Puppy, Feeding and Training

show dog has been originally and genuinely purchased as a pet. Many people feel that breeders have some magic formula for selecting a puppy and that they will never sell their best puppies; this, of course, is not true, although over the years one develops an 'eye' for picking a puppy. This is not a thing that one can teach; it is an acquired art. Therefore if you are in any doubt about your ability to choose a puppy, take an experienced fancier with you when the choice is to be made or rely on the breeder's integrity. The latter is probably your best course of action.

It takes no great skill to select a healthy puppy (the entire litter is probably so), but look for the puppy that has plenty of bounce, clear, sparkling eyes and a bold inquisitive nature. The skin should be loose and free from any form of irritation, and the bone should be of good substance. Avoid the puppy that appears shy and shrinks back (though these are few and far between in English Setters as they are, from a very young age, intensely friendly). A puppy with fine bone and a 'pot belly' in all probability has not been well-reared and is likely to be wormy. All young puppies have worms but the puppy should have been wormed two or three times before he is old enough to leave for his new home. It is wise to ask the breeder to show you the puppy's teeth to ascertain that the jaw is not malformed; at this age the top teeth should well overlap the bottom teeth. If the bite is too good, i.e. the top teeth touching the bottom ones, he may well end up undershot as the bottom jaw grows on longer than the top one, so a slightly overshot mouth is best. As puppies of seven or eight weeks will not have been vaccinated, many breeders will not allow strangers to handle them for fear of infection, but the breeder will always stand the puppy on a table for you to assess the various points. Do not expect the breeder to say 'This puppy is a certain future champion'. If they are honest, the furthest they will commit themselves is to say 'This puppy shows promise', and it sometimes happens that the smallest or 'runt' of the litter turns out to be the best, that in fact the ugly duckling sometimes becomes the swan.

The English Setter

Good Points

It is very difficult to predict from looking at a puppy what he or she will look like as an adult, but if one sees the dam and possibly the sire, one will have an idea of the type. The points to look for are a nicely rounded skull, a broad deep muzzle with a good stop, this being the indenture between the eyes, which should be dark and have a soft kindly expression. The nose and eye rims should be dark, but here let it be said that the pigmentation round the eyes sometimes does not fill in completely until a later age if the puppy is very lightly marked. The ears should be set on low and hang close to the cheek. Ensure that the shoulder placement is good; the blades should be set fairly close together and laid well back and there should be a good reach of neck. The ribs should be nicely rounded and the back of medium length. The hindquarters should be strong and capable of withstanding a firm pressure of the hand. Stifles should be well-bent with the hocks level, showing no sign of turning in or out. It is most important that the puppy should have good bone; the front legs should be straight with the elbows tucked well in. The tail should be set on in line with the back and in length should reach the hock. The feet should be round, catlike, thick-padded with arched toes.

Faults

Some faults to look for and avoid are light eyes, a pale or butterfly nose (except in the case of the light-lemon belton, when a flesh-coloured nose is permissible) and lack of pigmentation around the eyes (though small breaks can fill in at a much later age as previously mentioned). Other faults are bad mouth, especially an undershot jaw, which will never improve, high set ears and lack of stop or lack of depth of muzzle, which gives a snipey appearance. The head should never appear wedge-shaped; on the other hand the lips should not be too pendulous. Short neck, coarse, lumpy or straight shoulders are to be avoided as are lack of bone, long, weak pasterns and long hare-shaped or flat splayed feet. No spring of rib, long back, dipped

Choosing a Puppy, Feeding and Training

or roached back, low set tail, sloping croup, straight stifles cow- or sickle-hocks and loose elbows are all faults. These latter points, like straight shoulders, would impair good movement, which is so essential to a breed like the English Setter.

The next question to arise is whether one should have a dog or a bitch. Many people go for a bitch thinking they are quieter and more affectionate than a dog. In many breeds this is probably so, the males being more aggressive than the females, but this certainly is not the case with English Setters, the dogs being every bit as docile and loving as the bitches. One can make a case for and against either sex. The dogs are bigger, more 'showy' and eye-catching, as they invariably carry more coat. On the debit side, he is more likely to roam, especially if any members of the opposite sex attract him. The bitches are smaller and not so boisterous and there is the added joy of being able to breed from them if desired; if not, it is a simple matter these days to suppress their seasons with tablets or injections, though I should add that I do try to deter people who tell me that they want a bitch but will have her spayed. This operation not only causes the bitch to put on weight and the coat to grow very woolly but can have other side-effects such as incontinence and skin problems. On the whole, I feel the choice of sex is very much a case of personal preference.

The colour of the puppy's coat can be very misleading – all English Setters are born pure white with the exception of those showing any jet-black (an ear or eye patch). Some are born with these patches, and they occur more frequently in some strains than others, generally the very dark blue beltons and tricolours. The markings start to appear on the foreface at about two weeks and from that time onwards gradually appear on the legs and finally the body. One may be tempted to ask how the eventual adult coat-colour can be forecast, the answer being that to any definite degree it cannot, though if by the age of four or five weeks the puppy shows heavy dark smudgy facial markings, it is unlikely he will turn out to be very light. If he shows blue markings on his ears and face but none on his feet, it is more than likely he is going to be a tricolour (blue belton and tan), as the tan markings take longer to come through than the blue. The orange belton can be even more misleading, as a virtually white six- or seven-weeks-old puppy can turn out to be quite a deep orange in adult life. If, however, one runs a finger up the puppy's back against the fall of the coat, it is often possible to see the deeper coloured undercoat.

Paperwork

Once you have actually purchased a puppy, you must ensure that all his papers are in order. You should have a copy of the pedigree, and if the puppy has already been registered with the Kennel Club, the registration certificate. Make sure this has been signed on the back by the breeder. This you then sign yourself in the space provided and send to the Kennel Club in order to effect the change of ownership to your own name. It may be that the breeder has not registered (named) the puppy, but just registered the birth of the litter; if this is the case, you should be given a form to enable you to name the puppy yourself. This form when completed must also be sent to the Kennel Club with the appropriate fee, and in return you will receive a certificate of registration. If the dog is to be exhibited or bred from, he or she must be registered. Most breeders insure their puppies and will give you a month's cover note. You would be well advised to continue this.

Finally, and most important, is a diet sheet giving the amount and types of meat, biscuit, milk etc. that the puppy has been fed on. Like all youngsters, a puppy's tummy is easily upset by sudden changes of food, so it is as well to stick as near as possible to what he has been used to and to make any changes gradually. He will at this time be having four meals a day, roughly as follows:

Breakfast: ½ pint of milk, warm and sweetened with glucose, mixed with Weetabix or Readybrek,
or scrambled egg (not more than twice a week).

Choosing a Puppy, Feeding and Training

Lunch: 4–6 ounces of minced or finely chopped meat (or Pedigree Chum Puppy Food) mixed with a handful of soaked puppy meal. Add vitamins such as Stress, Vitapet or SA 37.
Tea: Repeat lunch.
Supper: ½ pint of warm sweetened milk, to which add a Farley's rusk or Readybrek.
Bedtime: A few biscuits or rusks (baked bread).

As the puppy grows, the amounts should be increased, and the amounts may vary according to the individual. A large dog-puppy will obviously need more than a small bitch. It is most important to continue with the vitamins, especially calcium, which helps form good bone and strong teeth.

For the journey home come prepared with an old blanket or towel for the puppy to lie on, preferably on your lap; the puppy will be much happier travelling this way, though do have some paper or kitchen roll handy as the chances are he will be sick on his first journey. If travel sickness persists on subsequent journeys, give a Sea-legs tablet several hours before the proposed journey and, of course, no food or water prior to the trip. On arrival, the puppy will no doubt wish to relieve himself, so take him into the garden for a few minutes and then bring him in and give him a small drink of warm milk. The kitchen is probably the best place to make his home, at least until he is housetrained, as long as it is warm and draughtproof. Supply him with a cosy bed. A cardboard box with the front cut down is ideal until he is older and over the chewing period; it can then be replaced by a basket or dog bed. Give him a hot-water bottle well wrapped up in an old blanket, or a soft cuddly toy to snuggle up to. He will miss his brothers and sisters and may well cry the first night or two, but he will soon settle down and adapt to his new way of life.

Inoculations

It is most important that the puppy be inoculated against distemper, hard pad, hepatitis, leptospirosis and parvovirus before he is allowed out of his own garden or comes into contact with other dogs, so it is advisable to make an appointment with your veterinary surgeon to commence the course of vaccination as soon as the puppy has reached eight weeks of age. The course is spread over an eight-week period, the first one given at eight weeks, the second at twelve weeks and a third parvovirus at 16 to 18 weeks. This last one is most important as parvovirus is a dreadful disease, the mortality rate being very high. The puppy should not be taken out until ten days after vaccination has been completed. He should have a yearly 'booster' thereafter.

Teething

Puppies lose their milk or first teeth at four to six months of age and these are replaced by the adult teeth; these should total 42 made up as follows:

Upper Jaw
Incisors   6
Canine   2
Premolars 8
Molars   4

Lower Jaw
Incisors   6
Canine   2
Premolars 8
Molars   6

It is essential during the teething period that an adequate supply of calcium be maintained in the diet, and this should come from supplements such as Stress, Canoval Palatable Calcium etc. Having completed his vaccinations and got over teething, it is recommended that the puppy be wormed. Worm tablets containing Piperazine Citrate (1 tablet per 10 pounds of bodyweight being the dose) are the most effective and can be obtained from your veterinary surgeon.

Feeding

We have dealt with the feeding of your puppy at eight to twelve weeks of age, for which you will have had a diet sheet obtained from the breeder. At the age of three months, the meals can be reduced to three a day, quantities being increased as before and a more adult and varied diet given. The meals should now be roughly as follows:

Breakfast: ½ pint warm sweetened milk with Weetabix (occasionally add a raw, beaten egg) or scrambled egg.

Lunch: ½ pound minced or finely chopped meat mixed with a cupful of soaked puppy meal. Add vitamins.

Tea: ½ pound minced tripe or Pedigree Chum Puppy Food, mixed with a cupful of soaked puppy meal or puppy-size mixer.

Supper: ½ pint warm sweetened milk, with a handful of biscuits (such as Biscroks).

There are many brands of powdered milk on the market, all of which are better and more concentrated than cow's milk, but the best of all, if obtainable, is goat's milk, which unlike cow's milk can be frozen. So a quantity can be purchased at any one time and the amount required for each day taken from the freezer and allowed to thaw. Similarly, one can obtain numerous brands of frozen meat for puppies in packet form; these are available at your pet shop. If using tripe and feeding it raw, do make sure it is ox tripe; if it is sheep tripe (generally referred to as paunch), it must be well boiled, as sheep nearly all suffer from hookworm and this will be passed on to your puppy.

By six months, the puppy can be placed on two meals a day with the quantities of the main meal being gradually increased. He could now have a pint of milk for breakfast (still with a beaten egg in it two or three times a week), a few hard biscuits or some dry Pedigree Chum Mixer. The main meal should consist of about one pound of meat and a similar amount of biscuit meal. Any household scraps may of course be added, but basically a dog does not need vegetables, as unlike man he is able to produce his own vitamin C, of which vegetables have a high content. He should have a few hard biscuits at bedtime and a large marrowbone given occasionally will give him enjoyment as well as helping to keep his teeth clean. Never give any other bones, such as chicken or chop, as these splinter easily and may puncture the intestine.

Complete feeds are freely available these days, and you may prefer to use one of these although, personally, I feel that meat and wholemeal biscuit take a lot of beating. It really boils down to a question of palatability. The average quantity of food required will vary tremendously. Some dogs are very much more energetic than others; one burning up a lot of energy will need considerably more food to replace it than the quiet content dog who tends to lie around. It is, however, difficult to overfeed an English Setter, especially a youngster, as they are not on the whole a greedy breed. You are more likely to have difficulties with getting him to eat. Quite a few English Setters are 'fussy' eaters, and you may need to resort to a number of ploys to get them eating well. I never have, nor ever will advocate 'force-feeding', persuasion being a far better course of action, though one must admit it can sometimes stretch your patience to the very limit. If you have more than one dog, it may help to 'kid' him that you will give the food to another dog, or hand-feeding may help; for some reason food appears to be more palatable to him out of your hand than out of his feeding bowl. Adding some tasty morsel such as chopped liver, heart or breast of lamb to the food will sometimes work the miracle, but if all else fails, there is a wonderful product available at most good pet shops called High Calorie Vitamin Concentrate; this dietary supplement stimulates the appetite and will get most 'bad doers' eating. Dog nutrition is a greatly discussed subject these days and there is a wide variety of foods from which to choose. There is no doubt that some dogs will appear to like one type of food better than another, though to be honest this is possibly of more concern to the owner than to the dog himself.

House Training

The first priority with a newly acquired puppy is to get him

Choosing a Puppy, Feeding and Training

housetrained. This is a comparatively easy task, providing you persevere for a few days before he has had the chance to develop any bad habits. First thing in the morning take him into the garden and be prepared to stay with him and teach him one short word he will come to understand; it doesn't matter what word you use (I always say 'pennies' to my dogs, and they almost squat to order!) but don't confuse him with several different orders. When you have achieved your object, give him plenty of praise and take him back indoors for his breakfast. This should be repeated at frequent intervals during the day, after each meal and whenever he wakes up. It is advisable to spread newspapers on the floor near the door as he is bound to have the odd 'accident', but you should still stick to your routine. It is no good saying 'It isn't worth putting him out – he has already done it.' Never scold him unless you actually catch him in the act; a puppy's memory is very short, and you will only confuse him. If you see him go to the door, take him out at once and praise him, even if he doesn't do anything and it is in the middle of your favourite TV show. He will very soon learn what he goes out for.

Whilst one should always have an adequate supply of drinking water available during the day, always remove this at night; if a puppy wakes up and decides to have a drink, a puddle will inevitably follow.

Basic house manners should also be taught. Do not allow him to scratch at doors and ruin the paintwork or clamber all over the furniture. No one wants to sit in chairs covered in hairs or mud. Provide him with a comfy bed or basket, or if you let him sleep in a chair, make that chair his alone and cover it with a blanket that can be frequently changed and washed. In wet weather he must be taught to wait at the door for his feet to be dried and if necessary rubbed down with a towel before coming into the house. A wet, muddy English Setter can soon make a terrible mess. He must also be taught not to steal food or put his face or feet on the table whilst you are eating meals. Do not feed him from your plate as this will only encourage him to beg for food. If you wish to save him some tasty morsels from your plate, these should be given to him afterwards in his own dish. Once your puppy has learned the rudiments of good behaviour, he will be a pleasure to own.

Lead Training

Commence lead training at about three months by placing a thin leather collar on the puppy for about an hour a day. At first he will scratch at it, but he will soon get used to the feeling of something round his neck. After a few days he will cease to take any notice of it. Now is the time to attach the lead, which should be held loosely. Walk a pace or two away and, calling the puppy by name, urge him to follow, encouraging him with titbits. Directly the lead becomes taut you will probably be treated to a 'Wild West' show; the puppy will start bucking, jumping and throwing himself all over the place, but he will eventually get used to the feeling of restraint. Keep talking to him with words of praise and giving him little titbits. He will then associate the lead with something pleasant and will very soon trot along quite happily. The next stage is to teach him not to pull whilst on the lead. For this a leather slip lead or a leather choke collar are best (do not use chain chokes as they are too harsh for a puppy). A point to be stressed is that it is no use entering a tug-of-war contest with your dog, for there will never be a winner, and your walks will be a misery for you and the dog. If the puppy starts pulling, give the lead a short, sharp jerk, at the same time saying firmly 'heel' or 'back'. This must be repeated many times until he associates the word with the jerk on his collar. Always remember to praise and reward him when he has learned a lesson; he will soon learn to walk without pulling on the lead, which will be much more pleasant for both of you.

Car Training

Most English Setters love car-travelling and will jump in the car on every possible occasion, but as puppies they are frequently car-sick. As soon as your puppy is able to go out, i.e. when all vaccinations have been completed, take him for very short car rides, preferably to a nearby park or field where you exercise. He will then associate going in the car with something pleasant. Should he be sick on these first few journeys, give a travel-sickness tablet (I find Sea-legs are the best) an hour or two before the proposed journey, and you will find that, once he has completed a few journeys without being sick, he will look forward to his daily outing. A good method of accustoming him to the car is to put him in it whilst it is stationary for a short time each day, making sure he has sufficient air; but, of course, never do this on a hot day as a car soon becomes like an oven in the sunshine.

A really bad traveller will travel better on the floor than on the seat or in the back of an estate car, and a device fixed to the rear of the car which should just touch the road to break the static electricity is thought to help. However, you will find that the majority of English Setters look upon the car as part of their home, and I am sure would quite happily live in it. With my own dogs the excitement starts directly they hear the car start, as they always associate going out in the car with something exciting, be it going to a show or out for exercise.

We will go into the subject of free running exercise in greater depth in the following chapter, as a puppy needs only limited free running.

5
Care and Accommodation

Until the age of five or six months your English Setter puppy will not require too much exercise. More harm is done by over-exercise than by the lack of it. Your puppy will do very well with short walks on the lead and romps in the garden or field, but from five months onwards this can be built up gradually, and he can be taken for somewhat longer walks, which are especially valuable for getting him used to the sight and sound of traffic.

He should always be kept on the lead no matter how obedient he has become; there is nothing clever about walking your dog on a busy road off the lead. Something can always attract his attention and not only endanger his life but cause an accident and endanger the lives of other people. He should by this time also be having at least half an hour (slowly building up to an hour) free running on grass every day. Choose a park, heath or woods well away from any roads. Once off the lead let him run off his natural exuberance, then call him to you. If he comes back to you right away, praise and reward him (always have a few tasty titbits in your pocket). If he does not come when called, you must catch him, scold him and replace the lead, trying again later. Continue with this lesson until he will return instantly. It is worth persevering with this. I know many people who say they dare not let their dogs off the lead as they would run off, which is a miserable state of affairs. What life do such dogs have, attached to a lead all the while and never allowed the joy of a good gallop? With plenty of affection and praise the dog should **want** to come back to you when called. The dog owner, especially of a breed like English Setters, who uses love and trust to achieve his goal is infinitely more successful than

Care and Accommodation

those who use harsh command and a heavy hand. There is seldom any need to be more than firm but gentle.

The mode of calling a dog is very much the option of the owner, some preferring to call the dog by name or to use the command 'come' or 'here', whilst others prefer a whistle or a combination of all these methods. Whichever you decide upon, the most important things to remember are to be consistent and **praise** him when he obeys a command.

Grooming

An English Setter requires regular grooming to keep his coat in good condition. A few minutes every day is ideal, otherwise knots or mats may form in the feathering. It is advisable to accustom the puppy to being brushed from an early age, starting with a fairly soft brush. He will probably think this is a great game to start with and try to run off with the brush, but he must be taught to stand still; otherwise this can become a very exhausting task. You should also comb through his coat with a fine-tooth comb to ascertain that he has no parasites of any kind. If you detect any evidence of such, he should be dusted with powder or sprayed with a flea repellent (make sure you do not get any in his eyes). He will soon come to look forward to this daily routine. In fact, most dogs love being brushed; mine always try to push each other out of the way in their hurry to make sure they are first in line, directly they see me get out the grooming equipment. This equipment should consist of the following items:

A fairly stiff-bristle brush of the dandy type.
A rubber-cushion brush for the feathering.
A pin brush (sometimes referred to as a slicker) or a wire glove, to get rid of dead coat.
A steel comb with fairly widely spaced teeth.
A fine-tooth or flea comb.
A pair of nail clippers.

Always brush the coat the way you want the hair to lie, i.e. from the head down the neck and shoulders, from the back over the ribs towards the brisket and from the rump down the quarters. Brush the feathering of the chest, brisket, thighs, legs and tail with your cushion brush. If you find any knots or bits of twigs etc. stuck in his feathering, brush through with your pin brush, and if any knots or mats have still not come out, these should be carefully 'teased' out with the comb, never cut.

If your dog is moulting, go all over him with your pin brush or wire glove; the sooner all the dead coat is out, the quicker new hair will replace it. At least once a week check his eyes, ears and teeth. Eyes can be bathed with a diluted solution of bicarbonate of soda, boracic crystals or Optrex. Benzyl benzoate is extremely good for keeping the ears clean. Pour a small quantity in the ear, massage it round, then wipe out with a dry twist of cotton wool. Great care should be taken when cleaning the ear, as it is a very delicate organ; never probe into the ear channel, and avoid using cotton buds. Teeth can be kept clean by brushing with a diluted solution of hydrogen peroxide, though if they get heavily coated with tartar they will require scaling with the correct instrument by the vet.

English Setters are notorious 'nibblers'. One flea will send them into frenzy of scratching and biting, so be sure to give them a thorough dusting with Lorexane or something similar every two or three weeks, especially during the summer months. However, sometimes no cause at all can be found for such irritations. It is advisable in such cases to treat any affected spots with benzyl benzoate, which should be rubbed well in every two or three days. Another good remedy is Piriton tablets, which are freely available from any chemist. If it should be found that where your dog has been nibbling the hair has turned a pinky brown (this is caused by the saliva), it can be rectified by bathing any such affected parts with a solution of two parts hydrogen peroxide to one part olive oil.

If the dog's coat appears at all dry, and this is often the case when he is moulting, a great help for restoring the desired shine is Royal Coatalin, which should be brushed well into the coat every two or three days after grooming.

Care and Accommodation

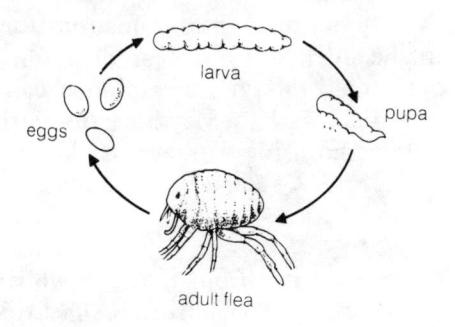

Figure 9 *Life cycle of the flea*

Bathing

If you are proposing to show your English Setter, he will require bathing before the show to make him look his best, but even if he is never to be shown and just kept as a pet, an occasional bath will be beneficial and prevent him ever smelling 'doggy', especially if he has indulged in a roll whilst out at exercise. I find most dogs take no objection to being bathed; in fact they appear to really enjoy it and will jump in the bath quite happily. Do, however, make sure you always place a rubber mat in the bath to prevent him slipping; also plug his ears with cotton wool to prevent any water getting in. If you have a shower or spray attachment, it will be be much easier than baling the water over him.

Start by wetting the coat thoroughly all over with the exception of his head, ensuring that the water is only warm and not hot, then work in the shampoo all over his body, legs and tail. Be sure when you are washing his thighs and tail that you do not get any shampoo under his tail. If any gets into the anus a 'dead tail' will result. When you have worked up a good lather all over, wash his face with a flannel, wiping round his eyes with care. Rinse the shampoo off thoroughly, making sure there is no shampoo left in the coat anywhere, or it may cause irritation. It is advisable to finish off with a conditioner or a tablespoonful of glycerine to a bucket of water for the final rinse, as this replenishes the oil in the coat that the bathing may remove. If the dog's coat was looking slightly yellowish, swish a Reckitts Blue Bag in the bucket of the final rinse until it is deepish blue; his coat should then dry a sparkling white. It is best to use any good quality shampoo, be it for humans or dogs, but you should avoid using detergents.

Drying

Squeeze the excess water from the coat whilst he is still in the bath, and then rub him all over with a Spontex cloth, squeezing it out frequently. This method will save a lot of mess as well as too many wet towels. The drying time will be cut down if you now give him a vigorous rubbing-down with a towel before finishing him off with a dryer. The turbo type of hair dryer is best, as they are very much more powerful than the normal type of hand dryer, but make sure that you do not have the heat too high. You should brush the coat with your pin brush the way you wish it to lie all the time you are using the dryer; otherwise it may well blow the hair up the wrong way. Make sure that he is thoroughly dry, finishing off with a light spray from a coat conditioner to put a nice shine on his coat. Of course, if it should happen to be a warm sunny day, the dog can be left to dry in the garden after he has been given a good brush as previously mentioned, but if he is going to a show the next day, more care and attention are needed. This will be dealt with in more detail in the chapter on showing.

Trimming

To keep your English Setter looking his best, his coat will need tidying up fairly frequently, as it will grow long and thick on his ears and neck while his feet will become very tufty (and extremely muddy in wet weather), and on the whole he will present a rather unkempt appearance. You may prefer to have him trimmed by an expert dog beautician, but if you decide to do this yourself, you should start at about five months, just doing a little at a time to start with, so your puppy does not become bored. You will need a kitchen-type table. If it has a formica top, place a rubber mat or something similar on it so that your puppy does not slip. Make sure it is steady; if it wobbles, it may frighten him, and it is essential that he should be happy and relaxed whilst you trim him or he may keep jumping off the table. The tools required are a pair of hairdressing scissors with sharp points, a pair of thinning scissors with one blade finely serrated, a Duplex Dresser or similar item (with some spare blades) and a fairly fine comb.

If you have more than one dog, or intend to breed or show, it would be wise to invest in an electric clipper. There are many makes of clipper on the market, any you choose should be fitted with a medium blade, about a 3 mm, as you do not want to take the hair off too close. It should be stressed that a clipper should be used only on the ears and hocks and *nowhere* else. In the USA they use the clipper right over the head and down the neck, but this practice is frowned upon in this country. However, if you run the clipper down lightly, always from the top of the ear down to the tip, and from the hock downwards, always keeping the blade flat, it does save a lot of time and is much more pleasant for your dog than the constant pulling entailed in trimming the ears with a stripping implement.

I have never found a dog who objects to the buzz of an electric clipper, but with a puppy or young dog it is advisable to let him get used to the noise for a minute or two. Switch the clipper on and let it run, gradually getting it nearer the dog, then gently lay the body of the clipper against his neck or shoulder, so that he may grow accustomed to the slight vibration caused. Talk to him gently all the time, and when he seems quite happy, you can commence the clipping operation.

Start with the thinning scissors to thin out the abundance of hair that grows from under the ears, around the neck and shoulders and down the throat to the breastbone. When using thinning scissors, it is essential to comb through the hair after every two or three cuts so you can see how it is progressing or you may end up with a bare patch. Always cut into the fall of the coat (with an upward stroke) or downwards with the fall of the coat, never across or you will leave ugly scissor marks. Great care has to be

The English Setter

taken when trimming the neck under the ears as it will be found that the hair grows in several different directions. The neck and shoulders should now present a nice, smooth, elegant appearance. The next step is to remove the long silky hair that grows on the ears; this can be pulled out with the Duplex trimmer, leaving a little hair on the front edge to give a soft look. Clean out under the root of the tail, again with the thinning scissors; the tip of the tail should be trimmed to give a nice curved effect. Always hold your fingers over the bone at the tip of the tail before cutting. Next, cutting downwards, take off the tufty hair that grows from the hocks down the back feet.

Finally, trim the feet themselves. It is much easier if your dog will lie down whilst you trim his feet. My dogs generally go to sleep at this stage of the proceedings. Using your sharp-pointed scissors, cut away the excess hair from between the pads, then with your finger and thumb pull up any hair that grows between the toes and trim it off. Finish off by cutting round the edge of all the pads to give the foot a nice rounded catlike appearance.

Always remember to check the nails; some dog's nails grow much quicker than others, the rate of growth sometimes depending on whether the dog has a lot of road work or more exercise on grass. The nails should be cut as shown in the diagram. If the nails are light coloured, the quick can clearly be seen; the length to cut can be gauged accordingly on the black nails, but be very careful not to cut the quick. Not only will it bleed profusely, but it will be very painful and make the dog very apprehensive the next time you attempt to cut his nails. As with bathing, the finer points

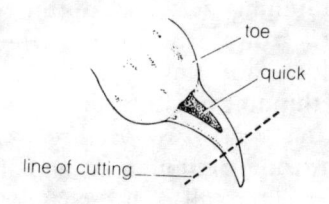

Figure 10   *Cutting a nail*

of trimming for show will be dealt with in the chapter on show preparation.

Kennels

You may decide that your dog or dogs are to be housed outside in a kennel. It is, of course, not essential to have a kennel even if you have two or three dogs as there is no doubt they prefer to be with you as members of the household. You may, however, find it useful to have a kennel in which the dogs may be put to dry if coming in wet and muddy from a walk. A kennel can be equally useful for housing bitches when in season and, of course, if you propose to go in for breeding in a fairly big way, kennelling is essential.

The kennel may be constructed of brick, breeze blocks, concrete, wood or the latest prefabricated material. Wooden kennels are probably the warmest but should always be lined with hardboard for extra insulation and the roof covered with a good quality roofing felt. It is essential that there be adequate windows to provide light and ventilation. Windows should open outwards to enable the aperture to be covered with weldmesh to prevent the dogs jumping up and putting their feet on the glass. The door should be of the stable door type, so that the top half may be left open in hot weather. Alternatively, an inner door constructed of weldmesh should be fitted so that the outer wooden door may be left open. The kennel should measure at least six feet by four feet to house two dogs comfortably. *I never recommend kennelling one English Setter on its own if at all possible.* It should be high enough for you to stand upright inside, as this makes cleaning out operations much easier than having to bend double and keep bumping your head. There should, of course, be a strong wooden floor covered with hardboard or a heavy duty linoleum. Make sure this fits tightly and does not leave any cracks, so that it may be washed over easily. The bed or sleeping bench should be raised off the floor and be the width of the kennel, i.e. four feet by two feet, to allow the dogs to stretch out, although they generally sleep curled up in a ball.

The English Setter

The choice of bedding is largely a question of personal preference and there is a wide choice: straw, wood wool, shredded paper or the new polyester pile bedding. If you decide on straw, it should be changed frequently as it becomes very dusty and should be well sprinkled with 'Cooper's Louse Powder' or some such gammexane preparation each time the bed is changed. A word of warning here – always ensure that it is wheat straw that is used for bedding as oat or barley straw will cause irritation, and never use hay as hay is a great breeding place for fleas.

Wood wool must be pulled out well as the bales are very tightly packed, so it should be 'fluffed up' frequently, otherwise it becomes very hard and lumpy.

Shredded paper is fine as it has the added advantage of being free from parasites. It too should be shaken up regularly to keep it soft and comfortable and should be changed when it gets too chopped up or dusty. Make sure that the paper is white and not shredded newspaper as the dye comes off newsprint and your dogs will never look clean. The floor of the kennel should be liberally covered with white sawdust as this will quickly absorb any wet patches. Do not ever use cedar sawdust as this is rather reddish brown in colour and when wet will badly stain a white coat.

Electricity should be supplied to your kennel or shed not only because it is useful for you to have light available but also because you may well need an infra-red heater during the very cold weather, especially if the kennel is to be used for puppies.

Runs

A run fitted to your kennel will save your garden from untold damage, especially the digging of holes in the lawn, an occupation of which English Setters appear to be particularly fond.

The run can be as large as you like according to the space available but certainly no smaller than 12 feet by 6 feet and obviously the bigger the better. It should be constructed of weldmesh or chain-link fencing at least five feet high with strong wooden posts or angle iron. The fencing and the posts should be well-sunk into the ground to prevent escape attempts by digging. A stout board six to eight inches high, fixed along the bottom and inside the wire, is a deterrent to digging.

If chain-link fencing is used, there should be two line wires running through it, one halfway up and one at the top to keep it taut as chain link tends to sag, especially when the dogs constantly jump up against it. Another sound idea is to construct one side of the run, depending on its location, with wooden fencing such as Larchlap. This will act as a windbreak as well as providing welcome shade on sunny days.

There is a wide choice of surfacing for your run such as concrete, bricks, paving slabs, pebbles (sometimes called beach), ash or grass. One can make a case for or against any of these. Concrete is the easiest to keep clean, but it is cold for a dog to lie on, so ensure that a wooden platform or pallet is situated somewhere in the run. Bricks are quick drying after rain and are not so cold as concrete, the disadvantage being that urine tends to seep into the cracks, making frequent disinfecting necessary. Ash or cinders drain very well and this surface, covered with pebbles, is very satisfactory. If grass is decided upon there should be a section of concrete or brick outside the kennel to facilitate cleaning out and a small footpath extending from this to the gate.

Fresh drinking water should always be available in the run (but always remember to empty it at night and to turn the drinking vessel upside down). A bucket wired or clipped to the fence is probably the most satisfactory – any shallow vessel will undoubtedly be used as a paddling pool or at least have the water 'pawed' out of it, a very common habit among English Setters. A strong heavy bowl of the greyhound type is good, if wedged in the corner with bricks so it cannot be tipped over, but **never** use a plastic bowl as it will be chewed in no time.

If space is available, an ideal arrangement is to have a large grass paddock where the dogs can be put to play and gallop about for periods during the day; this can be as large

The English Setter

as your space will allow, but should be at least 60 feet by 40 feet and, again, a wooden platform should be provided for the dogs to lie on should the ground be wet. The grass of the paddock should be kept mown; if it is allowed to get long and overgrown, you will find the dogs will just stick to one path through the weeds and not gallop about freely. Another sound idea is to have a concrete path about two feet wide running round inside the wire; this will not only prevent it becoming a muddy track where the dogs run up and down but will also prevent the dogs digging under the wire. If at all possible, a small kennel or shed should be sited in the paddock with its door propped open to provide access whenever desired.

6
Establishing a Line

If one intends seriously to start breeding English Setters for show, one needs to establish a line or strain, and if one is to be successful, the essential starting point is a good foundation bitch.

It may prove difficult to obtain a young adult bitch, as breeders are often loath to part with a good one, but if you do happen to find one, you must be prepared to pay a good price for such an animal. However, it is sometimes possible to obtain a bitch on breeding terms. These terms vary considerably, but generally it means that you pay about half the normal price which would be asked for such a bitch. She is then mated at a time agreed by both parties to a dog of the breeder's choice (possibly to one of the breeder's own stud dogs) and he or she would have first pick of the ensuing litter.

If you cannot find a bitch to meet your requirements, start off with a puppy. You will first of all have seen the dogs from this kennel, including of course the parents of the puppy. Having established that this is the particular strain that appeals to you, study the pedigrees of the dogs and find out all you can about any faults (and good points) that recur in the pedigrees.

Genetics is a very involved subject. Many characteristics are governed by the genes that the puppy carries, so although one looks for a puppy that has a good head, dark eyes, correct dentition, good bone and general conformation, one should always think of temperament and soundness and any hereditary defects.

The next consideration is the choice of stud dog and again one should study the pedigree carefully to ascertain that he 'ties in' with your bitch. It may be tempting to use

The English Setter

a dog that is winning at nearly every show, but unless he carries some of the same lines as your bitch, it is unlikely that they will breed true to type for several generations, although of course there is the possibility that something good may come of such a mating in the first instance. If this should be the case, the obvious course to take would be to mate back to a near relation to establish the line.

The most satisfactory method is line breeding, which means the mating of two dogs that are in some way related to one particular dog, the aim being to perpetuate his qualities, though one must be careful not to breed in anything undesirable.

Some matings in line breeding would be uncle to niece, aunt to nephew, grandfather to granddaughter, grandmother to grandson and more often, half-brother to half-sister. I would never advocate going closer than this, although years ago brother to sister, mother to son, father to daughter matings were quite common. One needs to have a deep knowledge of the breed before attempting such matings.

Below are listed some examples of line breeding:

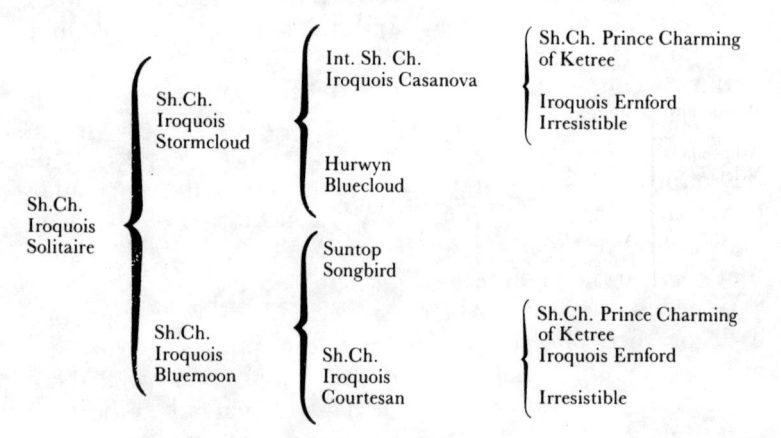

```
                                 ┌ Int. Sh. Ch.         ┌ Sh.Ch. Prince Charming
                                 │ Iroquois Casanova    │   of Ketree
                Sh.Ch.           │                      │ Iroquois Ernford
                Iroquois         │                      └ Irresistible
                Stormcloud       │
                                 │ Hurwyn
                                 └ Bluecloud
Sh.Ch.
Iroquois
Solitaire
                                 ┌ Suntop
                                 │ Songbird
                Sh.Ch.           │                      ┌ Sh.Ch. Prince Charming
                Iroquois         │ Sh.Ch.               │   of Ketree
                Bluemoon         │ Iroquois             │ Iroquois Ernford
                                 └ Courtesan            └ Irresistible
```

The above example shows that Int. Sh. Ch. Iroquois Casanova and Sh. Ch. Iroquois Courtesan were full brother and sister.

Establishing a Line

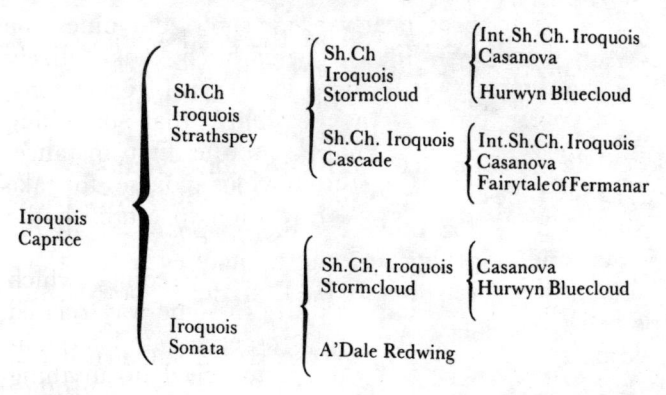

```
                        ┌ Sh.Ch          ┌ Int. Sh. Ch. Iroquois
                        │ Iroquois       │ Casanova
            ┌ Sh.Ch     │ Stormcloud     └ Hurwyn Bluecloud
            │ Iroquois  │
            │ Strathspey┤                ┌ Int.Sh.Ch. Iroquois
            │           │ Sh.Ch. Iroquois│ Casanova
Iroquois   ─┤           └ Cascade        └ Fairytale of Fermanar
Caprice     │
            │           ┌ Sh.Ch. Iroquois┌ Casanova
            │ Iroquois  │ Stormcloud     └ Hurwyn Bluecloud
            └ Sonata    │
                        └ A'Dale Redwing
```

In this example, Sh. Ch. Iroquois Strathspey and Iroquois Sonata were half-brother and sister through their sire, Sh. Ch. Iroquois Stormcloud, as were Sh. Ch. Iroquois Stormcloud and Sh. Ch. Iroquois Cascade through their sire, Int. Sh. Ch. Iroquois Casanova.

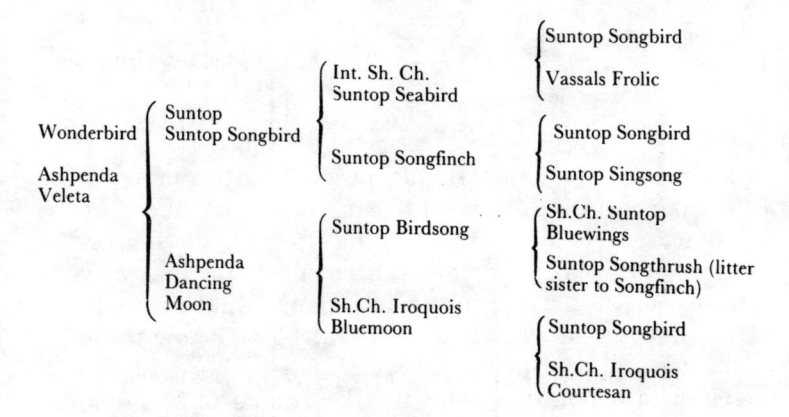

```
                         ┌ Int. Sh. Ch.    ┌ Suntop Songbird
            ┌ Suntop     │ Suntop Seabird  └ Vassals Frolic
            │ Suntop     │
Wonderbird  │ Songbird   │ Suntop Songfinch┌ Suntop Songbird
            ┤            └                 └ Suntop Singsong
Ashpenda   ─┤
Veleta      │            ┌ Suntop Birdsong ┌ Sh.Ch. Suntop Bluewings
            │ Ashpenda   │                 │ Suntop Songthrush (litter
            │ Dancing    │                 └ sister to Songfinch)
            └ Moon       │
                         │ Sh.Ch. Iroquois ┌ Suntop Songbird
                         └ Bluemoon        │ Sh.Ch. Iroquois
                                           └ Courtesan
```

This example shows very close line breeding to Suntop Songbird.

Line breeding is no doubt the best method of breeding true to type, although one must realize that faults are

75

likely to be transmitted as well as the good points one is seeking. However, with careful breeding over the generations, it is to be hoped that any inherent faults will be eradicated.

If close line breeding has been used for several generations, it is sometimes wise to bring in a fresh strain; this, of course, should be a dog that nevertheless possesses all the qualities that one is looking for, and he may even carry one line of your strain, even if it is back in the fourth or fifth generation of his pedigree.

Inbreeding is the mating of very closely related animals, such as father to daughter, mother to son, or full brother and sister and, as previously stated, is not advisable for a novice breeder, as it is necessary to have a full and deep knowledge of the breed before attempting such matings.

My foundation bitch was a result of a father to daughter mating, but her breeder, Mrs A. Broadhead, was a very knowledgeable lady. The breeding was as follows:

Iroquois Ernford Irresistible	Ernford Easter Parade	Fluellen of Fermanar
		Celandine of Haverbrack
	Ch. Ernford Evening Flight	Ernford Easter Parade
		Teal of Yaresyde

Great thought and care should be given to planning future litters, and the use of a split pedigree file can be of great assistance in enabling you to put together pedigrees of various dogs that you may want to use with that of your bitch. You will be able to see at a glance what the pedigree of the puppies of such a mating will be and how the lines of the dog and your bitch 'tie in'.

If you are not satisfied with the results of any mating go 'back to the drawing board' so to speak and think out an alternative breeding programme. The obvious aim is to breed from two animals that conform as nearly as possible to the standard, whose blood lines tie in, and who will reproduce all their good points. However, one must face the fact that no dog is without some faults, so try to avoid

Establishing a Line

mating together two animals carrying similar faults. If your bitch has a particular failing in some respect, choose a dog that is near perfect in that department.

Do not ever try to eradicate a fault such as a dipped back by mating to a dog that tends to roach his back, as the chances are that some of the puppies will take after the dam and some after the sire. By using a dog with a good level topline, you should at least get a proportion of puppies that have the correct topline. Similarly, if your bitch fails a little in head, do not choose a coarse-headed dog to counteract this fault. As previously stated, the stud dog should approach the ideal as nearly as possible.

It does not always follow that a top winning show dog becomes a successful sire. Many famous dogs through the years have failed to produce any offspring approaching anywhere near their own excellence; on the other hand, a not so famous dog may turn out to be a prepotent sire, so it is advisable to note the quality and uniformity of the puppies a dog is producing, rather than his show record. A prepotent sire generally sires puppies of good type strongly resembling himself and can often be mated to bitches of various strains. The offspring of such a sire can safely be line bred.

There is no magic formula for selecting puppies nor is it an art that can be taught, but if you look for all the points described in chapter 4 on 'Choosing a Puppy' it is to be hoped that the selected puppy will turn out to be a good one.

It is advisable to 'run on' a couple of puppies if at all possible, if you are in any doubt as to which one is the best. It is also much better from the puppies' point of view to have a companion to play with until four or five months of age, by which time the good points of one puppy will possibly surpass those of the other.

To summarize, to establish a successful kennel start with foundation stock of good type, who are sound and of good temperament.

Study the pedigrees and ascertain that your foundation stock approaches the standard as nearly as possible.

Plan your litters with care and thought and try to fix a

type. Select the resultant puppies with equal care and be prepared to dispose of as pets any that do not come up to expectations.

It is a foolish policy to keep a puppy after the age of six months, kidding yourself that it might breed you something good. If it does not turn out to be as good or better than its parents, it is not worth keeping. One has to take a firm view in this matter, or one will very soon end up with a lot of passengers, which is something that few of us can afford these days.

Colour Inheritance

When line breeding or inbreeding, thought should be given to colour inheritance. The black or blue gene is dominant, whereas the orange or lemon is recessive. Therefore, two blue beltons or tricolours mated together can produce orange or lemon beltons, as well as blues and tricolours, but two orange or lemon beltons mated together cannot produce blue or tricolour.

To take this a step further, a blue cannot be bred from parents, one of which is not blue.

Secondly, one will tend to get more blue puppies from a blue × orange or blue × blue mating.

Thirdly, a blue cannot be bred from two orange parents, but two blue parents can produce an orange or a lemon. If any orange or lemon puppies are born to two blue parents, it proves that both parents carry the recessive gene for orange or lemon belton.

There are many dogs that only throw blue or tricolour puppies, regardless of the fact that they may have been mated to an orange or lemon bitch. These 'pure for blue' dogs carry no recessive genes for orange or lemon and therefore cannot reproduce them.

Sh. Ch. Iroquois Whiteseal Silvermorn (light tricolour) was such a dog. He mated nearly 100 bitches of all colours and never produced an orange or lemon puppy. It is interesting to note that two of his sons, namely the litter brothers Sh. Ch. Iroquois Snowstorm of Sundeala and Sh. Ch. Iroquois Snowprince of Northgate, both light-blue

Establishing a Line

beltons, followed their father in being 'true for blue'; neither of these dogs ever produced an orange, though their litter sister Iroquois Snowfern, mated to a blue dog, did produce orange. A son of Sh. Ch. Iroquois Snowprince of Northgate, namely Sh. Ch. Northgate Grenadier (blue belton), produced no orange or lemon puppies even to bitches of this colour, so it would seem that this hereditary factor comes down on the male side. Sh. Ch. Iroquois Stormcloud (blue belton), sired by Int. Sh. Ch. Iroquois Casanova (orange belton) out of Hurwyn Bluecloud (blue belton), sired at least one and sometimes several orange puppies in every litter, whereas his son Sh. Ch. Iroquois Strathspey (deep-orange belton), who was out of Sh. Ch. Iroquois Cascade (orange belton), sired predominantly blues.

Similarly, eye colour, like coat colour, is either dominant or recessive. Light eyes (like the orange or lemon belton) are recessive, and two dogs with light eyes will not produce dark-eyed offspring. This is comparable to human beings where two blue-eyed parents will not produce a brown-eyed child, but where, however, two dark-eyed parents that carry the recessive gene could of course produce light eyes.

These hereditary genes do, of course, affect the entire structure of the dog, so great care must be taken when line breeding so as not to inbreed any inherent faults. A point in question is deafness, which does occur in English Setters as in any basically white-coated dog. Deafness can only occur if the gene is carried by both parents, so if any deafness is suspected in a dog's pedigree, be it two or three generations back, a wise precaution is to do a test mating, as the Irish Setter breeders did to eradicate P.R.A. (progressive retinal atrophy), often referred to as night blindness. For example, Sh. Ch. Iroquois Concerto produced several deaf puppies but, of course, never to any bitch that did not carry the gene, before we discovered that he obviously did. So I test-mated Sh. Ch. Iroquois Crescendo to a deaf bitch. There were no deaf puppies in the resultant litter, nor has he ever produced one, so he obviously does not carry the gene. This may sound a trifle complicated to the

The English Setter

novice breeder, especially if they are starting off with a couple of bitches whose pedigrees contain a 'hotch-potch' of lines. Pedigrees must be studied, and if a certain dog or bitch appears more than once in a pedigree and offspring of this dog or bitch are consistently sound and typical, try to build on this line. The aim is obviously to breed something better than the bitch herself, as there is little point in breeding if improvement is not the aim.

As previously stated, the mating of completely unrelated dogs may well throw the occasional 'flyer' in the first generation, but this standard is unlikely to be maintained over future generations unless a line or strain is established.

Countess – the first dual champion. Bred and owned by Edward Laverack

Ch. Maesydd Mustard – a leading pre-war sire, winner of 9 CCs

Ch. Ernford Evening Flight – one of the best bitches of all time

Ch. Shiplake Sincerity – a pre-war champion

Sh. Ch. Rombalds Templar – winner of 20 CCs

Noble

Ch. Shiplake Dean of Crombie, Reserve Best in Show, Crufts 1957.
Winner of 13 CCs

C. M. Cooke

Ch. Shiplake Dean of Crombie – working

C. M. Cooke

Sh. Ch. Shiplake Swift – winner of 21 CCs

Iroquois Ernford Irresistible (by Ernford Easter Parade ex Ch. Ernford Evening Flight) – foundation bitch of the Iroquois English Setters

7
Breeding

The most fascinating and rewarding aspect of dog ownership is no doubt the breeding of puppies. Having established your line (dealt with in the previous chapter), you are no doubt hopeful of breeding that elusive 'flyer', and if at first you don't succeed, try, try again. Do not ever become 'kennel blind' and think everything you breed is marvellous; be critical. A good rule to follow is never keep anything that isn't better or at least as good as the stock you already own; if you do, you are going downhill. You will find that the longer you are associated with the breed, the more of a perfectionist you will become, which is as it should be.

The greatest delight in breeding is not only selecting the puppy you wish to keep, rearing and training it up to the time you can try it out in the show ring, but also providing someone else, especially a novice, with a good one to show. I personally get just as much thrill in seeing another person win with one of my dogs as I do when winning myself. Of course, no one can be absolutely sure how a puppy will turn out; it would be foolish to say 'This one is a top class show puppy' – much wiser to say 'This puppy looks promising'. An almost discarded little runt can turn out to be the best. For example, Sh. Ch. Iroquois Strathspey weighed 5½ ounces at birth and was hand-reared, so do not despair of the little weakling; with patience and dedication miracles can happen.

Whilst it is most gratifying to see a dog that one has bred go on to win major awards, it must be said that many people go in for breeding with the sole idea of making money. To anyone who thinks breeding is an easy way to make a quick profit, it would be wise to forget it. One must take into account the stud fee, veterinary surgeon's fees, extra food for the bitch, food for the puppies, light, heat and, of course, your own time. As the puppies near saleable age, one has to consider the cost of registration, vaccination and insurance. However, having taken into account all these items, with good luck and good management a litter of puppies should at least pay their way, if not make you a small profit, depending on the size of the litter. However, do not expect vast profits.

The In-Season Bitch

The time of a bitch's first season can vary tremendously, but most bitches come in season for the first time between eight and twelve months, though occasionally it can be as late as fifteen months. The cycle is generally thought to be six-monthly, but it is much more usual for an interval of eight or nine months to elapse between seasons. The best time to mate your bitch is on her second or third season, which may be at any time between fifteen months and two years of age. It is evident that young bitches whelp far easier than older ones, so it is wise not to leave it too late.

The first sign of a season is a swelling of the vulva and a slight colourless discharge; this may last several days. She will also frequently pass water. After a day or two the discharge will become bloodstained, and it is when this commences that one should consider it to be the first day of her season. She must be watched carefully during this period as she may try to escape and seek a mate, and you may well have the local Romeos visiting you. Anti-mate sprays are available at pet shops, and these, if sprayed round the doorways and gates, help to discourage such visitors. However, if you own an experienced stud dog, these sprays are of little use as they come to associate the smell (generally oil of citronella) with a bitch in season. Dosing the bitch with Veterinary Amplex tablets is a more satisfactory course of action. If you are proposing to mate the bitch, you should stop the tablets forty-eight hours before the proposed service.

The correct day for mating varies from bitch to bitch,

Breeding

from the tenth day of showing colour to the fifteenth. One can not lay down any hard and fast rule, some bitches 'standing' earlier and some later, but the twelfth day is when most bitches are mated. A daily watch should be kept on the bitch as a good guide to her readiness for mating is when the discharge loses its bright red colour and turns more pinky; she will also flick her tail from side to side when touched with the hand around the area of the vulva and the base of the tail. By the third week of the season the discharge should have almost dried up and the vulva returned to normal. The season should not last more than twenty-one days, but it is advisable to leave her a couple of days more, then give her a bath to rid her of any lingering odours before taking her out again.

Misalliance

If by any chance you have been careless enough to let your in-season bitch escape, or perhaps not noticed a stray dog in the garden, remember it can take but a few minutes for a mismating to occur. This can happen any time during her season, although she is at the height of her season during the second week, and extra special precautions should be taken during this time. Should you suspect that any misalliance has taken place (you will find that she will be wet on her back where the dog has jumped on her) or indeed catch her in the act, the most sensible course is to get her to your veterinary surgeon to administer an injection within twenty-four hours of the event. This injection will have the effect of starting her season off again, and although she will have no puppies from the misalliance, do not run away with the idea that you can then mate her to a dog of your choice, as this induced season is an entirely false one and nothing will come of any mating.

Many people have a completely erroneous idea that if a bitch does get 'mismated' and has a cross-bred litter, this will affect any subsequent litters she may produce. This is utter nonsense. However, there is no doubt that dual conception can take place, so even if she has been mated to the desired dog and a few days later she manages to get herself mated to another dog, she may conceive as a result of either or both of these matings. I once knew of an English Setter bitch that was mated to the desired dog and on her way home from the mating was given a run. She promptly disappeared into some bushes and was found 'tied' to a black Labrador Retriever. The resultant litter were four apparently normal English Setter puppies and two jet-black, which rather proves the point. Another case was a litter of so-called English Springer Spaniels that were brought to me to have their tails docked. The instant I saw eight black puppies, I told the owner that these were not pure Springers and that the bitch must have got herself 'mismated'. She was quite incredulous and informed me that the bitch had been taken to be mated to a well-known dog. However, on close questioning it transpired that the bitch had been left in the garden after she had been mated to the Springer dog, so one presumed that the 'proper' mating had not taken and that she had conceived to the 'mystery' second mating. Great care must be taken throughout a bitch's season and nothing left to chance.

Mating

The choice of stud dog will have been selected in advance and the owner approached. They should then be notified immediately your bitch comes in season, i.e. the first day of showing colour, so that a suitable day for mating can be arranged. Do not leave it until the last minute before informing the owner of the stud dog that you require his services on a certain day as he may be quite heavily booked, especially if he is a popular stud and producing numerous winners.

The bitch must, of course, be taken to the dog; one could not expect the owner of a popular stud dog to take him to visit bitches all over the country. In these days of easy travel via motorways, this is generally no problem. However, if it is utterly impossible for you to take the bitch for mating, she can be sent by train. If this is the case, make sure that she travels in a roomy travelling box (never send her uncrated) and that the box is comfortable and well ventilated. Ensure

Breeding

that the owner of the stud dog knows exactly what train she is travelling on and particularly the time of arrival. You should request that she be kept overnight and returned the following day after the mating, again making sure which train she will be travelling on and the time of arrival so that you may be there to meet her.

Having booked the day and the time to take your bitch for mating, ensure that you arrive on time, as the stud dog will not have been fed if expecting a bitch and the owner will not appreciate it if you arrive hours late. On arrival, the bitch should be allowed to relieve herself, she should then be introduced to the dog, both being kept on leads at this stage. If the bitch appears at all 'flirty' and courts the dog, he can be released, but keep the bitch on the lead at all times as she may well resent the dog's advances and try to snap at him; this may not be due to ill-temper or mean she is not ready to be mated, but more likely that she is frightened, so whilst holding her firmly, soothe her with gentle words. Be sure to have a strong leather collar on her and stand in front of her, holding her very firmly. She may well try and snap at you or the stud dog. If she persists in this snapping, the safest thing is to tie her muzzle. I find a nylon stocking or crêpe bandage ideal for this purpose. It should be tied around the jaws, crossed underneath and then secured fairly tightly behind the ears. Once the mating has been effected and the dog turned, this can be removed. A smear of vaseline on the finger, gently inserted into the vaginal passage, often assists penetration by the dog, especially if it is a maiden bitch.

Another problem that may crop up is the height of the bitch. If she is very tall the dog may have some difficulty reaching her. If this is the case, it is advisable to give him some form of platform to stand on so that the bitch is on a lower level than he (a thick coconut doormat is often sufficient). If she is a very small bitch, it is she who may have to stand on a slightly higher level. The owner of the stud dog will no doubt assist the dog by placing two fingers round the bitch's vulva and guiding the dog into the correct position. The dog will be quite used to being handled. A dog that will only mate bitches if left to his own devices is most unsatisfactory, and if left alone, injury to either party might result.

When the 'tie' is effected, the dog may well try to jump off quickly, but it is better just to lift his front legs off the bitch so as to relieve her of his weight and allow them to stand side by side for five or ten minutes, after which you can allow him to lift one hindleg over and stand back to back. The 'tie' itself may last only a few minutes or anything up to an hour, though between 15 and 30 minutes is most usual. Be prepared to stay with the two during the tie. If left alone, injury may be incurred, as previously mentioned. Once the mating has been completed, the bitch should be removed at once and put somewhere to rest quietly and the dog left to tidy himself up. He should then be wiped down under his tummy and hindlegs, especially around the genitals, with a solution of weak disinfectant, before returning to his kennel mates.

A final word in respect of mating is that the fee you pay is for the service of the dog and in no way does this guarantee puppies. Should it be the case that the bitch has no puppies, breeders will generally offer you a further service free of charge, but it should be understood that this is in no way obligatory.

Pregnancy

During the first few weeks of pregnancy, the bitch should be treated quite normally and given plenty of exercise to keep her in good hard muscular condition, which will be of assistance to her when whelping time arrives. Three weeks, and no later after mating, she should be wormed. All puppies have worms, but worming your in-whelp bitch will prevent them being heavily infested. From the end of the fifth week her food should be increased. She should be given plenty of high-protein foods such as eggs, milk, fish, meat and, of course, extra vitamins, especially calcium. By the sixth week she should show if she is in whelp, the signs being a slight enlargement and pinkness of the teats and an enlarged abdomen. She may develop a voracious appetite or become very pernickety. Bitches vary in their

Breeding

MATED JANUARY	DUE TO WHELP MARCH	MATED FEBRUARY	DUE TO WHELP APRIL	MATED MARCH	DUE TO WHELP MAY	MATED APRIL	DUE TO WHELP JUNE	MATED MAY	DUE TO WHELP JULY	MATED JUNE	DUE TO WHELP AUGUST	MATED JULY	DUE TO WHELP SEPTEMBER	MATED AUGUST	DUE TO WHELP OCTOBER	MATED SEPTEMBER	DUE TO WHELP NOVEMBER	MATED OCTOBER	DUE TO WHELP DECEMBER	MATED NOVEMBER	DUE TO WHELP JANUARY	MATED DECEMBER	DUE TO WHELP FEBRUARY
1	5	1	5	1	3	1	3	1	3	1	3	1	2	1	3	1	3	1	3	1	3	1	2
2	6	2	6	2	4	2	4	2	4	2	4	2	3	2	4	2	4	2	4	2	4	2	3
3	7	3	7	3	5	3	5	3	5	3	5	3	4	3	5	3	5	3	5	3	5	3	4
4	8	4	8	4	6	4	6	4	6	4	6	4	5	4	6	4	6	4	6	4	6	4	5
5	9	5	9	5	7	5	7	5	7	5	7	5	6	5	7	5	7	5	7	5	7	5	6
6	10	6	10	6	8	6	8	6	8	6	8	6	7	6	8	6	8	6	8	6	8	6	7
7	11	7	11	7	9	7	9	7	9	7	9	7	8	7	9	7	9	7	9	7	9	7	8
8	12	8	12	8	10	8	10	8	10	8	10	8	9	8	10	8	10	8	10	8	10	8	9
9	13	9	13	9	11	9	11	9	11	9	11	9	10	9	11	9	11	9	11	9	11	9	10
10	14	10	14	10	12	10	12	10	12	10	12	10	11	10	12	10	12	10	12	10	12	10	11
11	15	11	15	11	13	11	13	11	13	11	13	11	12	11	13	11	13	11	13	11	13	11	12
12	16	12	16	12	14	12	14	12	14	12	14	12	13	12	14	12	14	12	14	12	14	12	13
13	17	13	17	13	15	13	15	13	15	13	15	13	14	13	15	13	15	13	15	13	15	13	14
14	18	14	18	14	16	14	16	14	16	14	16	14	15	14	16	14	16	14	16	14	16	14	15
15	19	15	19	15	17	15	17	15	17	15	17	15	16	15	17	15	17	15	17	15	17	15	16
16	20	16	20	16	18	16	18	16	18	16	18	16	17	16	18	16	18	16	18	16	18	16	17
17	21	17	21	17	19	17	19	17	19	17	19	17	18	17	19	17	19	17	19	17	19	17	18
18	22	18	22	18	20	18	20	18	20	18	20	18	19	18	20	18	20	18	20	18	20	18	19
19	23	19	23	19	21	19	21	19	21	19	21	19	20	19	21	19	21	19	21	19	21	19	20
20	24	20	24	20	22	20	22	20	22	20	22	20	21	20	22	20	22	20	22	20	22	20	21
21	25	21	25	21	23	21	23	21	23	21	23	21	22	21	23	21	23	21	23	21	23	21	22
22	26	22	26	22	24	22	24	22	24	22	24	22	23	22	24	22	24	22	24	22	24	22	23
23	27	23	27	23	25	23	25	23	25	23	25	23	24	23	25	23	25	23	25	23	25	23	24
24	28	24	28	24	26	24	26	24	26	24	26	24	25	24	26	24	26	24	26	24	26	24	25
25	29	25	29	25	27	25	27	25	27	25	27	25	26	25	27	25	27	25	27	25	27	25	26
26	30	26	30	26	28	26	28	26	28	26	28	26	27	26	28	26	28	26	28	26	28	26	27
27	31	27	May 1	27	29	27	29	27	29	27	29	27	28	27	29	27	29	27	29	27	29	27	28
28	Apl 1	28	2	28	30	28	30	28	30	28	30	28	29	28	30	28	30	28	30	28	30	28	Mar 1
29	2	29	3	29	31	29	July 1	29	31	29	31	29	30	29	31	29	Dec 1	29	31	29	Feb 1	29	2
30	3	—	—	30	June 1	30	2	30	Aug 1	30	Sept 1	30	1	30	Nov 1	30	2	30	Jan 1	30	—	30	3
31	4	—	—	31	2	—	—	31	2	—	—	31	—	31	2	—	—	31	2	—	—	31	4

Figure 11   *Gestation table showing when a bitch is due to whelp*

87

The English Setter

behaviour tremendously but whichever, the order of the day is little and often rather than one or two big meals. The emphasis should be on quality of food and not quantity.

During the last two weeks of her pregnancy, avoid over-exercise. It is wise just to let her potter about and take what exercise she desires. The normal gestation period is 63 days, but be prepared from the 58th day onwards (see Figure 11). English Setters seldom go full time and even more seldom overtime, so if she has not whelped by the 65th day, consult your veterinary surgeon, who should in any case have been forewarned of the event. A week before she is due to whelp she should be introduced to her whelping quarters.

Many people prefer their bitch to whelp indoors where it is far easier to keep an eye on her. Wherever you decide, it should be warm, dry and draughtproof. The

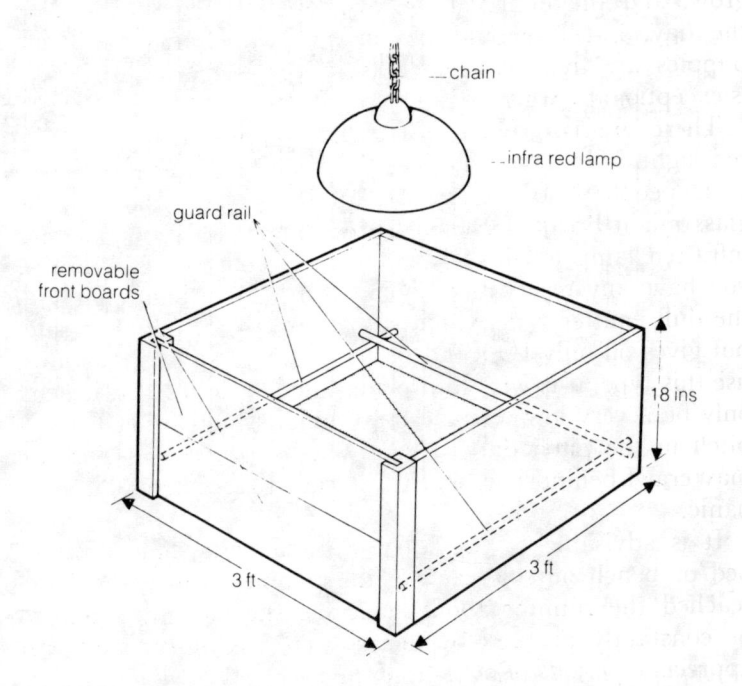

Figure 12 *Whelping bed*

Breeding

whelping box should be roomy enough for the bitch to stretch out, at least three feet square, with the sides and back being no less than 18 inches high to ensure it is free from draughts. The front should have removable boards so that the puppies can be kept confined in the early stages and the boards removed to allow them to clamber in and out of the box as they grow. A rail should be fitted round the inside of the box about four inches from the floor and the same distance from the sides as a safety precaution, to prevent the bitch trapping a puppy behind her back against the side of the box when she lies down.

It is essential to have an infra-red lamp suspended over the box; newborn puppies need to be kept very warm and the temperature should certainly never drop below 70°F. The lamp should be suspended three feet over the whelping box. This height can be increased as the puppies grow, and the light can be turned off for periods during the day, but it should be turned on at night until the puppies are five or size weeks of age unless the weather is exceptionally warm.

There are two types of infra-red lamps available. The red light bulb gives off light and heat. There are, however, people who are nervous of using these in case the glass might break. I hasten to add I have used this form of infra-red lamp for 40 years with no problems. If, however, you have any reservations about this type of lamp, there is the dull emitter type which is, of course, 100 per cent safe, but gives off only heat and no light. If you should decide to use this type, it is wise to provide some form of light; it need only be a very low-wattage bulb, but I would never leave a bitch in the pitch dark with a new-born litter, as puppies may crawl behind her, and if she cannot see them, she may panic.

It is advisable to provide the bitch with some form of bed or bench out of reach of the puppies when they have reached the running-about stage, as she will not want to be constantly plagued by her boisterous children and will appreciate periods of peace and quiet.

Whelping

The bitch will generally give several signs of entering the first state of whelping. She will become restless, constantly getting up and down, digging or scratching up her bed, accompanied by fits of panting. During the last 24 hours or so before whelping starts, her temperature will drop from normal to as low as 98°F; this drop in temperature is the surest guide that whelping is imminent.

Now is the time to prepare for the confinement. Have everything ready so that there is no last-minute panic. Remove any blankets or bedding from the whelping box and replace them with several layers of clean newspaper. You will need a plentiful supply of newspapers to replace those in the box as they become soiled during the whelping. You will also need several towels, a sterilized pair of scissors, some strong thread, a set of scales, a bowl of weak disinfectant and some cotton wool. Have a notepad handy to record the times of the puppies' birth and any other data you may wish to keep, including the weight of each puppy. Should it be necessary to call out your veterinary surgeon at any time during the whelping, he will require this information. You should have a strong cardboard box with the front cut down, into which the newly born puppies can be placed once they are clean and dry. Place it near to the bitch so she can see the puppies, but it will prevent her trampling on them during the actual whelping. A hot-water bottle wrapped in a piece of blanket or towel should be placed in the box for the puppies to lie on.

During the whole of the whelping period, sit quietly with her; most English Setters hate to be left alone and tend to panic but will be much more relaxed if you are nearby.

The first stage of whelping can last for an hour or two or continue for as much as 24 hours, but the puppies will not start being born until she enters the second stage. You will notice the onset of this as periodic trembling, followed by slight straining which at the onset appears as a ripple down the back. The contractions will gradually grow stronger and more frequent. The time taken for a puppy to be born varies very much; some bitches literally 'pop' them out

Breeding

after just one or two strains, whilst others may go on for up to an hour. However, if the bitch continues straining for over an hour with no results, you should call your veterinary surgeon. Similarly, there is no regular time between the birth of the puppies, sometimes one or two arriving within a five or ten minute interval of each other. The bitch may then have a rest and even a little sleep for an hour or two before starting to strain again. I have known bitches produce six to eight puppies in three or four hours, but the majority would take much longer than this to produce a litter of this size, eight to ten hours being nearer the mark. It is often difficult to be certain that the bitch has actually finished whelping, as there is usually the longest interval, sometimes of several hours, before the birth of the last puppy. Also the bitch may continue to strain from time to time after the last puppy has arrived, but this may be due to a retained afterbirth. It is then advisable to call your veterinary surgeon to administer an injection of pituitrin or oxytocin, which will cause her to expel it.

Each puppy is born in a sac or bag with an afterbirth or placenta attached to the umbilical cord. The bitch will break the sac open with her teeth, and will then eat the placenta and bite through the umbilical cord. Care should be taken to ascertain that she does not sever the cord too close to the puppy's tummy, or severe bleeding may occur. If this should happen, tie the cord with a piece of thread quickly to prevent further bleeding. Sometimes the sac is broken just before the puppy is born; the puppy will then literally float out into the world in a gush of clear fluid. Puppies are normally born head first, though it is quite common for them to be born the wrong way round; this is called a breech birth.

Most bitches have little problem in dealing with the delivery of their puppies, but if she appears to be at a total loss about what to do, you must intervene. It is vital that the bag containing the puppy should be broken as quickly as possible, since until this membrane is broken, the puppy cannot breathe. This should be done with your finger and thumb around the head. Using your sterilised scissors cut the umbilical cord about three inches from the puppy's

The English Setter

tummy, dispose of the afterbirth and then proceed to dry the puppy. Rub it well with a towel to stimulate the breathing, continuing until the puppy squeaks, which will mean that it has air in its lungs. Weigh the puppy; it can then be placed in the cardboard box on the hot-water bottle.

Should the bag be broken before birth, it is even more important that you act very quickly, as with these very 'wet' births the puppy may be half drowned. In this case, wrap a towel round it and holding it very firmly, head downwards, give it several firm shakes to rid the lungs of the fluid; then continue rubbing with the towel. If it still seems limp and lifeless, you can administer mouth-to-mouth resuscitation, but a word of warning here. Be sure that all the fluid has been cleared before attempting this; otherwise you may blow the fluid back into the lungs.

Puppies are quite often born without an afterbirth attached, but this need not be any cause for concern, it merely means that it has parted prior to birth; the retained afterbirth will usually be passed later. If not, you must call the vet.

Offer the bitch a drink of warm milk and glucose from time to time or, if she refuses this, water. She may wish to go out and relieve herself some time during the whelping. Take this opportunity to remove any soiled paper and replace it with clean, always making sure it is several layers thick for her comfort and to prevent the bed itself from getting wet.

When you have ascertained that the bitch has finished whelping, you should give her a drink of egg and milk or a baked egg custard, and allow her to settle down to rest. You can then put all the puppies to the milk bar, though the first born or older ones will no doubt have already had a little feed. It is as well to get them all feeding together; you can then see if any are getting pushed out or need a little assistance. You can often help a small or backward puppy by holding it on to the teat until it is strong enough to hang on itself. Failing this, supplementary feeding may be necessary; we will deal with this under the section on 'Rearing Puppies' (page 94).

After Whelping

The bitch will continue to have a vaginal discharge for some time after whelping. This discharge is, to begin with, dark green in colour, but this should quickly cease and turn red and may continue in lessening degrees for up to two weeks. It is advisable on the first day after whelping, when you take her out to relieve herself, to wash her down, as her tail and breeches will have become very soiled with the whelping. Have a bucket or bowl of warm water with a few drops of mild disinfectant added and a soft cloth. Wash her down thoroughly, then rub her dry with a clean towel and finish off by combing through the feathering to make sure there are no knots. The last is most important as puppies can easily 'hang' themselves by getting their heads through a loop of knotted feathering. The washing may have to be repeated for a few days depending on how heavy the discharge is. By keeping her clean, you will be able to tell exactly the extent of the loss. Should this become abnormally heavy and the blood bright red (it is usually quite dark), she may be starting to haemorrhage. This can occur any time during the first week after whelping. If this is the case, you should contact your veterinary surgeon without delay to administer Vitamin K (a blood-clotting agent). If the haemorrhage is not stopped, a hysterectomy may be necessary.

If the bitch is not losing heavily and is keeping herself clean, the papers in the whelping bed can be replaced by a Vetbed, which will be more comfortable both for the mother and the puppies. This bed should be changed and washed daily to start with and every few days thereafter or as it becomes soiled.

The bitch should be kept on a light diet for the first 48 hours: fish, chicken, rabbit, mixed with a little boiled rice, eggs, milk, and as much water as she will drink to help induce her milk supply. She should have three or four meals a day and as she returns to her normal diet, her meat and biscuit may well need to be increased if she is not to lose condition. Be sure to continue with her vitamins, especially calcium.

During the first week, make a daily examination of the bitch's teats to make sure the milk is being drawn off them all, and none are getting hot, hard or lumpy. If this should be the case, hot fomentations will help to take the inflammation down and the milk, which will appear thick and 'cheesy', should be drawn off with the finger and thumb. This treatment should be continued two or three times a day until the milk runs clearly. It is essential to persevere with this treatment or mastitis will ensue and the bitch will run a high temperature and appear very off-colour. Your veterinary surgeon must be called to administer antibiotics if this should happen.

A careful watch must be kept on all the puppies to make sure they are all doing well. A well-fed, warm, contented puppy will be peaceful, making little or no noise when it is not feeding. If a puppy constantly cries or wails, it is either hungry, cold or has tummy ache. Have a feeding bottle handy, check that the temperature in the whelping box is warm enough and be ready to administer a dose of gripe water. Puppies should be round and chubby, with thick necks and nice round tummies. If any appear long and scrawny, it probably means that they are not getting their fair share at the milk bar, so you should supervise the feeding to ensure all get their share.

Rearing Puppies

An English Setter bitch should cope quite easily with a litter of seven or eight puppies. However, should there be more than this number or if there are any small or backward ones, you should be prepared to supplement the feeding. There are numerous brands of powdered milk on the market to choose from. I personally always use full cream baby milk mixed to the following proportions: one scoop to one ounce boiled water and one scoop glucose. This mixture must be poured through a fine strainer or sieve, or it may block the teat on the bottle. I use a normal baby's bottle and a teat with a medium-size hole. I have found that with a large hole the milk comes through too fast for a very young puppy, whereas a small hole makes it much too hard for them to suck, and they get tired before they have taken enough. Equally good, if not better than powdered milk, is goat's milk as of course it requires no mixing or straining and is always consistent in strength. It also has the added bonus of being freezable so you may purchase a quantity at a time and store it.

When the puppies are four days old, the dew claws should be removed. These extra claws not only look unsightly, they serve no useful purpose and are liable to get torn at exercise in adult life. It is advisable to get a breeder to do this simple operation with your first litter. If you assist and watch carefully, you can easily undertake the task yourself in future. Always remove the bitch, as she may become perturbed. Have a sterilized pair of sharp scissors, some cotton buds and some Kwik-stop or permanganate of potash. The scissors should be held flat against the inside of the puppy's leg (it is much easier if someone holds the puppy for you) and the dew claw cut off together with the piece of flesh to which it is attached. Dip the cotton bud in the Kwik-stop and dab it on the cut. There should be no bleeding, the whole operation taking just a matter of minutes. The bitch can then be returned to lick and comfort the puppies.

Weaning should commence at three weeks. The puppies will still be getting a plentiful supply of milk from mother, so it is best to start them off with a little meat. Buy best quality fine ground mince. This should be rolled into little meat balls about the size of a hazelnut, one ball for each puppy. Start by putting a little in the puppies' mouths, and they will soon get the hang of it; in fact, once they have got the taste of meat, they will eat it in no time. After they have mastered the art of this, try putting the mince in a flat dish, pour some warm tasty gravy over it so that it is fairly sloppy and get them lapping this. (Make sure they are all still getting an adequate quantity.)

Now you can start them on a milk feed. Mix up some baby cereal or baby rusks with warm milk sweetened with glucose, again made fairly sloppy so that it is easy for them to lap.

When the puppies are on solid food, they should have

their first worming. This should be repeated in 10 to 14 days and again at eight weeks just before they go off to their new homes.

By the time the puppies are five weeks old they should be settled into a routine feeding of two milk feeds and two meat meals, to which can be added some soaked fine biscuit meal or Weetabix. Vitamins such as Vitapet or Stress should always be added to one of the meat meals. The feeding should now be as follows; the quantities given are for each puppy:

8 a.m.: ¼ pint of warm sweetened milk with baby cereal, rusks or Readybrek.
12 noon: 2 ounces of mince with a similar quantity of fine biscuit meal soaked in Oxo gravy or meat stock. Add vitamins.
4 p.m.: Repeat 12 noon feed omitting vitamins.
8 p.m.: Repeat morning milk feed.

The bitch will not want to be with the puppies during the day from five weeks onwards but should be with them at night for another week. By six weeks she should be taken away from the puppies altogether, though it is advisable to let her in with the puppies for just five minutes night and morning for a few more days to rid her of the last of her milk. Check her milk glands daily to ascertain that she has dried up satisfactorily. Now that the mother is not feeding them at all, it is advisable to give them a milk drink mid-afternoon between the two meat meals and to make the 8 p.m. feed rather later, say 10 p.m.

Should the weather not be too cold or wet, the kennel door can be left open from time to time during the day so that the puppies can run in and out, but make sure they go in for periods of rest and do not lie about on cold concrete or wet grass.

The food should naturally be increased as the puppies grow, and they may be given something hard to chew such as baked bread, biscuits or a marrow bone. They should also have plenty of things to play with; the hard rubber bones or toys are fine. Avoid the soft type of rubber toy as these get chewed up very quickly. I find an old pair of socks

Breeding

or the sleeves of an old jumper knotted firmly a cheap and very acceptable plaything.

When the time arrives for selling the puppies, vet your prospective buyers with great care. As previously mentioned, English Setters are not the easiest dogs to cope with, and the new owner needs to be fairly dedicated to the breed. If the new owner has very young children, make sure they will not be allowed to pull the puppy about and tease it unduly. Never sell a puppy to anybody who goes out to work all day. Apart from the miserable life the puppy would lead shut up in a house or garage all day, the poor thing would probably bark or cry all day and chew things up and soon become a candidate for re-homing. Try as far as possible to ensure that the right people get the right puppy. Explain what owning an English Setter entails, how it does need regular grooming and exercise and lots and lots of love. It is not just a decorative ornament.

The pedigree, registration certificate, diet sheet and insurance should also be handed over at the time of purchase, and impress upon the new owner the importance of vaccinations and yearly boosters. If the puppy is to be sent by train or air, make sure the travelling box is of ample size and well ventilated, and that the person concerned is informed of the times of the train or flight so that the puppy may be met at the other end of his journey. If he is to go abroad, you will need a Veterinary Certificate of Health issued within a few days of his departure and an export permit which is obtainable from the Ministry of Agriculture and Fisheries.

8
Shows and Showing

Should you decide to embark on a show career for your dog, you would be well advised to visit one or two shows as a spectator. You will then see for yourself what is entailed. Watch the English Setters being judged, note how the dogs are trimmed and presented and see how their owners handle them.

Dog shows are the shop window of the dog world, a meeting place for all breeders and people from all walks of life who are interested in dogs. At the bigger shows you will find numerous stalls selling all sorts of dog requisites, numerous dog foods and a large selection of books and collectors' items, so you will be able to spend an interesting as well as instructive day.

The weekly papers *Dog World* and *Our Dogs*, devoted to dogs and dogdom, are available at the larger newsagents, and you will find all forthcoming shows advertised in them. They will list the breeds catered for and the name, address and telephone number of the Secretary, to whom application should be made for a schedule.

There are numerous types of shows to choose from:

1) **Exemption Shows** These shows are generally run in conjunction with local fetes or gymkhanas. A dog does not have to be registered at the Kennel Club to compete in this type of show, hence the name, and awards won are not recorded at the Kennel Club. They are held purely for fun and generally have classes such as 'The dog with the most appealing eyes' or 'The dog with the waggiest tail'.

2) **Sanction Shows** The smallest type of show for which

dogs must have been registered with the Kennel Club and duly transferred from their breeder's name to their present owner. These shows do not generally have classes for separate breeds but cater for 'any variety' classes, which means they are open to dogs of all breeds. No dog who has won five or more first prizes in post-graduate or higher classes is eligible for entry at a sanction show and of course any Challenge Certificate winner or champion is excluded.

3) **Limited Shows** This type of show is confined to members of the society who are running the show and limited to dogs who have not won a Challenge Certificate. These shows sometimes schedule classes for breeds popular in that particular area, but like the sanction shows they consist mainly of 'any variety' classes.

4) **Open Shows** These shows are open to anyone. You need not be a member of the Society to enter, and any dog (providing it is registered with the Kennel Club) may be exhibited. They vary widely in size, most of them scheduling numerous breeds, with between four and six classes for each breed, as well as the usual 'any variety' classes. This type of show is very popular, and you will undoubtedly find one which is held in or near your locality. They are ideal for starting off a young dog, as the competition is not quite so stiff as one encounters at a championship show. A win in a breed class at an open show counts one point towards a Junior Warrant (wins in 'any variety' classes do not count). For details of a Junior Warrant, see under Kennel Club Titles on page 101.

5) **Championship Shows** These are the biggest and most important type of show, often held over a period of three or four days, each day being allocated to one or more of the different groups (dogs are divided into the following groups by the Kennel Club: Working, Utility, Terriers, Hounds, Toys, Gundogs). Nearly every

The English Setter

breed, with the exception of a few rare breeds, has classes scheduled, which may number anything from 12 to over 20. The sexes are always divided at championship shows, and the classes allocated to English Setters are generally much as follows:

Minor puppy dog	Minor puppy bitch
Puppy dog	Puppy bitch
Junior dog	Junior bitch
Novice dog	Novice bitch
Graduate dog	Graduate bitch
Post-graduate dog	Post-graduate bitch
Limit dog	Limit bitch
Open dog	Open bitch

As well as all the general championship shows up and down the country, there are all the breed specialist clubs which hold championship and open shows solely for English Setters. At all championship shows Kennel Club Challenge Certificates are awarded to the best of each sex. Three Challenge Certificates won under three different judges give the dog the title of Show Champion.

Kennel Club Titles

Challenge Certificates These are awarded to the best of each sex at a championship show, providing the judge is clearly of the opinion that the exhibit concerned is of such outstanding merit as to be worthy of the title of Champion.

Show Champion This title is given to a dog who has won three or more Challenge Certificates under three different judges. This is a title solely for gundogs as a gundog cannot become a champion until he has won a Show Gundog Working Certificate or an award at a recognized field trial. Prior to 1958 no such title existed; consequently, no matter how many Challenge Certificates a dog had won, if he had not obtained a Gundog Working Certificate, he was not permitted to use any title.

Shows and Showing

Champion A dog who has won three Challenge Certificates under three different judges and has also won at least a Certificate of Merit at a recognized field trial or has been awarded a Show Gundog Working Certificate, one of the judges of which must be on the 'A' panel of the official list of judges, is entitled to be called a champion. No dog may run for a Show Gundog Working Certificate more than three times and not more than twice in any one field trial season.

Field Trial Champion This title is given to the winner of the Setter and Pointer Champion Stake and also to a dog which wins two first prizes at two different Field Trials in Open Stakes for Setters and Pointers in which there are no fewer than 16 runners. One of these wins must be in a stake open to all varieties of setters and pointers.

Dual Champion A title that is indeed rare these days, for the dog must be outstanding both in the field and the show ring to be a Field Trial Champion and a Show Champion.

Obedience Champion This is not a title that one associates readily with English Setters. The breeds that spring at once to mind are, of course, Border or Working Collies and German Shepherds. However, the qualification is that the dog is entitled to the title of Obedience Champion if he has won three Obedience Challenge Certificates under three different judges, although the winning of the Obedience Certificate at Crufts automatically gives the dog its title. At Crufts only dogs that have won Obedience Certificates during the previous year are eligible to compete and Obedience Certificates are not awarded to any winning dog if he has dropped more than 10 points.

Junior Warrant This is the only title or award made by the Kennel Club for which application must be made. The points needed to obtain a Junior Warrant are as follows:

> One point for a first in a breed class at an Open Show.
> Three points for a first at a Championship Show; wins in 'any variety' classes do not count.

The English Setter

25 points are required before reaching the age of 18 months to qualify.

When you have decided which show you wish to enter and have received your schedule, read this through carefully, especially the definition of the classes, to ensure that your dog is eligible for the classes you decide to enter. Don't go mad and enter him for every class for which he is eligible. Always go for the lowest class to start with; for instance, for his first show you can enter in the Novice class, which is for dogs not having won more than two first prizes. When and if he has won his way out of this class, you can progress to the higher classes. If it is an open show that has scheduled classes for English Setters, having entered the appropriate breed class you can also enter an 'any variety' class, which is good experience for you and your dog. You will also have the opportunity of showing under two different judges. No two judges think exactly the same, so even if you do not do well under one judge, you may do wel'zll under another. Never get downhearted if you do not win; your dog may not have moved or shown himself to his best advantage, and as a beginner you may not be doing him justice. Remember there is always another day, another show, and another judge to look forward to.

Show Preparation

Preparing your dog for show is as important as the show itself. He must be in good condition, not too fat or too thin, and he must be fit and muscular from his exercise and in full coat. Do not attempt to show him if he is in the process of moulting; better to stay at home until he has grown a new coat.

He will require some basic training to stand still without moving his feet or tossing his head about. The best method of doing this is to stand him for a few seconds each day after you have groomed him. Never overdo this by trying to make him stand too long or too often, or he will become bored. The essence of a good show dog is to keep him happy and enjoying it. Always praise and reward

Shows and Showing

him, and you will gradually be able to get him to stand for longer periods. It is important to ensure that he is standing comfortably and not in an unnatural stance, or he will fidget. If you can get a friend to stand him for you, it will enable you to study the stance and to pose him to his best advantage. Failing this, stand him up in front of a long mirror; you will then see him as others do.

The front legs should be straight and in line with the top of the shoulder or withers, with the feet three or four inches apart, whilst the hind legs should be slightly spread and placed somewhat backward of square. He should have a nice, level topline, and if the hind legs are placed too far back it will cause him to have a sloping topline like that of an Irish Setter or German Shepherd, which in an English Setter is incorrect.

The head should be held gently, not in a vice-like grip, round his muzzle; you will find he has a very convenient V-shaped bone under his muzzle which is, in fact, the lower jaw bone. If you place your fingers in this V you will be able to hold his head quite comfortably and coax him to stretch his neck forwards which will show his neck and shoulders off to advantage. If he pulls his head back, let go and start again; it is useless to struggle. Do not hold his head too high as it will spoil the topline and make him appear short in neck even if he is not. Hold the tail by the tip to form a straight line with the back; this should also be done with a light touch.

He must learn to move as he will have to in the show ring, that is, in a straight line at a trot and on a slack lead. Any tendency to break into a gallop, jump about or pull sideways must be checked firmly with the word 'No'. Start again, and when he does it correctly, praise him and reward him with a titbit. He may also tend to put his head down to sniff at the ground, especially if being moved on grass. This habit can be discouraged by slipping the show lead up behind his ears and lightly holding his head up. Alternatively, have something very tasty such as baked liver in your pocket; show him a piece of this, and when he moves correctly with his head up, reward him with it. A dog who holds his head high and strides across the ring proudly is said to be a good showman, and such a dog is likely to catch the judge's eye. Although, of course, he must move soundly as well as having good conformation and quality, an extra dash of style and personality often just carries the day. In most districts the local Canine Society holds ringcraft classes. These are well worth attending for the novice exhibitor and not only for the social side. It will accustom your dog to having other dogs around him and to being handled by strangers, and it will be most beneficial to you in learning to handle and move your dog correctly.

Trimming

We covered basic trimming in Chapter 5, but for preparation for showing a little more care and attention are needed. You cannot make a dog look his best in five minutes, so make a start a few weeks before the proposed show. Trim the ears, neck and shoulders, hocks and feet as previously described, then go all over his coat and, using your thinning scissors, thin out any excessively wavy coat or any that tends to stick up the wrong way, until it is all lying flat. Daily brushing is important at this stage and twice a week treat the coat with a liberal application of Royal Coatalin, which is a wonderful aid to growing, improving and toning up the texture.

Three or four days before the show, go over him again, paying special attention to any little bits of hair that may have grown and are sticking up where they should not; check that his ears and teeth are clean and that his nails do not require cutting.

The day before the show he should be bathed, again paying special attention to brushing his coat the way it should lie all the time you are drying him. When he is quite dry (and not before), spray his coat with a conditioner to add that extra bit of shine; then pin a large bath towel round him to keep the coat flat and lying the correct way. If you allow a dog to lie down whilst his coat is still damp, it will curl up the wrong way, and you will get an ugly shelf which will be impossible to rectify the next day.

Shows and Showing

The Show Day

You will need a fairly large holdall to take the various items you will require which will be as follows:

> Bench blanket. Your dog may be on the bench for seven or eight hours, so he needs to be made comfortable.
> Benching chain and leather collar (not of the slip variety) and a show lead.
> A bowl for food or drink.
> Brushes and combs.
> Towel and tin of talcum powder in case he gets wet and needs drying.
> Bottle of water or milk.
> Jar containing his favourite titbits (baked, diced liver is best) for rewarding him.
> First aid kit. This should include TCP, Savlon, wound powder, bandage and cotton wool.

You should also take a thermos flask for your own drink and some sandwiches. Make sure you have your ring clip for your ring number, a biro to mark your catalogue and, most important, your exhibitor's pass. This will have been sent to you on receipt of your entry, and it is as well to put it in your show bag as soon as it arrives.

This may seem a lot to have with you, but all these things are essential for the welfare of your dog. Try to keep your personal belongings down to a minimum as you may well find that you are faced with quite a long walk from the car park to the showground. Even so, it is often advisable to take a light folding chair with you, or you may also be faced with a long day on your feet.

Allow yourself plenty of time to get to the show, including a stop *en route* to exercise him if it is a long trip, and plan to arrive at least an hour in advance of your class. It can take considerable time to park the car, get into the show, find your bench, give your dog a drink and then a final groom to ensure he is looking his best, before going to find the ring in which your breed is being judged.

The English Setter

Thought should be given to your own clothes. High-heeled shoes and tight skirts are not suitable. You may have to run over rough grass. Nor should you wear anything too frilly or fussy; a neat loose skirt, slacks or a trouser suit are ideal. Do not let your dog down, having spent so much time on his preparation, by turning up in old jeans.

Your show lead should be as narrow and unobtrusive as possible. Choose a colour that blends in with the colour of your dog's coat and always make sure your leads are kept in nice, clean condition. The leather ones should be treated with saddle soap to retain a supple feel; the nylon type should be washed after each using. If you are not in one of the first classes, sit at the ringside and watch how the more experienced exhibitors are handling their dogs and standing them to their best advantage. Go and collect your own dog in plenty of time for your own class; be sure to have a small brush or comb in your pocket as well as your titbits. Never rush your dog from the benches straight into the ring, or he cannot be expected to give of his best.

The ring steward will give you your number, which should be attached to your ring clip, and will tell you where the judge wishes the dogs to stand. Listen carefully to whatever the steward or the judge tells you, but make no attempt to enter into any conversation with the judge.

Do not let your dog annoy or impede other exhibitors, and do try and keep your composure as any sign of nerves will certainly be passed on to your dog. It is hoped that the outcome of all your preparations and hard work result in a prize card, but win or lose, you will have learned a lot and hopefully enjoyed it all.

After the show, check your bench carefully when packing up to leave to be sure you have left nothing behind. Give your dog a drink and a walk before setting off on the journey home.

Judging

When you have been exhibiting for some time and have perhaps established yourself as a breeder of some repute and have consistently shown good stock, you may well be offered a judging appointment. This in an honour and should not be undertaken unless you are satisfied that you can do a competent job. It is wise to act as a ring steward several times before taking on a judging appointment. Most canine societies are always glad of stewards, and this task will enable you to work closely with a judge, compare his decisions with your own and give you an idea of the general organization of a class of exhibits. A good steward can be of great assistance to a judge. Once you have built up some experience, a judging appointment can be accepted.

As a judge, be decisive and have the courage of your own convictions. There is nothing worse than a judge who keeps the dogs standing for an interminable time whilst he wanders up and down trying to make up his mind.

Do not judge a dog on his past reputation. He is there for *your* opinion of him on the day, and everything must be assessed – head, mouth, eye colour, expression, body construction, coat, movement and presentation – as you are trying to pick the dog that approaches most nearly to the ideal.

Handle the dogs gently when going over them. A heavy-handed or rough judge can soon put a young dog off showing. Be patient with novice exhibitors. Be clear and concise when telling them what you require them to do, i.e. move in a triangle or straight up and down.

When you have gone over and moved all the dogs in the class, call into the centre of the ring those you have selected, at the same time thanking the less fortunate ones before dismissing them. A quick second look at your selected dogs or even moving them once again would not come amiss at this stage, before making your final decision. If you are quick and sure of yourself, the exhibitors will have confidence in you and your decision.

9
Gun-Training and Field Trials

Some show dogs can be trained, if they have natural hunting ability, but do not waste time trying to train one who does not put his nose down and hunt if there is game about. The ability to use nose, to be keen to hunt and to have natural quartering sense is inherited, and these are the first essentials if you wish to gun-train or trial your English Setter.

Obviously you must first instil some obedience in your potential worker – he must obey the command 'No' and be taught always to stop what he is doing on this command. Almost as essential is coming back to his trainer as soon as called. No dog is of any use for work if he is out of control, for he can put up birds far too far ahead of the guns. If he naturally 'freezes' when setting game, well and good, but one who flushes without command is useless, for invariably he will then chase the game over the horizon!

So train the dog in complete obedience to your commands before you ever teach him the rudiments of gunwork. Then, having ensured that he will be reasonably responsive to the recall (either by whistle or voice) and the command 'No', take him out and introduce him to game scents, preferably on ground which has plenty of cover to hold birds.

It is advisable, particularly if the dog is a keen hunter and appears to range wide, to put him on a thin nylon check cord and to work him in a zigzag course across the field, encouraging him to quarter the ground. Always work the dog up wind, so that he is helped to scent the game. Let him hunt to the left of you; then when you want him to

Gun-Training and Field Trials

turn, call his name and blow your whistle, and if he should not respond, pull sharply on the check cord, repeating the whistle call. Give a hand signal to direct him to the right, having praised him, and repeat the process. He will soon associate the whistle with the need to turn. Generally if the youngster sees you change course, he will do so also, so this helps with the lesson of quartering.

The next thing to learn is dropping on command. This should really be taught away from the training field, as it is much easier to teach away from interesting scents. However, if you have failed to do this before the gun-training as such starts, then, when he is quartering the ground and passing in front of the handler, a quick movement should be made to face the dog, your right hand waved in front of the dog, and the command 'drop' given, together with a blast on the whistle. Should the dog not obey the signals, he should be held and placed in a sitting position, and the command should be given again. As with the other lessons, this exercise will need to be repeated several times before being perfected. By keeping the dog in the sitting position and walking away from him, then calling him up to you, he will soon become steady to the 'drop', which you should be able to make him do from a distance if game is flushed when he is not on point.

The time has now come to perfect his 'set'. It is instinctive in this breed to acknowledge game in this way, but the dog must be taught steadiness, i.e. not to flush or chase. When the dog is on point, the trainer should slip a leash on him, so that, when the bird is flushed and shot, he is restrained from chasing. Nothing is more annoying than to have a dog disappear into the distance in hot pursuit of game!

The dog should be accustomed to gunfire long before he is taken out to the shooting field, so he should have a gun fired at a distance from him, while his attention is fixed on something interesting. Gradually the distance is reduced until the dog is quite happy with very close gunshot.

If it is not possible to train the dog to hunt on ground known to contain game, then it is possible to place birds in pens in various covers and work him into the wind up to them, ensuring that he quarters the ground thoroughly.

The English Setter

Show Gundog Working Certificate

A gundog which has won a challenge certificate may be entered for a Show Gundog Working Certificate at a field trial meeting for its breed, providing the society holding the meeting is recognized for the championship for its breed, and that one of the judges is on the 'A' panel of the official list of judges.

A dog may not run for a Show Gundog Working Certificate more than three times and may not run more than twice in any one field trial season.

Before awarding such a certificate, the judges must test the dog in the line. He must make sure that the dog is not gun-shy and is off the leash during gunfire. In the case of a pointer or setter, the judge must make sure that the dog hunts and points.

Field Trials Field trials are run for different breeds, and those for English Setters are mostly run jointly with pointers and all setter breeds. The requirements for these breeds are that the dogs shall quarter the ground with pace and style in search of game birds, working correctly to the wind, and that they shall be steady to fur and feather, that they drop to shot and, where necessary, to falling game.

When a dog has worked ground, and game birds have been left, then the dog will be eliminated, and if a dog leaves the point and continues hunting he will also be discarded. It is an eliminating fault if the dog barks or whines.

The dogs are run in pairs and handlers must walk within a reasonable distance of one another, as though shooting together.

Before gaining any award the dog must have been shot over and proved not to be gun-shy.

Field Trial Regulations

Open Stakes This is a stake in which dogs have the opportunity of gaining a qualification (whole or part) for the Field Trial Champion title or for entry in the championships or

Champion Stake for its breed, in which entry is open to all dogs of a specified breed or breeds. It may be limited to a prescribed number of runners, in which case these shall be decided by a draw, where preference must be given to previous performances.

All-Aged A stake which is open to all dogs of a specified breed or breeds without restriction as to their age but which may be restricted by any other conditions which may be determined by the society.

Novice A stake which is confined to dogs which have not gained the following awards – First or Second or Third in Open Stakes or First or Second or Third in other stakes.

Puppy A stake confined to dogs whelped not earlier than 1 January of the year preceding the date of the field trial. (For such Stakes run in January a dog which was a puppy in the previous year shall be deemed to be still a puppy.)

Title of Field Trial Champion (a) The winner of the Pointer and Setter Championship Stake (b) A dog which wins two first prizes at two different field trials in Open Stakes for Pointers and Setters, in which there are no fewer than 16 runners. One of these wins must be in a stake open to pointers and all breeds of setters.

10
English Setters Overseas

There have been English Setters exported to numerous countries throughout the world over the years, but in many cases they have gone as pets or purely as gundogs, and show dogs are so few in number that they have not warranted recognition by the Kennel Clubs of these countries.

I have collected as much information as possible about English Setters overseas and thank the people concerned for their help in providing this information.

Australia

English Setters were mentioned as being in Australia as long ago as 1897, and the first English Setter recorded was a bitch by the name of Venus who was bred by a former Premier of Tasmania, the Hon. Thomas Reibey. He imported a dog name Jack, who had some fame at the time. Perhaps this Thomas Reibey inherited his sporting ways from his well-known grandmother; as Mary Haydock in Lancashire, she had been transported to the colonies after having, as a teenager in England, stolen a horse and ridden it dressed as a boy. For this crime she was sent to Australia for life. In years to come she was to marry a Thomas Reibey, and they were to produce a long line of successful descendants.

Many years on, in 1919, Mr Sam Shallard inherited three fine English Setters from a Mr Don Wells of Hobart to add to his already excellent 'Elmo' stock. After the Great War in 1924 Mr Shallard imported from the British Primley Kennels. Later, in the '30s, Maesydd stock were imported by Truro Kennels in Bendigo, Victoria. Irish Ch. Banner

Sh. Ch. Silbury Soames of Madavale. Bred by Mr and Mrs P. Gardiner-Swann and owned by Mrs A. Williams

C. M. Cooke

Int. Sh. Ch. Iroquois Casanova – winner of a gundog group and a great sire

C. M. Cooke

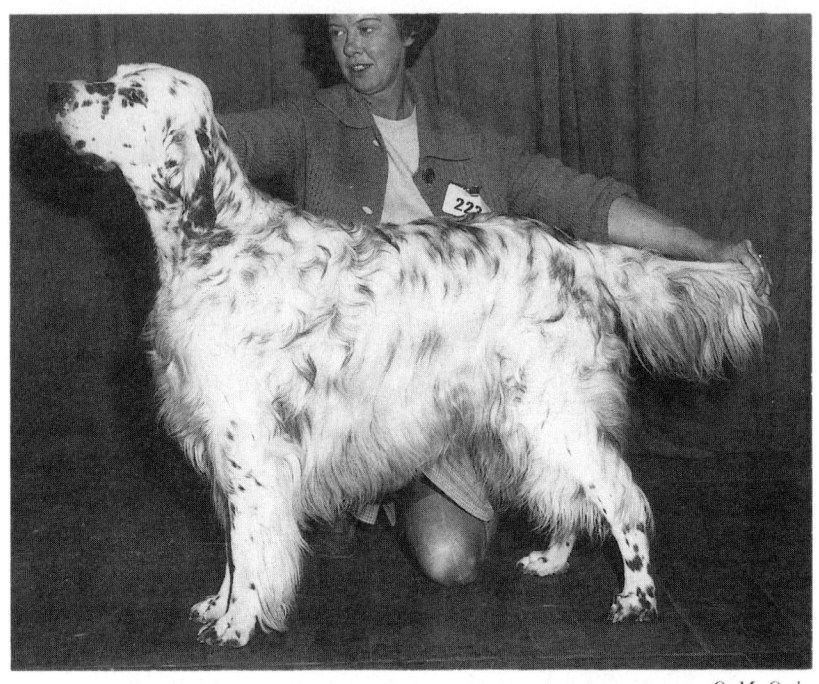

Sh. Ch. Iroquois Stormcloud, Casanova's son and another great showdog and sire

Sh. Ch. Bournehouse Enchantress, winner of 28 CCs and 16 Reserve CCs

Diane Pearce
Sh. Ch. Bournehouse Dancing Master, Best in Show, Supreme Champion at Crufts 1977

Sh. Ch. Hurwyn Wigeon, winner of 28 CCs

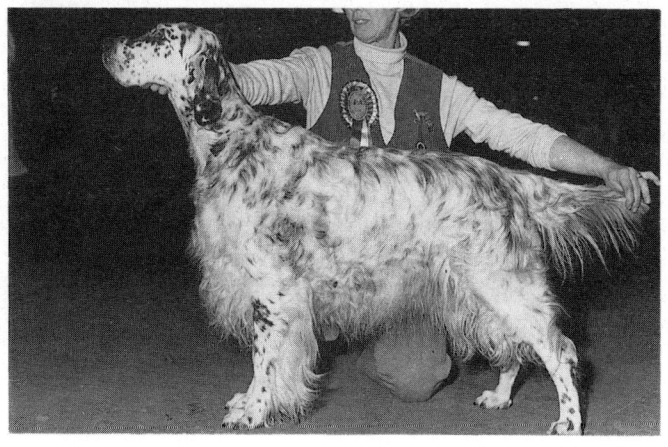

Diane Pearce
Sh. Ch. Iroquois Rainbow – Reserve Gundog Group, Crufts 1972

Frank Garwood

Sh. Ch. Iroquois Whiteseal Silvermorn – a great sire and winner of 10 CCs. He was Best of Breed at Crufts in 1973 and 1975

Sh. Ch. Snowstorm of Upperwood – a big winner of the '80s

of Crombie was imported by Pat Smith (now Mrs Nance-Kivell) of the Manoah prefix, and Mr Graham Head of the Granada prefix imported Ch. Rombalds Cardinal. The de Groen family of New South Wales brought New Zealand lines into the country. Ch. Weeley Fortune Hunter was to sire some excellent stock and so commenced the well-known Australian Kennels, Whernside, based in Melbourne. In the hands of the late Millie and Alex Price this kennel was to dominate the English Setter scene through the '60s, and it is now in the control of their daughter, Mrs Judy Price Williams.

Gilberton Kennels imported Ch. Silver Lining of Ide, a 17 C.C.s winner in the UK and well-known to all. This dog was originally purchased from Shiplake along with a sister, Silver Cloud; these two were to contribute much to the breed. More Shiplake were imported by Whernside, Shiplake Shimmer, Sungold and Sungleam. Sungold and Sungleam carried British, US and Canadian lines, and these were to have a powerful effect on the breed in Australia. Wenella Kennels also were well-established by this time by the Tormey family of Melbourne. Meanwhile, a Dr Massey of the Coddington prefix in New South Wales imported Trodgers Lucerne, who when mated to Shiplake Shimmer helped to strengthen the British type again. Suntop imports were to arrive in the mid-60s for Mr J. Sherri of Sydney; Seabird, Royal Sunglint and Noyna Rockette were all champions. There is a move today in Australia to mix the breeding of the past with the new US blood, mainly to gain a better ring temperament and coat quality. It remains to be seen whether such a move will improve the breed in the future. There are many breeders who are trying to keep the British type and lines.

Judging and Championships

In Australia judging is to the British KC Standard, but with so much of the judging carried out by non-specialists in the breed, the top bzwinners generally carry a coat of exceptional quality and also have an exceptional show personality.

The English Setter

Many good specimens may be missed because these essentials are lacking. This does not help the breed and does not bear comparison with the US and British system of choosing specialist judges for all breed shows. The breed entries in Australia are usually too small to warrant separate judging, except in the case of speciality shows. In many cases, where we have some of the larger entries for royal shows, the judging may be carried out by a judge not qualified to judge the breed in that person's country of origin.

Challenge Certificates are awarded on the basis of a point system. The winner of the best of each sex is awarded six points plus one point for each animal of the same sex over six months of age who is defeated. A maximum of 25 points may be awarded. The same point system is used to determine the points to be awarded to a Best in Group winner, but never more than 25 at any one show. One hundred points makes a champion. Very few judges refuse challenges, even if there is only one of the breed at an all breeds championship show. With very little competition, a champion can be made up with ease. In New South Wales there can be as many as 350 championship shows held in any one year. In the state of South Australia, however, there would be only approximately 90 championship shows held, and since it has a smaller population, this makes more sense. This state holds many parades and open shows which give aspiring judges many opportunities to practise the art of dog judging. Victoria has a similar show pattern, and it is to be hoped that New South Wales will one day follow this system. Victoria and New South Wales both have an English Setter Breed Club and hold championship shows. There are royal shows held in each state and territory once every year. The Royal Melbourne Show in Victoria carries the greatest prestige. Receiving the largest entry, it takes place over a period of 11 days, and the Sydney Royal Show taking place over 10 days is next in order of prestige.

Over the past 10 years the kennels that have made their mark in Victoria are Ambershah, Eireannmada (importing three from Iroquois), Glendalyn, Kingsett, Tarquin, Temeraire and Tyburn (importing from Engsett). In South Australia Arongay and Bridgewood have led the way, the latter with the Whernside/Fildmor (Mrs Milford) combination. The Holding family brought to Australia a Hurwyn bitch. In New South Wales Blackwall Kennels imported three Suntops; Brownlea imported a Hurwyn, and in 1987 Brookfire imported a Tragus dog. Avvier Kennels contributed with Victorian stock, and Nottingham have imported in recent years from Engsett and Mindenday Kennels. In Western Australia, Amhurst imported two Suntops, and Sheranne imported from Engsett. Glenelbert brought out a Willowsett, and Mr and Mrs Paul Marshal came to Australia with a Silbury dog. In Queensland two Kennels contributed some breeding; these are Mossett and Waratah. Pamploma have made their mark in Tasmania.

The umbrella ruling body is the Australian National Kennel Council (ANKC), based in Melbourne. There are eight canine controls, one for each state and territory, listed below. It is hoped by many that in future years the ANKC may be able to adopt the sensible system of one control as in the United States and the United Kingdom.

Canine Controls

The Ras Kennel Control,
PO Box 74, Paddington, NSW 2021
Tel. (02) 331 9111

The Canine Control Council (Queensland),
Exhibition Grounds, Gregory Terrace,
Fortitude Valley, Queensland 4006
Tel. (07) 852 1831

The South Australian Canine Association Inc,
25 Holland Street, Thebarton,
South Australia 5031
Tel. (08) 43 7899

The Kennel Control Council,
Royal Showgrounds, Epsom Road,
Ascot Vale, Victoria 3032
Tel. (03) 376 3733

The English Setter

The Canine Association of Western Australia,
PO Box 301, Gosnells,
Western Australia 6110
Tel. (09) 455 1188

The North Australian Canine Association,
PO Box 37521, Winnellie, 5789,
Darwin, Northern Territory
Tel. (089) 84 3570

Canberra Kennel Association,
PO Box 815, Dickson, ACT 2602
Tel. (062) 41 4404

The Kennel Control of Tasmania
Box 116, PO Glenorchy,
Tasmania 7010
Tel. (002) 72 9443

Canada

English Setters have been recognized and shown in Canada since the inception of the Canadian Kennel Club in 1888; the first registration was of an English Setter bitch. Interest was maintained in the breed for both field work and show on a limited basis until the 1980s when the breed received prominence as Group and Best in Show winners. Am. and Can. Ch. Sunstone's Sturdy Patch won Top Sporting Dog for 1980, Am. and Can. Ch. Storybook's Marauder won Top Dog (all bzbreeds) in Canada in 1981, and Am. and Can. Ch. Fantail's Sunshine Man won Top Dog in 1982, also bettering the record for the number of dogs defeated in any year.

Due to Canada's vast land area and the nearness to the United States, breeding and showing activities tend to concentrate on north-south corridors rather than being nationwide. Often individual animals will only be in direct ring competition with each other in a national specialty show, designed to be a gathering of dogs, breeders and owners for competition, comparison and education. The national show is held in different areas of the country each year, in order to allow as many exhibitors to attend as possible.

Prominent Canadian breeders include John and Frances Mills (Maidstone Kennels), James and Marie Tinlin (Burgandyrun), Robert and Irene Gilham (Brandyrun), Don and Kathy Hawker (Maldawn) and Nairne Sittig (Kelvingrove). Sally Vertulia, a life member of The English Setter Club of Canada and of the Canadian Kennel Club, is still breeding at Wragge Run a line from her foundation bitch, Am. and Can. Ch. Ludars Ludette. Rick and Honey Glendinning (Fantail) are the breeders of the top-winning Canadian show dog of all time.

Wayne and Diana Rodgers (Briarsette) maintain a line of winning field trial English Setters. Other Canadians, including Greg and Isabelle Stewart and Norma Allen, have imported American-born dogs and won numerous awards in the show ring.

Conformation showing takes place on two levels, at sanction matches and at championship shows. Matches are held for dogs of at least three months of age, who have not obtained five championship points, as a training for dogs, handlers and judges. No official record is kept of wins at this level. These shows may be entered at the ringside.

A dog must receive a minimum of 10 championship points under at least three different judges at 'championship' or 'Recognized' shows to be awarded the title of Champion and to be allowed to enter 'specials only' competition. Classes are divided according to sex and age: Junior Puppy (six to nine months), Senior Puppy (nine to 12 months) plus Bred-by-Exhibitor, Canadian-Bred and Open. Dogs placed first in each class compete for the titles of Winners Dog and Winners Bitch, Reserve Winners Dog and Reserve Winners Bitch! The dog and bitch awarded Winners titles will receive championship points to a maximum of five each show, according to a scale based on the number of dogs directly or indirectly defeated on the day. Winners Dog and Winners Bitch then enter competition with the champions of record entered in the Specials Only

The English Setter

Class to compete for Best of Breed and Best of Opposite Sex. A Best of Winners is also awarded to either the Winners Dog or Winners Bitch. Additional championship points might be added to the number already won (still keeping to the limit of five in any one show) by placing Best of Breed, Best of Opposite Sex or Best of Winners. The animals awarded Best of Breed and Best Puppy in Breed go on to compete at the group level. Placings are given to fourth place in group and a Best Puppy in Group award is made. The first-place finishers in each of the seven groups advance to Best in Show competition.

The 'Specials' compete for 'Top Dog' honours as well as awards at the individual shows; one point is awarded to each dog for all dogs defeated directly or indirectly in Best of Breed, Best of Group, and Best of Show competition. The dog in each breed that amasses the greatest number of points in the show year—January to December—is declared Top Dog of its breed and is presented with a certificate from *Dogs in Canada* magazine. There are awards for Top Sporting Dog and Top Dog—All Breeds. A special issue of *Dogs in Canada* is reserved to honour the Top Dogs, with the best All Breed honoured as the cover dog of the month. This high honour has been won twice by English Setters.

Recent major show wins include the Canadian Centennial Show, with English Setters judged by breeder Robert Gilham. Best of Breed went to Ch. Shadren's Stellar Serenade (Ch. Guys N' Dolls Boss Tweed ex Ch. Ebtide's Sweet Senerade), bred and owned by Jim Knudsen. This female was also Best of Opposite Sex at the English Setter Club of Canada National Specialty held the day before, also in Toronto, under breeder Honey Glendinning. Best of Breed at the Specialty was Am. and Can. Ch. Carob Keystone Cabot (Ch. Rogresta Lord Deveraux ex Gold Rush Alliance), bred by Carol Ulrich in the USA and owned by Carol Ulrich, R. Gleason and J. Borchardt.

Following the Centennial Show the London Kennel Club held their show in honour of the Canadian Kennel Club's Centennial; the CKC was formed as a result of a meeting held in London in 1888. Best of Breed at this show was Am.

and Can. Ch. Kelyric California Sun (Am. Ch. Colthouse Count Basil ex Am. Ch. Gold Rush Gold Digger Blues), bred by Dennis and Karen Kennedy and owned by Lise Trottier.

Canadian Official Breed Standard for the Setter (English)

Origin and Purpose: Although even our oldest authorities are not entirely in agreement as to the origin of this breed, it is generally agreed that the earliest English Setter had its origins in some of the older of the land spaniels that originated in Spain, or were the product of careful crosses of the Spanish Pointer, the large water spaniel, and the Springer Spaniel. By careful cultivation, the English Setter attained a high degree of proficiency in finding and pointing game in open country. The major credit for the development of the modern English Setter goes to two men of the middle 1800s, Mr Edward Laverack and Mr R.L. Purcell Llewellin.

General Appearance: An elegant, stylish and symmetrical gundog of good substance that projects a heritage of well-developed hunting instinct and bird sense. He suggests the ideal blend of strength and stamina combined with grace and style. Flat-coated with feathering of adequate length. Gaiting freely and smoothly with long forward reach and strong rear drive. Males should be decidedly masculine in appearance without coarseness. Females should be decidedly feminine in appearance without over-refinement.

Temperament: A true gentleman by nature, he has a kind and gentle expression and is constantly expressing a willingness to please with an affectionate, happy, and friendly attitude. He has a lovable, mild disposition and is without fear or viciousness.

Size: Dogs about 25 inches (63 centimetres); bitches about 24 inches (61 centimetres) in height, when measured at the withers. Symmetry: the balance of all parts is to be

The English Setter

considered. Symmetrical dogs will have level toplines or will be slightly higher at the shoulders than at the hips. They will have well-angulated fore and rear-quarters that work smoothly together. Balance, harmony of proportion, elegance, grace and an appearance of quality, substance and endurance to be looked for.

Coat: The coat should be flat without curl or woolliness. The dog should be adequately feathered on the ears, the chest, the belly, the underside of the thighs, the back of all legs and on the tail. The feathering, however, should not be so excessive that it hides the true lines and movement of the dog, nor should it affect the dog's appearance or function as a sporting dog.

Colour: Black-and-white, orange-and-white, liver-and-white, lemon-and-white, white, black-white-and-tan, orange belton, liver belton, lemon belton, tricolour belton, blue belton. The belton markings may vary in degree from clear, distinctive flecking to roan shading. Dogs without heavy patches of colour on the body but flecked all over preferred.

Head: The entire head should be in proportion to the body. It should be long and lean with a well-defined stop. Skull: the skull when viewed from above should be oval. The skull should be of medium width, without coarseness, and should be only slightly wider at the base than at the brows. The widest part of the oval should be at the ear set. There should be a moderately defined occipital protruberance. The length of the skull from the occiput to the stop should be equal in length to the muzzle. Muzzle: brick-shaped, and the width to be in harmony with the skull. It should be level from the eyes to the tip of the nose. When viewed from the side, the line of the top of the muzzle should be parallel to the line of the top of the skull. A dish face or a Roman nose is objectionable. The flews should be square and pendant. The nose to be black or dark brown in colour except in white, orange-and-white, lemon-and-white or liver-and-white, where it may be lighter. The nostrils should be wide apart and large in the openings. Foreface: the skeletal structure under the eyes should be well-chiselled with no suggestion of fullness. The cheeks, like the side of the muzzle, should present a smooth, clean-cut appearance. Jaws: the lower jaw should extend in length so that the lower teeth form a close scissors-bite with the upper teeth, the inner surface of the upper teeth in contact with the outer surface of the lower teeth when the jaws are closed. An even bite is not objectionable. The teeth should be strongly developed with upright incisors. Full dentition is desirable. Eyes: the eyes should be bright, and the expression mild and intelligent. The iris should be brown, the darker the better. The eyelid rims should be fully pigmented. Ears: the ears should be set low and well back. Preferably, the set should be even with the eye level. When relaxed the ears should be carried close to the head. They should be of moderate length, slightly rounded at the ends, and covered with long silky hair.

Neck: The neck should be rather long, muscular and lean. The neck should be slightly arched at the chest, and cleancut where it joins the head at the base of the skull. The neck should be larger and very muscular toward the shoulders, and the base of the neck should flow smoothly into the shoulders. The neck should not be too throaty or pendulous and should be graceful in appearance.

Shoulder: The shoulder blade (scapula) should be laid back to approach the ideal angle of 45 degrees from the vertical. The upper foreleg (humerus) should be equal in length to the shoulder blade (scapula) and form an angle of 90 degrees with the shoulder blade. This enables the elbow to be placed directly under the back edge of the shoulder blade and brings the heel pad directly under the pivot point of the shoulder, thus giving a maximum length of stride. The shoulders should be fairly close together at the tips, but with sufficient width between the blades to allow the dog easily to lower its head to the ground. The shoulder blades should lie flat and meld smoothly with the contours of the body. This structure permits perfect freedom of action for the forelegs.

The English Setter

Forelegs: When seen standing from the front or side, the forelegs or arms (radius and ulna) should be straight and parallel. The elbows should have no tendency to turn either in or out when standing or gaiting. The upper arms (humerus) should be flat and muscular. The bone should be fully developed and muscles hard and devoid of flabbiness. The pastern should be short, strong and nearly round, with the slope from the pastern joint to the foot deviating very slightly forward from the perpendicular.

Feet: The feet should be closely set and strong, pads well-developed and tough; toes well-arched and protected with short, thick hair.

Forechest: The forechest should be well-developed and the point of the sternum (prosternum) should project about ¾–1 inch, (2–3 centimetres) in front of the point of the shoulders.

Rib Cage: The chest should be deep, but not so wide or round as to interfere with the action of the forelegs. The keel should be deep enough to reach the level of the elbow. The ribs should be long, springing gradually to the middle of the body, then tapering as they approach the end of the thoracic cavity.

Topline: The topline of the body of the dog in motion or standing should appear to be level or to slope very slightly from the withers to the tail, forming a graceful outline of medium length without sway or drop. The tail should continue as a smooth, level extension of the topline.

Back: The back, the area between the withers and the loin, should be straight and strong at its junction with the loin area. The loins should be strong, moderate in length, slightly arched, but not to the extent of being roached or wheel-backed, and only discernible to the touch.

Hips: The slope and length of the croup determines the tail set, and the degree of slope should not be more than 15 degrees from the horizontal for an ideal tail set. The hip bones should be wide apart with the hips nicely rounded and blending smoothly into the hind legs. The pelvis should slope at an angle of 30 degrees from the horizontal. The pelvis governs the forward reach and the backward follow-through of the hind legs, and this angle permits a maximum length of stride. Again, for efficiency and balance, the length of the pelvis and the upper thigh (femur) should be equal, and they in turn should be equal in length to the shoulder blade (scapula) and upper arm (humerus).

Hind Legs: The upper thigh (femur) should be well developed and muscular. The well-developed lower thigh (tibia/fibula) in a well-balanced Setter should be slightly longer than the upper thigh (femur) and should become wide and flat as it approaches the hock joint. The knee joint (stifle) should be well bent and strong. The pastern from the hock joint to the foot should be short, strong, and nearly round and perpendicular when viewed from the side. The hind legs, when seen from the rear, should be straight and parallel to each other and the hock joints should have no tendency to turn in or out either at rest or when the dog is in motion.

Tail: The tail should be straight and taper to a fine point with only sufficient length to reach the hock joint or less. The feather must be straight and silky, hanging loosely in a fringe and tapering to a point when the tail is raised. There must be no bushiness. The tail should not curl sideways or curl above the level of the back (sickle tail).

Gait: An effortless graceful movement demonstrating rapidity and endurance while covering the ground efficiently. There must be a long forward reach and strong rear drive with a lively tail and a proud head carriage. Head may be carried slightly lower when moving to allow for greater reach of the forelegs. The back of the dog should remain strong, firm and level when in motion. When moving at a trot, the properly balanced dog will

The English Setter

have a tendency to converge toward a line representing the centre of gravity.

Faults:

1. Any deviation from the affectionate, happy, friendly attitude which makes the English Setter the true gentleman of the dog world.
2. Undershot or overshot bite.
3. Any dog over 27 inches (69 centimetres) or under 24 inches (61 centimetres). Any bitch over 26 inches (66 centimetres) or under 23 inches (58 centimetres).
4. Incorrect tail set or tail carriage, such as a steep drop from the hips to the tail set or a tail which curls sideways or curls above the level of the back (sickle tail).
5. Incorrect soft or woolly coat texture that will not protect the dog while working in the field.
6. Light eyes. Loose eyes.
7. A lack of long forward reach and strong rear drive.
8. A hackneyed, paddling gait and a rolling, stilted, or lumbering motion.
9. Flat, splayed, or long feet or feet that turn in or out.
10. Too narrow or too wide a front.
11. Barrel-like or slab-sided ribcage.
12. A down-faced or snipey muzzle.
13. Flews in excess of that required to present a square muzzle.
14. A lack of backskull.
15. Cowhocks.
16. Any deviation from a topline that is level or very slightly sloping.

Finland

The English Setter scene in Finland is much the same as the other Scandinavian countries of Norway and Sweden, where they very much favour the working or field trial type, and the breed is mainly kept for hunting, though they are also shown.

English Setters Overseas

There have been a few English dogs exported to Finland, the best known of recent times being Yeo Silver Sequin and Yeo Silver Top, bred by Mrs Lucille Sawtell, who also bred Windsong of Yeo (Suntop Birdsong ex Sh. Ch. Noyna Sunfairy) owned by Mrs Bloechliger-Gray of Switzerland. Windsong became a Monagasque Champion. Mrs Sue Wilkinson sent out the aptly named Hurwyn Flying Finn, and Mrs Lynette Bacon (Origo) exported a bitch who won two CACIBs under Swedish judges.

France

In France, English Setters are primarily gundogs and are bred for their working ability rather than for beauty.

The English standard is officially recognized, as France is a member of the F.C.I. (Fédération Cynologique Internationale) which requires all breeds to be judged to the breed standard of their land of origin. However, as the dogs are mainly of the field trial type and therefore somewhat smaller than the show English Setter, they have amended the height standard amidst great controversy. The standard now reads: height, dogs 56–62 centimetres (22½ – 24½ inches), bitches 53–60 centimetres (21 – 23 inches). There is no distinction between field trial English Setters and show English Setters.

No gundog in France can become a show champion without passing a test in a field trial and no gundog can become a field trial champion without being shown in the ring.

Germany

The following account, told to me by Frau Margaret Klemp of Berlin, is worth relating, as it would appear that this was the beginning of a line of post-war English Setters in West Germany.

In 1944, during a bombing raid over Berlin, one of the bombers suffered a direct hit; the crew all baled out,

The English Setter

including the captain who in his arms had a little English Setter bitch. They landed safely and the officer was taken prisoner and sent to a prisoner-of-war camp. The little bitch was taken to a dogs' home. A Berlin Setter fancier heard about this and took the bitch and kept her until the end of the war. She was then registered in the German Stud Book as English Setter bitch—name, Senta; estimated date of birth, February 1944; land of origin, England; pedigree, unknown. At the end of 1946 an English Setter stud dog from Denmark was located in Berlin, and Senta was mated to this dog, the result being that she became the foundation bitch of a long line. She was of field trial type, small, lightly flecked, with little feathering. Many of her offspring showed much talent in the field. Frau Klemp, whose Semper Idem affix was very well known in the early post-war years, in fact owned a niece of Senta whom she bred to her Italian dog Ch. Oddo del Brembo, and they produced many good puppies who won well both at shows and in the field, amongst them Ch. Semper Idem Davinia.

This field trial Italian type persisted for many years, but efforts have been made over the last decade to improve the type by importing English and American bloodlines. Today the field trial type are seldom shown.

There are many rules and regulations one has to comply with before breeding in Germany, and a qualification must be obtained. First the dog must be shown once, and the judge must award a minimum of 'Very good'. The judge must look at the dentition, as one is not allowed to mate two dogs with missing teeth and many of the English imports have two missing premolars. If this is the case, a dog with complete dentition must be used for the partner when mating. The judge must also look for any other faults that they might consider detrimental for breeding purposes. A potential breeding dog or bitch must also pass a simple field trial test, really just to show they are capable of hunting as setters and pointers should do and that they are not gun-shy. If this should be the case they are labelled *wesensschwach*, which is considered a grave fault, and one is not permitted to breed from such an animal. They must also be X-rayed for hip-dysplasia and a reasonable pass must be obtained. Unless a dog can pass all these tests, a pedigree will not be supplied.

There is also a regulation regarding the age of breeding dogs and bitches. Dogs must be a minimum of 18 months of age before being allowed to mate a bitch. Bitches must be two years of age before being bred and must not be bred from after nine years of age. A bitch must not have more than two litters in two years, and if she is mated on two seasons running, she must have a minimum of 12 months break before being bred again. A bitch is allowed to have five litters during her lifetime, but each kennel is restricted to three litters a year.

The German Show System

Here again there are many more restrictions in Germany than one is accustomed to in England. A dog or bitch cannot be exhibited in more than one class. There are two classes for young dogs, i.e. Youngsters, which is puppies between six and nine months of age and Youth Class, nine months to 18 months. These two classes do not compete for the Championship; they are really to give youngsters showing experience.

The earliest age at which a dog can compete for any championship is 15 months. They must have then been entered in the Open Class. To enter the Working Class the dog must have had a pass in a field trial, or some form of test where the essentials of pointing and setting are necessary. The last is the Champion Class, which as its name implies is open only to Champions.

Champion Qualifications

There are five different kinds of Champion, as follows:
1. Bundessieger: this title is awarded at an international show where the CACIB is on offer; one win at this show entitles the dog to be called Champion.
2. Europasieger: similar to the above, one win and the dog is entitled to be called Champion.

The English Setter

3. VDH Champion: the VDH is similar to our Kennel Club. They award VDH Champion to any dog or bitch that has won Excellent (first) four times at a national or international show. There must be a minimum of three different judges who have awarded the dog a VDH Champion Certificate out of the necessary four judgings.
4. Deutscher Schönheits Champion: this is the German Show Champion, to be won at national shows for setters and pointers (similar to our breed championship shows) or international shows where the CAC and CACIB are to be awarded. Three are needed for the Show Champion title and must be gained under at least two different judges. They must have been received over a period of more than one year, and the dog must also have done a working test or field trial.
5. International Schönheits Champion: as the title implies, has the same qualifications as for the Deutscher Schönheits Champion, but in more than one country.

There are 12 national shows a year and 12 international shows, where the CAC VDH CH and the CACIB can be won. The judging is to the English Standard.

The top breeders in Germany of the last decade include Mrs Lilli Ahnert, whose McElwyn Kennel has been winning for 30 years, and most of the English Setters in Germany today carry McElwyn bloodlines. Mr and Mrs Prager, whose Von Crailsheim is a big kennel, have also been breeding a long time and have produced many champions. Most others are smaller breeders who have bred two or three litters at the most, and these are 90 per cent McElwyn or Von Crailsheim bloodlines.

The top winning dogs of the late 1980s are: Fairfields Bennet, orange belton, bred in Germany by Mr and Mrs Gerzman, by Tisbury Gold Rush Ike (American import) ex Fairfields Ambra. Yosemites Alpares and Yosemites Arriba, blue belton litter brothers, bred in Germany by Mr and Mrs Brudt, by Glen Aire Morgan Hill (an orange belton American import, and himself a big winner) ex Dam of the Ranges. Fenton Bohemian, blue belton, bred in Germany by Mr Schwikardi, by Canon von der Asseburg ex Spring Fashion of Hurwyn (English import). Freddy Boy Von Fasanenbuschel, orange belton, bred in the Netherlands, now owned by Mr and Mrs Prager, by Suntop Shining Breeze (English import) ex Blue Glory of the Turning Point. The top winning bitches are: Fairfields Belle, orange belton, litter sister to Fairfields Bennet. Fenton Bumblebee, blue belton, sister to Fenton Bohemian. Liz McElwyn and Lapis McElwyn, tricolour litter sisters, bred in Germany by Mrs Ahnert, by Dash McElwyn ex Clariho Cinnamon Cookie (American import). Agatha von Schönhof, tricolour, bred in Germany by Mrs Fels, by Oldholbans Wigeon (English import) ex Trendset Fantasy (English import).

Holland and Belgium

I have grouped these two countries together as it is somewhat difficult to separate them, many Belgian-owned dogs being exhibited more in Holland than in Belgium. This is mainly due to the fact that to become a Champion in Belgium a working certificate is required, whilst in Holland it is not.

The first recorded dog shows in Holland were organized by the Dutch Society of Agriculture. These were held in Amsterdam and Rotterdam in 1874. All the setter breeds were grouped together under the title of *Engelse Langhaarige Patrijshonden* (English Longhaired Partridge Dogs).

These days the Winners Show at Amsterdam is very well known, and indeed every year parties of British visitors travel over to visit this largest of the European Shows. It was first held in 1892 when most of the English Setters entered were imports or their direct descendants, many of them by the imported dog Dick of Kippen.

It seems that the first breeder and exhibitor of English Setters in Holland was Mr G.J. Van Vliet who was credited with the first litter to be registered in the Dutch Kennel

Club Stud Book and who was the top breeder from 1875 to 1900.

During the years prior to the First World War, the leading owner was Mrs Paine-Stricker with her My Fancy Kennel; she had many first-class dogs, including Ch. Mallwyd Mumm, bred by Mr Tom Steadman.

There was naturally a lull during the war years, but in the late 1920s a bitch was imported from England by Mrs A.J. Timmermans, by name Julia of Kingstree. She was considered to be a very typical bitch and besides becoming a Champion in 1930 was an influential brood bitch. It is interesting to note that from this bitch, Mr Dan Verbaan of Natal, who then lived in Holland, acquired his now famous kennel name of Kingstree.

In 1930 the *Vereniging van Liefhebbers van de Engelse Setter* (Society of Lovers of the English Setter), hereinafter referred to as the VES, was formed and this heralded a steady stream of English imports to supplement Dutch stock.

In Belgium the emphasis was very much on the working side, and much of their stock came from such countries as France and Italy. The leading kennel of the '30s was Heathflower, the affix of C. Gips, who bred the Champion bitch Antoinette of Heathflower, by Ch. Chaplin ex Irma. The Chaplin Kennel (not to be confused with the dog who was bred in Belgium) added their affix to the litter brothers bred in 1932 by the Heathflower Kennel, namely Chaplins Charioteer of Heathflower and Chaplins Charley of Heathflower, who were by Ch. Chaplin ex Ch. Julia of Kingstree. Both received their titles in 1934. Other leading kennels were Mrs Timmermans' Abbotsford, Mrs Blaauw's Van Elandslaagte, and J. Mattemaker's Van Reesthof.

Up to the outbreak of the Second World War, these kennels imported many English dogs, among them Lorette of Fermanar, Monks Patrol, Punch of Ballymoy, Jennifer of Fermanar, Killian of St Rocco, Roco Racer and Sandra of Swo. As with other countries, breeding virtually came to a standstill during the war years, though a few shows were held and several dogs, all bred in Holland, attained their titles.

English Setters Overseas

One of the most respected owner/breeders was Mrs P.J.A. Van Leyenhorst Van de Zwan who was a member of the VES for more than 45 years. She purchased her first English Setter in 1940 and made up her first Champion, Lilly of the Valley of Beverley Hills, in 1949. Her son, Keep Heart's Archie, by Rombalds Spey, was made up in 1952; her last title holder was in 1954. She became Secretary of the VES in 1946, resigning in 1987 shortly before her death. She retained a great interest in the breed even after she stopped showing and indeed imported Suntop Royalfinch, for use at stud. She could always be relied on for help and advice, and her passing was a sad blow to all lovers of the breed as well as to the VES.

The 1950s saw the recommencement of English imports, with Archdale Foretop, imported by Mrs Timmermans, and Shiplake Goldflower, bred by Mrs J. English, by Ch. Shiplake Stonechat of Truslers out of Sh. Ch. Shiplake Shining Chance owned by Mr W. Knappers. These two bitches both gained their titles; other imports made up to champions in Holland during the '50s were Inia Boy (Sh. Ch. Ripleygae Mallory ex Wendover Gay) and Shiplake Spring Blossom (Sh. Ch. Shiplake Swift ex Sally of Radnage), bred by Mrs C. Ercolani. Three others had English bloodlines in the first generation.

Twelve dogs received their Dutch titles during the 1960s, this being the beginning of the popularity of the show-type English Setter in Belgium. Seven of these were English imports, another four having English bloodlines. The English imports were Shiplake Supersonic (Int. Sh. Ch. Ernford Highflyer ex Ch. Shiplake Daystar of Crombie); Suntop Snow Bunting (Sh. Ch. Shiplake Swift ex Suntop Spotlight of Torbol); Suntop Bluestar (Paymaster of Ketree ex Suntop Starlight) – both Snow Bunting and Bluestar were owned in Belgium; Shiplake Marygold (Sh. Ch. Shiplake Swift ex Boisdal Bogmyrtle); the litter brother and sister Boisdale Angus and Boisdale Averil (Boisdale Kestor ex Boisdale Butterpuff); and Suntop Seamew (Int. Sh. Ch.-Suntop Seabird ex Suntop Songfinch). The last four were owned by Mrs Liestert who was Dutch but whose kennel was situated in Belgium. Of the four with English bloodlines, one dog was of all-English breeding, being by Dutch Ch. Shiplake Supersonic ex Dutch Ch. Shiplake Spring Blossom; another was a bitch, Silver Song Morning Star, bred in Belgium by Fencefoot Fast Packet out of a German bitch, Breeze McElwyn, bred by Mrs Ahnert, owned by Mrs W. Augustyn-Brumsen, who was a very successful breeder/exhibitor of this era and who also made up Suntop Blue Daisy (Flatford Blue Duck ex Suntop Winterwine) and the Dutch-bred bitch, Waterwonder.

Another breeder to make her mark in the '60s was Mrs Liestert, who imported Wistful of Weaversdown as early as 1935 and made her up to a Dutch Champion in 1938. In the early '60s she established her Fantails Kennel based on Shiplake and Boisdale bloodlines. She exhibited with great success in Holland and Belgium; her first champion bearing the Fantails affix was Fantails Nightstar, others of English breeding being the litter brother and sister, Fantails Punchinello and Fantails Picture (Ch. Boisdale Angus ex Sh. Ch. Sea Fairy of Noyna), and Fantails Raff (Ch. Redtops Rompster ex Fantails Mercedes).

Redtops Rompster was imported by Mrs P. Gerster and bred by Mrs N. Treharne by Redtops Rajah ex Redtops Penycae Bronze Silk. A very influential bitch was Fantails Xenia, who was the foundation bitch of the Van de Volmolen Kennel. The last Fantails champion was Fantails April Morn, made up in 1981. However, several kennels were based on Fantails breeding, amongst them the aforementioned Van de Volmolen Kennel from Belgium of Mr and Mrs Genechten and Mrs J.D. Hygens in Holland, whose foundation bitch of her Van de Zuidwesthoek Kennel was Fantails Valeska; this bitch, mated to Fantails Twinkle, produced three Dutch Champions in Baronet, Alure and Amber Van de Zuidwesthoek, the last named being top-winning bitch in 1979 and Best in Show at the VES Club Show 1982.

Several Suntop-bred dogs were imported during the early '70s; those gaining their titles were Suntop Winterwind (Suntop Winterbird ex Sh. Ch. Suntop Bluethrush) Suntop Snow Flair (Suntop Birdsong ex Suntop Snowy Owl) and Suntop Blue Daisy. Mr Henk Wunderink from

Arnhem, hence the kennel name of Arnhemset, was very successful during the '70s with his imports, Attleford Silverbutton (Sh. Ch. Iroquois Whiteseal Silvermorn ex Attleford Silver Lining), Ashpenda The Red Witch (Sh. Ch. Ashpenda Red Robin ex Wolvershill Hester) and Monksriding Cinderella (Sh. Ch. Monksriding Ernford Flamingo ex Sh. Ch. Monksriding Baroness). Mr Wunderink also made up two home-bred Dutch Champions, both out of Ashpenda The Red Witch; these were Arnhemset Fast Baronet by Suntop Regalwings and Arnhemset Pirate Bird by Attleford Silver Button.

By the end of the '70s, owing to a gradual dwindling of imports, the choice of good stud dogs was limited, so Mr H. Sleegers, a Dutch student, decided to import a completely new strain in the form of a bitch from Canada, Leighton's Cinema Star. She gained her Dutch title in 1979. Another import followed in Culmstock Leighton Blaze, and these two bitches were the foundation of Mr Sleegers' successful Fairray Kennel of American-type English Setters. The mating of Ch. Culmstock Leighton Blaze to another American import, Prairies Peaches and Cream, produced no less than four Dutch champions; these were the dogs Fairray Charming Orange Camargue and Fairray Charming Orange Calypso, and the bitches, Fairray Charming Orange Daisy and Fairray Charming Orange Fana. At the gundog show at Hertogenbosch in 1988 where I was judging, I was pleased to award the CACIB to yet another dog of this same breeding, Fairray Gallant Orange Velvet owned by Grace Sanstra.

The American type continued to do well and was further boosted by Mr N. Lamb of the American Air Force bringing his dogs with him from America when he was posted to West Germany. In 1983 Mr Lamb's Am. Ch. Tisbury Gold Rush Orange Ike gained his Dutch title, and in 1985 his Am. and Can. Ch. Seamrog Glory Hallelujah added Dutch title to her other two. These two outstanding champions were mated together to produce another pair of Dutch Champions in Mariners Alpheus, whom Mr Lamb took back to the USA with him, and Mariners Acadia, owned by Mr and Mrs Busscher, who also owned

Ch. Fairray Dreaming Orange Ike, bred by Mr Sleegers by Am. and Dutch Ch. Tisbury Gold Rush Orange Ike out of that great brood bitch Ch. Culmstock Leighton Blaze, who produced two more title holders in the litter brother and sister, Fairray Gallant Orange Baron and Fairray Gallant Orange Glitters.

Others with American bloodlines to gain their Dutch titles in 1987 were two dogs and a bitch bred by Mrs Van Westering – Finesett Lord Fana, Finesett Bucks Fizz and Finesett Bloody Mary. Bred in America and imported by Mr M. Brown was Lynnans Hart of Gold.

Late in 1986 Mr P. Halstead, who was with the British Army stationed in West Germany, took two of his dogs out to stay with friends in Belgium. These two, the dog Northgate Sandgold of Hammoon (Northgate Copper King ex Northgate Silver Brocade) and the bitch Northgate Rhapsody of Hammoon (Sh. Ch. Iroquois Concerto ex Northgate Orange Velvet), both bred by Mrs T. Fuller, had resounding success, attaining their Dutch titles, winning 12 CACs and eight Best of Breed between them. Unfortunately, neither was bred from. However, the friends that so kindly cared for them whilst they were being campaigned, Mr and Mrs H. Kuyper of Belgium, have a very lovely blue bitch bred by Mr and Mrs Halstead in Hammoon Madrigal, by Ownways Jubilee Event ex Hammoon Charlie Girl by Sh. Ch. Iroquois Concerto. Madrigal has gained both her Dutch and Luxembourg titles, and it is hoped to mate her to a leading English stud dog to perpetuate this line.

There are English imports bearing the affixes of Valsett, Tragus, Hurwyn and Bellesett as well as the American bloodlines.

To gain the Dutch Champion title requires four CACs under at least two different judges, but at certain shows, such as the Winners Show and the Club Championship Show, the CACs are worth double. The Reserve CAC at these shows is also worth double and effectively becomes a CAC. It is also possible to count four Reserve. CACs as one CAC, the maximum permitted to count in this case being 12.

Unlike in Britain, judges in Europe are required to pass an exam before being permitted to judge. They must have a general knowledge of dogs, including anatomy and genetics, and pass a practical exam before a jury of judges and a member of the Kennel Club in which five dogs and five bitches have to be assessed, a report written on each dog and questions asked by the panel answered.

Some problems arise as the Dutch Kennel Club, being a member of the F.C.I., requires that all breeds should be judged to the breed standard of their country of origin, and, as will be appreciated, not only are there the English and American types, but in any Continental country one may find Italian, French and German types as well. To add to the confusion, the judge may well be Swiss or Spanish. The reports must be translated into Dutch and then written out in English. On the credit side, however, the Dutch breeders and exhibitors are very dedicated and devoted to the breed, so the future for English Setters in Holland and Belgium looks extremely healthy.

Ireland (Eire)

The championship shows in Eire are all one-day events, much like our bigger open shows. They are all unbenched, with no wet weather rings at the outdoor shows, so if it rains, which it so often does in Ireland, everyone is in for a soaking.

The season starts with St Patrick's Show, which is always held on 17 March; this show is the equivalent of our Crufts. All breeds are guaranteed a five-point Green Star, and this carries a qualification for Crufts. There are 22 all-breed championship shows a year, St Patrick's being the biggest indoor show, whilst Swords is the biggest outdoor show. There is an English Setter Society of Ireland and also an Irish Gundog and Field Trial Society.

The highlight of the show season is the Munster circuit held in August, which consists of four championship

The English Setter

shows held within a week. The first is Clonmel, which is followed by Killarney and Limerick and finally by Tralee.

Classification is designated by a group letter between A and H, depending on the number of classes, which range from 16 down to two. Most classes are divided according to sex, but the smaller ones include both sexes. Each group is allotted one- or two-point Green Stars, but these are decided according to the number of dogs shown on the day; absentees do not count when totalling the entry. The entries are much smaller than in England; in English Setters 30 dogs would be considered a big entry.

Field trial English Setters are shown in the same classes as their show type counterparts, though when the shooting season starts in August, little is seen of the field triallers in the show ring.

Many of the show type were originally imported from England, but most are now bred in Ireland.

All gundog breeds in Eire must pass a Working Certificate to become Irish Champions. There is no Show Champion title.

To make up an English Setter to Champion you need to have 40 Green Star points, which must consist of at least four 5-point Green Stars all under different judges; the remaining 20 points can be of any number from one to five. Having duly won the necessary 40 points, the dog must then obtain a qualifying certificate in the field. He will be required to quarter the field, flush the pheasant or grouse and stay steady to the gun (he must not be gun-shy or mouth the bird). If you are not successful the first time, you are entitled to two more attempts, but not more than three with any one dog.

Some well-known English dogs who gained their Irish title were Irish Ch. Banner of Crombie, Irish Ch. Shiplake Skymaster and Irish Ch. Trodgers Yarrow. Mr S. Adair, whose affix is Portvogie, bred Ch. Hurricane of Craiglands and Sh. Ch. Raycroft Jewel, both being by Marker of Crombie ex Spindrift of Portvogie. Jewel was later owned by Miss Kelly, who from Jewel bred Sh. Ch. Cill Dora

Yvonne by Raycroft Orange Boy. Miss Kelly also bred Ch. Ernford Cill Dora Felicity (Grouse of Capard ex Minx of Medehamstede).

A very successful English-bred sire in Eire was Oldholbans Lysander, bred by Mrs Ann Findlay by Trodgers Oregon ex Oldholbans Golden Magic. He sired Ch. Faymyr Sapphire, bred by M. Quigley out of Faymyr Dusty Bluebell and Miss Mary Jarry's Carncombe Stroller, who was a C.C. winner in England.

Mr and Mrs Schoneville have done well in recent years, with Balvenie Sunglow (Northgate Masterpiece ex Gaewill Cornish Gillyflower) winning numerous Green Stars.

New Zealand

New Zealand has a long tradition of dogs kept for work and field sports, and there is evidence that English Setters of Laverack's strain were imported from England around the mid-to-late 1800s, followed in the early 1900s by those of Adare, Mallwyd, Maesydd, Beechgrove, Downsman and Craigsland.

Kennel Club records were not kept until the end of the last century, when a stud register was implemented. This register continued until 1930 when a card system came into operation, and in the 1960s an individual register came into force. The first New Zealand Kennel Club recorded champions were two bitches Papanui Belle and Weeley Fan Light in 1928. Championships were, however, certainly awarded before this time, as one unofficial record shows that in 1912 an English Setter, Ch. Burkeland Rock, was exhibited at Manawatu Show. One record mentions that 'Setters' were entered at a show held in Dunedin in 1887; however, the first New Zealand Kennel Club show was held in Christchurch in 1887, where there were classes for English Setters. Two imported dogs that feature with great regularity in the records are Beechgrove Phil and Beechgrove Jean, whilst the first recorded English Setter in the New Zealand Stud Book was Gleepark Don in October 1887, bred by P. Hunter. Paul Hunter was President

The English Setter

of the NZKC from 1905 to 1926; he bred and exhibited many English Setters during the late 1880s, and it was not unknown for him to attend a show with up to 20 English Setters.

There is no doubt that a number of imports have influenced the breed in New Zealand from the turn of the century up to the present day. The earlier imports originated mainly in England, but in recent years a number have come from Australia. Both before and after the war there was an influx of English Setters from the United Kingdom, the pedigrees of whom contained such famous affixes as Withinlee, Bondhu, Rombalds, Bayldone, Ripleygae and Crombie. The more familiar names, however, which may be recognized by today's breeders, were the quartet from Shiplake's, namely: Shiplake Sheila of Sharvogue, Sh. Ch. Shiplake Shot Silk, Ch. Shiplake Stonechat of Truslers and Shiplake Swagger. Two other influential imports worth mentioning were the two Fermanars, Fairchance, whose sire was Ernford Easter Parade, and Fairlady.

Moving on to the present day, among the imports that have most influenced the breed during the last 10 years is Aust. and NZ Ch. Engsett Extra Promise, imported by Mr and Mrs Heskett from Mr and Mrs Wheeler. This bitch produced the big winning litter brother and sister Ch. Setterlands Sensation and Ch. Setterlands Sunseeker, both of whom are multiple Best in Show winners. Sensation has been tremendously successful both as a show dog and as a sire. He not only is an all-breeds Best in Show winner but is also the sire of the current top all-breeds Best in Show winning Ch. Ballymore Call Me Blue, whilst Sunseeker is the dam of several Best in Show winners. Mr and Mrs Heskett also imported, from Mr and Mrs Wheeler Engsett, Par Enterprise (litter brother to Sh. Ch. Engsett Par Excellence). He sired, in one litter, four champions, all of which were made up by Mr and Mrs Culverwell of the Chilworth Kennels. Two of these were group winners, but the most well known is Ch. Chilworth Fusilier, a dark-tricoloured, very typically 'English', English Setter. Fusilier is a multi-group winner as well as a Best in Show winner at several breed specialist shows. Fusilier has in turn sired numerous group and Best in Show winners for the Pamploma Kennels in Australia, as well as Mountshannon and Setterlands. His outstanding son, Ch. Pamploma Chilworth Lad, is in turn siring winning stock, amongst whom are the group winner, Chilworth Colonals Lady, and, in Australia for the Pamploma Kennels, her litter brother Chilworth Just William.

Another English import of influence, Farmacy Flycatcher of Suntop, imported by Helen Lyles of the Barnstop Kennels, produced Aust. and NZ Ch. Barnstop Clockwork Orange, and for the Fifields Cricklewood Kennels, Ch. Cricklewoods Snow Cloud, who was a beautiful light-tricoloured dog who was a Best in Show speciality winner with numerous groups to his credit. Snow Cloud's son Aust. and NZ Ch. Hawkwood Lennox did his share of winning, both in Australia and New Zealand, for Mrs Gill's Hawkwood Kennels. Flycatcher sired Ch. Hawkwood Portia, whose daughter is the currently winning Ch. Hawkwood Singer. Flycatcher was the grandsire of Ch. Cricklewood Hunters Moon, a dark-tricoloured dog owned by Mr and Mrs Goodall, and Ch. Celia of Weston Lodge, who is the dam of Ch. Chilworth Fusilier. Ch. Celia of Weston Lodge is a granddaughter of Int. Sh. Ch. Suntop Winterbreeze, and she has produced five champions.

Mr and Mrs Ormandy (Glengordon) imported from Mr and Mrs Preece of Australia the Engsett Emery daughter, NZ Ch. Pamploma Tantivy, who was the dam of the Champions Glengordon My Charmaine, Glengordon Melody Maker, Glengordon Bell Amber and Glengordon Giovanni, amongst others. Another bitch to be imported from Australia was Nottingham First Lady, who produced for her owners', Mr and Mrs Velvins, Velenetter Kennels Aust. and NZ Ch. Velenetter English Lord, a multiple Best in Show speciality winner, and his sister, Ch. Velenetter April Lady. Perhaps the most prolific Australian import was Ch. Sidella Starshine, who was imported by Mrs Brockie from Mr John Thompson's kennel. He was a multiple Best in Show winner who sired 13 Champions for, amongst others, Shelta, Talbots, Hendry,

Saxilby, Stylish and Fleckwood Kennels. Some of his group- and Best in Show-winning progeny were Ch. Talbots Independence, Ch. Stylish Paper Lace, Ch. Shelta Lorna Doone and Ch. Blue Heaven of Hendry to name but a few, and now six generations later his descendants, Ch. Shelta Seaswift, Ch. Stylish Colombo and Aust. Ch. Shelta Sho Em Style, are winning well.

It is worth noting that out of all the winning dogs mentioned above, 13 are directly descended from Suntop Songbird, Suntop Birdsong and Sh. Ch. Engsett Electrode and carry lines that trace back to Sh. Ch. Iroquois Whiteseal Silvermorn, Shiplake Sungold and Shiplake Shimmer.

The top-winning English Setters in New Zealand in recent years have been the orange belton trio bred and owned by Mrs Ormandy, Ch. Glengordon Gay Cavalier, Ch. Glengordon Muskateer and Ch. Glengordon Colonel Bogey, each of whom won over 100 Challenge Certificates. Mrs Brockie's Aust. and NZ Ch. Shelta Snowchief, another orange belton, was also a multiple Best in Show winner; a grandson of Int. Sh. Ch. Suntop Royal Sunlight, he produced Ch. Shelta Chieftainess who in turn produced Ch. Shelta Bold Chieftain amongst many other top winners.

Ch. Glengordon Chatterbox, owned by Mr and Mrs Velvin, holds the distinction of being the only English Setter to have won Best in Show at the Tux National Show. I have already mentioned Mr and Mrs Heskett's glorious orange belton, Ch. Setterlands Sensation, and his son, owned and bred by Miss James, Ch. Ballymore Call Me Blue. Another big winner of this era was Mr and Mrs Swift's Ch. Sunswift of Sunbury, a lemon belton, who was a great showman. Currently one of the top-winning dogs is the aforementioned Ch. Pamploma Chilworth Lad, owned by Mr and Mrs Culverwell, who holds the breed record for the youngest English Setter to be awarded a Best in Show all-breeds at the age of 13½ months, no mean feat. He has recently also won his Australian title.

Mr and Mrs Heskett's orange import Aust. and NZ Ch. Engsett Extra Promise amassed over 80 Challenge Certificates and Mr and Mrs Linklater's Ch. Glengordon My

Charmaine won over 70, which included group wins. Mr and Mrs Davidson's Ch. Glengordon Melody Maker, a striking orange belton, has the distinction of winning Best of Breed three years in succession at the Tux National Show. Miss James's Ch. Ballymore Neat 'n' Sweet, a blue belton sister to Ch. Ballymore Call Me Blue has numerous Best in Show wins to her credit, whilst Mr and Mrs Inwood's Ch. Stylish Paper Lace is a multiple group-winner and has a Breed Speciality Best in Show to her credit. Lastly, two more bitches worth a mention are Mr and Mrs Velvin's Ch. Velenetter April Lady and Mrs Thompson's Ch. Glengordon Lady Sarona.

The current top winning kennels are as follows: Mr and Mrs Ormandy (Glengordon), Mrs Brockie (Shelta), Mr and Mrs Velvin (Velenetter), Mr and Mrs Heskett (Setterlands), Mr and Mrs Culverwell (Chilworth), Mrs Gill (Hawkwood) Mrs and Mrs Inwoods (Stylish), Mrs Baylis (Fleckwood), Miss James (Ballymore), Mr and Mrs Davidson (Talbots) and Mr and Mrs Swift (Saxilby).

The New Zealand Show System

All classes are divided by sex, and the best of the sex in each class competes with the appropriate opposite sex to establish Best Puppy, Best Junior etc. These winners can then go on to compete for Best Puppy etc in the group. The dog and bitch challenge winners also compete against each other for Best of Breed and the winner goes forward into the group.

The Best of Group is judged at the conclusion of the breed classes, followed by Reserve Best of Group, Best Baby Puppy, Best Puppy, Best Junior and Best Intermediate in Group. Following the group judging, the Best in Show judging commences, followed by Reserve Best in Show, then Best puppy etc, as for the Group.

Nearly 100 all-breed championship shows are held a year, where over 140 breeds are scheduled. There are also of course the specialist breed club shows and various other functions.

The English Setter

New Zealand Championship Title
The title of Champion is awarded to a dog or bitch when it has gained a total of eight Challenge Certificates under at least five different judges. One Challenge Certificate must be won after the dog has attained the age of 12 months. No exhibit under the age of six months is eligible to compete for a Challenge Certificate.

South Africa

English Setters in South Africa go back some considerable time, though there appear to be few or no records prior to the war. However, it is known that in 1897 a cup was presented to the Queenstown Kennel Club for 'Setters', and two years later a further two cups were presented to the same club, one for English Setters and one for Irish Setters. These three cups are still in existence and were presented to the Gundog Club in 1964 by Mrs Kingsleigh, who described them as heirlooms. They certainly were, for the Queenstown Kennel Club itself has disappeared together with all the records, but these valuable cups are still competed for annually.

The Davisworth family of Natal have been involved with English Setters since Harold Davisworth obtained his first dog in 1911. His son, Harold Junior, worked Setters for many years, and the third generation, Ian, owned from 1957 to 1972 a Laverack bought for him by his father. In 1975 he was persuaded by Trevor Tinker to start again. Mr Trevor Tinker whose affix Casalino is associated with many top-winning dogs, was the first President of the Western Province Setter Association founded by Mark and Bridget Simpson in 1982, which is the only breed-specialist club in South Africa.

In the early '50s Mrs Taylor had a kennel in Port Elizabeth and Major Wright in Rivonia. A few years later Dan Verbaan started his now famous Kingstree Kennel in Durban. He has imported over 30 dogs from the UK and the USA. I well remember sending out a bitch, Bibima Annalee, to him, in whelp to Sh. Ch. Iroquois Whiteseal Silvermorn, and amongst the resultant litter were Ch. Kingstree Shade of Challeycroft, Ch. Kingstree Selenium and Ch. Kingstree Silver Moonlight of Casalino, who was to become Trevor Tinker's foundation bitch. From her stemmed all the stock in the Cape at that time. She had two litters which produced three champions in each litter. Dan Verbaan is currently showing and breeding American-bred stock, in partnership with the aforementioned Ian Davisworth; these are from the Clariho line.

In 1955 Sheila Fitchett was introduced to dog-showing by Buster Browning, and shortly afterwards founded her Oudenhoutdraai Kennel. In 1962 she imported Ch. Sedge Blazing Star in whelp to Ernford Kingfisher; the resultant litter was 10 puppies. She later imported Int. Sh. Ch. Suntop Royal Sunrise, who, handled by Buster Browning, twice won Best in Show awards.

Major Oscar Wilde (Brigade) imported a daughter of Sh. Ch. Silbury Soames of Madavale, Ch. Springhead Sheena of Madavale. Her daughter was mated to Ch. Renmark Simon (UK import), and this produced the greatest winner of the '70s, Ch. Sylvester of Antigua, who won no fewer than seven Best in Show awards. Sylvester was owned by Eric Collier, who at this time lived in Zimbabwe (then Rhodesia). Mr Collier later moved to Johannesburg, where he had many successes with both imports and homebred dogs under the Colsett affix. He later returned to England, changed his affix to Settcol, and continued showing for several years before retiring from the show ring to run the Ada Cole Memorial Stables. Michael and Linda Philip (Collaton) imported Engsett Royal Emmissary by Sh. Ch. Engsett Par Excellence ex Willowsett Whoopsie of Engsett, who carries Clariho lines.

Val Stinson (Perrylee) imported Bournehouse Exile of Perrylee, an orange belton dog, again by Sh. Ch. Engsett Par Excellence ex Sh. Ch. Bournehouse Floral Dancer. He has been most successful at stud, producing no less than five champions in one litter, one being Sunjon Sandalwood, who was top-winning bitch in 1986 and 1987.

Frank and Betty Swift (Sunjon) have also produced Ch.

The English Setter

Sunjon Sundancer, Ch. Sunjon Sabre Dance of Mirton and Ch. Colsett Carnival of Sunjon (bred by Eric Collier), top-winning setter in 1980 amongst many other big winners.

The most influential brood bitch of recent years has no doubt been the foundation bitch of the Winscott Kennels of Jim and Sarah Scott, Ch. Hurwyn Yum Yum of Winscott. She is by Hurwyn Flight Master ex Hurwyn Madam Butterfly, and went out to South Africa in whelp to Hurwyn Chorus Boy. Her 'imported' litter produced four champions, and a further two litters produced four more, all bearing the Winscott affix.

Another influential kennel is Ulvenhaut of Mr and Mrs Peter Faes, who purchased in 1969 two orange belton bitch puppies, bred by Major Oscar Wilde (Brigade), sired by the Int. Sh. Ch. Suntop Royal Sunrise out of Ch. Silver Wraith of the Brigade, who was a granddaughter of Sh. Ch. Silbury Soames of Madavale, and these two bitches were virtually the foundation of the Ulvenhaut Kennel. One of them, Ch. Silver Angin of the Brigade, mated to the imported Ch. Renmark Simon, produced Ch. East Africa Ulvenhaut Mr Soames, who won more Best in Show awards all breeds in Nairobi than any other dog in living memory.

Challenges Certificates are awarded to all breeds at all championship shows; as soon as a new breed is imported and the pedigree registered with the South African Kennel Union, Challenge Certificates become available for that breed. However, there are not that many shows in each area. For instance in the Cape there are six all-breed Championship Shows within a 100-mile radius of Cape Town and two 'specialist' (gundog) shows, the next closest shows being three to four hundred miles away. After that one has to travel to Johannesburg or Durban, which are both about a thousand miles away. There are four 'specialist' gundog shows in all of South Africa; these are the Gundog Club, Natal Gundog Club, Cape Gundog Club and Western Province Setter Association.

South Africa is divided geographically into five centres: Western Province, Eastern Province, Free State, Natal and Transvaal. To become a South African Champion a

NZ Ch. Chilworth April Love, litter sister to NZ Ch. Chilworth Fusilier – Engsett breeding

Diane Pearce

Sh. Ch. Hurwyn Cupie Doll – one of a line of great winning bitches

Dalton
Sh. Ch. Tragus Night Breeze – a top winner of the '80s

Frank Garwood
Sh. Ch. Northgate Blue Brocade – a beautiful top winning bitch

Dalton

Sh. Ch. Northgate Grenadier – Blue Brocade's son by Sh. Ch. Iroquois Snow Prince of Northgate, line bred to Sh. Ch. Iroquois Whiteseal Silvermorn

Anne Roslin-Williams

Sh. Ch. Suntop Starling – another great sire from this kennel

Frank Garwood

Sh. Ch. Iroquois Concerto (*left*) and Sh. Ch. Iroquois Sansovino of Sundeala at Bath 1981. Concerto won CC Best of Breed and the gundog group and Reserve Best in Show. Sansovino was the winner of the Championship stakes

Bill Francis

Am. Ch. Guys 'n' Dolls Annie O'Brien – the top winning English Setter bitch in America with 13 Best in Show awards and 102 Best of Breed

dog must win five Challenge Certificates under different judges, with at least one awarded after the dog has attained 18 months of age and one to be awarded in a province or centre other than the one from which the dog has come. Due to the high temperatures prevailing in South Africa, the show year starts in February and ends in October; most shows are unbenched. The classes are much the same as in the UK, i.e. Minor Puppy, Puppy Junior, Graduate, Open and Champion. All unbeaten dogs are brought back to the ring to challenge for the C.C. and Res. C.C. except in the Champion class where the dog or bitch may only compete for Best of Breed.

Spain

The first English dogs to be exported to Spain were from the Suntop Kennel. Unlike several other European countries, where the American type is becoming increasingly popular, Spain has remained with the English type, though they have been interbred with the continental field-trial type, mainly from France. The breed is used extensively for field work and hunting, and not many are shown. Most of the dogs are in the north of the country.

The Setter Club of Spain caters for English, Irish and Gordon Setters, and there are about 30 members who own English Setters; of these only about a third show them, and it is indeed rare to see more than three or four in any class at a show. There are about forty shows held annually, including the two big shows held in Madrid in June and October, and the Setter Club show.

The best known English Setter breeder in Spain is Jose Luis Mazo Gainza, who is also an international judge, but in the late 1980s a new young breeder in Valencia is starting to make his mark. He purchased two puppies, a dog and a bitch, from Mr J. Requena of Gibraltar from his litter by Sh. Ch. Upperwood Flash Dance out of Koiya Liberty Belle, litter sister to Sh. Ch. Koiya the Highflyer from Bournehouse. A further two puppies from this litter have gone to Portugal, whilst one has remained in Gibraltar, so it is hoped that Mr Requena's efforts will improve the type in Spain and Portugal.

To become a Spanish Champion the following is required: a C.C. to be won at the Madrid show, Excellent at the Setter Club show, plus 3 other C.C.s., or a C.C. to be won at the Setter Club show, Excellent at the Madrid show, plus 3 other C.C.s. The C.C.s must be awarded by three different judges, and a minimum period of one year must elapse between the first and last C.C. To become an International Champion a Field Trial Certificate must also be obtained.

Sweden

The first Laverack or show-type English Setters were imported from England in the early 1970s. Until then all the English Setters in Sweden were of the Llewellin or field trial type. The tricolour bitch Hurwyn Carissima, bred by Mrs S. Wilkinson by Suntop Songbird ex Hurwyn Ennford Fairybird (litter sister to the Sh. Ch. brothers Falcon and Flamingo), was the very first import owned by Elizabeth Matell, and later sold to Agneta Pettersson. Hurwyn Carissima enjoyed fabulous success and was the most successful English Setter ever in Sweden. In 1974 she was the third most winning dog all breeds; in 1975 she was second most winning dog all breeds. She won 13 CACIB, 19 Best of Breed, eight Best of Group awards and two Best in Show awards; she died in 1986 at the age of 13 years.

The next most successful dog was undoubtedly Sh. Ch. Suntop Nightingale; he was certainly the most influential sire. Owned by Christer Jansson, he was exported to Sweden by Miss M.D. Barnes, sired by Int. Sh. Ch. Suntop Winterbreeze (who was exported to Mrs P. Johnson in Australia) out of Wonder Star of Suntop. Nightingale was the seventh most successful dog among all breeds in 1980 and also placed third in the Best in Show competition at the Stockholm International (the Swedish equivalent of Crufts). He won four Best in Show awards in breed speciality shows and died in 1984, aged 10.

Other imports from England were Suntop Whispering

English Setters Overseas

Wind, bred by Miss Barnes, by Suntop Songbird ex Suntop Regal Finch; the full sisters Hurwyn Snow White and Hurwyn Mary Poppins, bred by Mrs Wilkinson, sired by Hurwyn Apollo ex Hurwyn Dawn Glory; Hurwyn Stormcloud (Int. Sh. Ch. Suntop Winterbreeze ex Hurwyn Dawn Chorus); Moon Magic of Yeo Suntop (Int. Sh. Ch. Suntop Winterbreeze ex Sh. Ch. Noyna Sunfairy), bred by Mrs L. Sawtell; Suntop Truly Proud (Sh. Ch. Suntop Freckled Star ex Suntop True Silk), breeder Miss M. Barnes. All the above have since died. Other imports include Suntop Sunbeam (Sh. Ch. Suntop Starling (litter brother to Nightingale ex Sunbeam of Yeo); Suntop True Ripple (Suntop True Glow ex Suntop Truewings); Goldstone of Suntop (Sh. Ch. Annsett Dark Night ex Peacloud Bluefinch); Suntop True Ripple's litter brother Suntop True Welcome and the litter sisters Suntop Freckled Thrush and Suntop Speckled Thrush (Suntop Truly Speckled ex Suntop Bonny Thrush).

The most influential and successful kennels in Sweden are those of Susanna Chapman (Glowing), Christer Jansson (Moon Magic), Agneta Pettersson (Royalwings), Benny Svensson (Crown-point). These kennels have exported dogs to Finland and Holland. Christer Jansson won Best in Show at the ESA of Sweden Club Show for two successive years, 1987 and 1988, with Suntop Speckled Thrush, whilst in 1985 and 1986 Susanna Chapman achieved the same feat with Suntop True Ripple. Christer Jansson has also done very well with his home-bred Moon Magic Design By Me and Moon Magic Ever So Nice (Sh. Ch. Suntop Nightingale ex Moon Magic of Yeo Suntop). Susanna Chapman has likewise done very well with Glowing Pot of Jam (Caleydene Gilded Gale ex Marmalade Sky) and Agneta Pettersson has continued breeding and winning with descendants of Hurwyn Carissima.

The first litter of English-bred show-type English Setters (as opposed to the field-trial type prevailing in Sweden) were born in 1978. Up to the present time 30 litters have been born, a total of 160 puppies. The Swedish Kennel Club holds about 30 championship shows a year and to become a Swedish Champion you need to win three C.C.s and not less than a third prize at a recognized field trial. The Kennel Club of Sweden considers the English type untypical, preferring their field trial type, and therefore in 1980 they made a rule that English Setters were not eligible for C.C.s unless they had qualified in the field. For this reason none of the aforementioned winning dogs is a Champion all their winning being confined to breed club shows. The Swedish Kennel Club also recommends that only Scandinavian judges judge the English-bred gundogs. The English Setter Association of Sweden is an unofficial breed club not recognized by the Swedish Kennel Club. It was formed in 1983 to promote the true English type. One show a year is held and a year-book published. At the present time it has about 100 members. It is hoped that the work of these few dedicated breeders to promote the true English show-type of English Setter will pay dividends in the long run.

United States of America

The greatest difference between American and British dog shows is probably simple geography. Though most English Setters are owner-handled, some people find it more economical to hire professional handlers when they live where there are long distances between shows.

Nearly all Americans are hobby-breeders and, indeed, most are working full-time to pay the expenses of showing their dogs. That leaves little time for conditioning large numbers of dogs, much less for driving long distances and taking vacation days from work.

Many cities limit the number of dogs one may have on the premises and for this reason, as well as because of the desire to control breeding practices, an increasing number of American dogs are being co-owned. Breeders sell their pups on co-ownerships, reserving the right to exhibit the animal, the right to supervise breeding and perhaps sharing the expenses or whatever arrangement is mutually acceptable. Co-owners may be novices who benefit from the experience of the breeder, or they may be breeders who simply have a common interest in the animal.

According to the American Kennel Club's statistics for the year 1987, the Santa Barbara Kennel Club in California had 3,520 dogs in competition and was the largest all-breed show held that year. By contrast, the Metro Mile Hi Kennel Club show in Longmont, Colorado, had only 137 dogs in competition and was ranked 1,060th in size. Usually, however, the smallest shows are in Hawaii or in Alaska, again simply because of the geography.

Santa Barbara is a very prestigious show, but the better-known showplace for American dogs is Madison Square Garden in New York City where there were 2,136 Westminster Kennel Club entries in 1987.

The development of 'cluster shows', several shows held on the same site, has over the past decade produced larger shows in some of the more sparsely populated areas of the country. The Mid-Continent Kennel Club show in Tulsa, Oklahoma, for example, had an entry of 2,122 dogs at the 1987 show. The clustering of shows brings large numbers of professional handlers but, also, larger numbers of owner-handlers, who can justify vacation from work when they can enter up to 11 or so shows within a two-week period.

Among speciality shows (for one breed only) those for English Setters rank among the largest. The English Setter Association of America National Speciality was ranked 18th in 1987 with 339 dogs in competition, out of 1,495 speciality shows.

There are about fifteen English Setter Clubs across the country, each of which is independent, but all of which belong to the parent ESAA and to the AKC. The national show is held in a different region each year, hosted by one or more of the local clubs. That local group usually hosts its own specialty show immediately following the two-day national and so has a correspondingly high entry. During other years, their local speciality would have entries ranging from about 45 in some parts of the country to 115 in others.

There are also the Combined Setter Specialty held in

The English Setter

conjunction with the Westminster Kennel Club, and the Far West Setter Specialty in California, both of which draw fairly large entries as they are for English, Gordon and Irish Setters and a number of setter fanciers in the USA do own all three breeds. A win at these shows is prestigious.

The AKC confers the title Champion on a dog who has been awarded a total of 15 points. Points awarded at each show are determined by the AKC based on the entries for that sex and breed in the previous year in each of the six divisions of the country (Alaska and Hawaii are each divisions). One dog and one bitch in each breed are awarded from one to five points at each show. Among the 15 points necessary, two wins must be at shows where three or more points were awarded and those wins must be under different judges. These shows are referred to as 'majors'.

Classes are divided by sex and include: Puppy (which may also be divided by age where entries are large); Novice for dogs which have not previously won three or more first places; Bred by Exhibitor; American Bred, and Open (open to any dog, including champions of record, though this is never done). The first-place winner in each class then competes in the Winners class for the title of Winners Dog and that dog is awarded the points. The winner of each bitch class competes likewise. The Winners Dog and Winners Bitch then compete with the champions of record for Best of Breed and Best of Opposite Sex. In addition, the Winners Dog and Winners Bitch compete against each other for Best of Winners; the one the judge chooses as Best of Winners is entitled to the number of points awarded the other if the other has won a greater number, as Best of Winners is considered to have defeated the opposite sex as well.

The Best of Breed dog proceeds to group competition and the winner of each of the seven groups (Sporting, Hound, Working, Terrier, Toy, Herding and Non-Sporting) then compete for Best in Show. If, perchance, the Best in Show dog or the winner of a group is not already a champion, he is entitled to the highest number of points awarded to either sex in any breed which he has defeated.

It sounds complex when one tries to explain it on paper,

and this is not the complete list of possibilities, but it all becomes clear when one reads the AKC's publication, *Show Awards*, which includes titles awarded as well as the results of all shows, obedience trials, tracking tests, field trials and the hunting tests. The *Events Calendar* lists all forthcoming competition held under AKC auspices, and the *Gazette* includes such things as feature articles, the minutes of AKC meetings, new judges who have been approved, and a column for each breed.

The ESAA publishes a monthly newsletter for its members and each year publishes a hard-bound book including the Association's annual history, local clubs' histories, national results, Annual Award winners and kennel pages paid for by individual members.

British English Setters have come to figure among American dogs primarily through the dogs belonging to many Canadian ESAA members. One finds the affix Suntop in some pedigrees, and one can also find the name of the imported Ch. Ernford Oriole. I suspect that those are the most common kennel names found in any pedigrees.

Americans were so impressed by the abilities of the dogs imported over a century ago from R.L. Purcell Llewellin that they are registered as English Setters but are referred to as 'Llewellins'. Though a great many 'Laveracks' are used as personal gundogs, one usually sees the 'Llewellin' at field trials. For the most part it is a smaller, more slightly built dog, often lacking the distinctive English Setter head and often with heavy patches of colour.

Heathrow's Rainbow Robber owned by Mike and Barbara Fletcher and Peter and M.A. Samuelson of California is the first English Setter to become both a bench and field champion. Neither championship was attained by a narrow margin. He did well at the field trials and then won a Best in Specialty Show under a breeder-judge (the late Nancy Dobson) and he did it from the Field Trial class, another first!

ESAA's Annual Awards for the year 1987 included:

English Setter of the year—to the English Setter winning over the greatest number of other English Setters as

The English Setter

Best of Breed: Ch. Foxtrack's The Invincible One, owned by Dick and Ingrid Fox of Cortland, New York, bred by Barbara Oakes, Five Oakes Kennel. Runner-up: Ch. Edition's By Invitation Only owned by Conny and Karen Helms of Indian Trail, North Carolina.

Best of Opposite Sex to the English Setter of the Year—to the English Setter, opposite in sex to the English Setter of the Year, who defeats the greatest number of other English Setters as Best of Breed or Best of Opposite Sex: Ch. Allspice Sesame Street (Ch. Guys 'n' Dolls Delancey Street ex Allspice Calendar Girl) bred by Harry Uva, Jr and Marlene and Darrin Uva, owned by J. and K. Kraemer and H. and M. Uva. Runner-up: Ch. Checkmate Flow Blue, owned by Ellie Kieme, Nan Olson Beeler and Shirley Hoeflinger, bred by Nan Olson Beeler and Shirley Hoeflinger.

Stud Dog—to the living English Setter dog who has sired the greatest number of AKC champions to date; the dog must be living as of 30 April of the award year: Ch. Guys 'n' Dolls Barrister Beau, bred by Lloyd and Lynda Talbot and Neal and Nancy Weinstein, owned by Ray-Lynn McAlpine of Mobile, Alabama. Runner-up: Ch. Seamrog Tyson of Palomar, bred by Shirley Hoeflinger, owned by Shirley Hoeflinger.

Brood Bitch—similar requirements to those for Stud Dog: Ch. Kadon Smart 'n' Sassy, bred by Kay Monaghan, owned by Pamela W. Lefever. Runner-up: Ch. Sunburst Hasten Down the Wind, bred and owned by Yvonne Ward of Arizona.

Sire of the Year—to the English Setter sire, living or dead, whose progeny win the greatest number of championship points during the award year: Ch. Gold Rush Gold Miner Blues, bred and owned by Jerry and Diane Beal of California. Runner-up: Ch. Guys 'n' Dolls Barrister Beau.

Dam of the Year—similar requirements to those for Sire of the Year: Ch. Kadon Smart 'n' Sassy. Runner-up: Ch. Silverline Sunsong o' Star-Vue, bred by Nancy Praiswater and Kathryn Gaut, owned by Kathryn Gaut.

In addition there are well-known kennels such as

Wickett, owned by Byron and Mary Margaret Ruth in Pennsylvania; Timbertrail, owned by Bob and Peggie Dunsmuir in Illinois; Willglen, owned by Tom and Roberta Williams in California; Windem, owned by Jack Gohde in Virginia; Five Oakes, owned by Barbara Oakes in New York; Heathrow, owned by M.A. and Peter Samuelson in California. There are probably several others which deserve mention for consistently producing quality animals and which have bred some of the big winners.

The English Setter breed clubs in the USA are: English Setter Association of America, English Setter Club of Greater Denver, California English Setter Club, English Setter Club of Ohio, English Setter Club of New England English Setter Club of Phoenix Arizona, Gateway English Setter Club, Golden Gate English Setter Club, Hudson English Setter Club, Iroquois English Setter Club, Michigamme English Setter Club, Minnesota English Setter Club, South Florida English Setter Association, Three Rivers English Setter Association and Western English Setter Club.

Revised American Kennel Club Standard (Approved 11 November 1986)

General Appearance:
An elegant, substantial and symmetrical gundog suggesting the ideal blend of strength, stamina, grace and style. Flat coated with feathering of good length. Gait free and smooth with long forward reach, strong rear drive and firm topline. Males decidedly masculine without coarseness. Females decidedly feminine without over-refinement. Overall appearance, balance, gait and purpose to be given more emphasis than any component part. Above all, extremes of anything distort type and must be faulted.

Head: Size and proportion in harmony with body. Long and lean with a well-defined stop. When viewed from the side, head planes (top of muzzle, top of skull and bottom of lower jaw) are parallel. Skull: oval when viewed from above, of medium width, without coarseness, and only slightly wider at the ear set than at the brow. Moderately defined occipital protruberance. Length of skull from occiput to stop equal in length to muzzle. Muzzle: long and square when viewed from the side, of good depth with flews squared and fairly pendant. Width in harmony with width of skull and equal at nose and stop. Level from eyes to tip of nose. Nose: black or dark brown, fully pigmented. Nostrils wide apart and large. Foreface: skeletal structure under the eyes well-chiselled with no suggestion of fullness. Cheeks present a smooth and clean-cut appearance. Teeth: close scissors-bite preferred. Even bite acceptable. Eyes: dark brown, the darker the better: bright, and spaced to give a mild and intelligent expression: nearly round, fairly large, neither deepset nor protruding. Eyelid rims dark and fully pigmented. Lids fit tightly so that no haw is exposed. Ears: set well back and low, even with or below eye level. When relaxed, carried close to the head. Of moderate length, slightly rounded at the ends, moderately thin leather and covered with silky hair.

Neck and Body: Neck: long and graceful, muscular and lean. Arched at the crest and clean-cut where it joins the head at the base of the skull. Larger and more muscular toward the shoulders, with the base of the neck flowing smoothly into the shoulders. Not too throaty. Topline: in motion or standing appears level or sloping slightly downward without sway or drop, from withers to tail forming a graceful outline of medium length. Forechest: well-developed, point of sternum projecting slightly in front of point of shoulder/upper-arm joint. Chest: deep, but not so wide or round as to interfere with the action of the forelegs. Brisket deep enough to reach the level of the elbow. Ribs: long, springing gradually to the middle of the body, then tapering as they approach the end of the chest cavity. Back: straight and strong at its junction with loin. Loin: strong, moderate in length, slightly arched. Tuck up moderate. Hips: croup nearly flat. Hip bones wide apart, hips rounded and blending smoothly into hind legs. Tail: a smooth continuation of the topline. Tapering to a fine point and of only sufficient length to reach the hock joint or slightly less. Carried straight and level with the back. Feathering straight and silky, hanging loosely in a fringe.

Forequarters: Shoulder: shoulder blade well laid back. Upper arm equal in length to and forming a nearly right angle with the shoulder blade. Shoulders fairly close together at the tips. Shoulder blades lie flat and meld smoothly with contours of body. Forelegs: from front or side, forelegs straight and parallel. Elbows have no tendency to turn in or out when standing or gaiting. Forearm flat and muscular. Bone substantial but not coarse and muscles hard and devoid of flabbiness. Pasterns: short, strong and nearly round with the slope deviating very slightly forward from the perpendicular. Feet: face directly forward. Toes closely set, strong and well-arched. Pads well-developed and tough. Dewclaws may be removed.

Hindquarters: Wide, muscular thighs and well-developed lower thighs. Pelvis equal to and forming a nearly right angle with the upper thigh. In balance with forequarter assembly. Stifle well-bent and strong. Lower thigh only slightly longer than upper thigh. Hock joint well-bent and strong. Rear pastern short, strong, nearly round and perpendicular to the ground. Hind legs, when seen from the rear, straight and parallel to each other. Hock joints have no tendency to turn in or out when standing or gaiting.

Coat: Flat without curl or woolliness. Feathering on ears, chest, abdomen, underside of thighs, back of all legs and on the tail of good length, but not so excessive as to hide true lines and movement or to affect the dog's appearance or function as a sporting dog.

Markings and Colour: Markings: white ground colour with intermingling of darker hairs resulting in belton markings varying in degree from clear distinct flecking to roan shading, but flecked all over preferred. Head and ear patches acceptable, heavy patches of colour on the body undesirable. Colour: orange belton, blue belton (white with black

The English Setter

markings), tricolour (blue belton with tan on muzzle, over the eyes and on the legs), lemon belton, liver belton.

Movement and Carriage: An effortless graceful movement demonstrating endurance while covering ground efficiently. Long forward reach and strong rear drive with a lively tail and a proud head carriage. Head may be carried slightly lower when moving to allow for greater reach of forelegs. The back strong, firm, and free of roll. When moving at a trot, as speed increases, the legs tend to converge toward a line representing the centre of gravity.

Size: Dogs about 25 inches; bitches about 24 inches.

Temperament: Gentle, affectionate, friendly, without shyness, fear or viciousness.

11
Leading Kennels

Chapter 2, 'The Breed Post-War', dealt with those owners and breeders who played such a big part in establishing the breed in the post-war years. Sadly some of those stalwarts are no longer with us; some have given up breeding and/or showing for one reason or another, and since I started writing this book we have lost one of our oldest and most respected breeders, Mrs Mary Darling, as well as one of our younger members, Mr René Goutorbe, who was very much involved in the field trial side as well as in showing and judging. This chapter chronicles those kennels that are still actively breeding and showing, which over the years have consistently bred influential stud dogs and brood bitches and produced top-winning stock. They are listed alphabetically under kennel affixes.

Arnsett, Mrs L. A. Child

This kennel is based on pure Suntop bloodlines. Great foundation bitch Suntop Summer Belle, dam of litter brother and sister Sh. Ch. Arnsett Alfa and Sh. Ch. Arnsett Afaya by Int. Sh. Ch. Suntop Winter Breeze. Sh. Ch. Arnsett Dark Night and litter sister Sh. Ch. Arnsett Night Daisy of Fencefoot owned by Mesdames Marsden and Croft, by Sh. Ch. Suntop Nightingale. C.C. winners Arnsett Fays Flirt of Brockthwaite (Mr and Mrs E. Evans), Arnsett Fays Frolic (Mr and Mrs Collier), Arnsett Fays Fable (Mr and Mrs Anderson) all by Sh. Ch. Suntop Starling out of Sh. Ch. Arnsett Afaya.

The English Setter

Bournehouse, Mr and Mrs G. Williams

First champions were ex foundation bitch Iroquois Jasmine, Sh. Ch. Bournehouse Meadowfern and full sister Sh. Ch. Bournehouse Ballerina by Evening Flight of Frejendor, followed by Sh. Ch. Barranco Bournehouse Diorama (Mr and Mrs V. Haynes), by Sh. Ch. Royal Mark of Etherwood ex Bournehouse Honeydew, who was another sister of Meadowfern and Ballerina. Record holder for the number of C.C.s won by a bitch (22), until beaten by Sh. Ch. Starlite Express of Valset, was Sh. Ch. Bournehouse Enchantress, a daughter of Sh. Ch. Bournehouse Meadowfern, owned by Mr and Mrs H. Wheeler and sired by Sh. Ch. Engsett Electrode. Next came yet another litter brother and sister in Sh. Ch. Bournehouse Figaro (Mr T. Rooney) and Sh. Ch. Bournehouse Flirting Freda by Sh. Ch. Monksriding Ernford Flamingo out of Bournehouse Bluemoon.

Winner of Best in Show at Crufts in 1977 was Sh. Ch. Bournehouse Dancing Master by Sh. Ch. Monksriding Ernford Flamingo ex Sh. Ch. Bournehouse Ballerina, superbly handled, as were many of the Bournehouse dogs at this time, by Mrs Marion France. He went on to achieve the unique distinction of becoming Top Sire for six consecutive years, 1978 to 1983. His daughter Sh. Ch. Bournehouse Solo Dancer, out of Suntop Dewberry and owned by Miss J. Reed, won 15 C.C.s, and her full brother Sh. Ch. Bournehouse The Waltz King (Mrs B. Davies) also attained his title.

Also sired by Dancing Master were a further pair of litter sisters, Sh. Ch. Bournehouse Quickstep and Sh. Ch. Bournehouse Floral Dancer, ex Marus Sea Holly, followed by their full brother, Sh. Ch. Bournehouse Dancing Boy. Yet another son, Sh. Ch. Latest Dance of Bournehouse, ex Mrs Williams's (formerly Mrs D. Knight) Sh. Ch. Limestone Liberty, is fast emulating his famous father as a leading sire. Further title holders sired by Dancing Master were Sh. Ch. Mindenday Music Master owned and bred by Mr and Mrs Armstead. Music Master won 13 C.C.s, two gundog groups and Best in Show Midland Counties

1978; Sh. Ch. Wistaston School Scallywag of Triora and Sh. Ch. Wistaston School Snowdrift, both bred by Miss G. Williams; Sh. Ch. Scratchwood Tattycorum, owned and bred by Mr and Mrs Grassby; Sh. Ch. Invogue Headliner, Best in Show ESA 1987, bred by Mr and Mrs S. Henderson; Mrs L. Sawtell's Sh. Ch. Dancing Partner of Yeo and Miss J. Reed's Sh. Ch. Derriford Don Giovanni (see Derriford).

Mrs (Penny) Williams who retains her Penmartan affix bred Sh. Ch. Penmartan Opal.

The most recent title holders to date are Sh. Ch. Bournehouse Dark Prize, a daughter of Floral Dancer by Sh. Ch. Dancing Partner of Yeo, a son of Dancing Master, and Sh. Ch. Koiya the Highflier from Bournehouse, by Latest Dance ex Sh. Ch. Hawthorn Lady Grace, herself yet another daughter of Dancing Master.

Chelmset, Mr and Mrs J. Bowen

Commenced showing in the early 1970s with a bitch purchased as a pet who became Sh. Ch. Rebway Heron by Renmark Edgar ex Mursett Azure Anne. Jack Bowen became Secretary of the English Setter Association in 1976, a post he still holds at the time of writing. Awarded the MBE for services to industry in 1986. Has owned and bred numerous winning bitches including the C.C. winner Chelmset Meg Merrilees. Has never kept dogs. Latest title-holder Sh. Ch. Shadowood Blue Moon of Chelmset bred by Mr and Mrs M. Winch by Invogue Minstrel Boy ex Bournehouse Dancing Melody, a daughter of Dancing Master.

Derriford, Miss J. Reed

First big winner Sh. Ch. Ashpenda Red Robin purchased from Mrs Carol Duffield when she gave up breeding and showing. Biggest winner to date, Sh. Ch. Bournehouse Solo Dancer (for breeding see Bournehouse), winner of 15 C.C.s, mated to Red Robin produced Sh. Ch. Derriford Ondine and C.C. winner Derriford Copelia whose daughter, Derriford Pavane, mated back to Sh. Ch. Bournehouse

Dancing Master, produced Sh. Ch. Derriford Don Giovanni. Ten C.C.s to date and a gundog group winner. Winner of the two Res. C.C.s, Derriford Solo Flyer (Sh. Ch. Bournehouse Dancing Boy ex Sh. Ch. Derriford Ondine) dam of Derriford Morgan le Fay by Sh. Ch. Latest Dance of Bournehouse.

Elswood, Mrs V. Foss

This kennel, founded in the early 1940s, had successes in the early post-war years but dropped out of the picture for a few years following the death of Mrs Elsie Foss. After Mr Bill Foss's remarriage in the mid-60s the kennel reappeared, with the purchase of a blue dog-puppy who was to become Sh. Ch. Elswood Renmark Baronet by Sh. Ch. Senglish Early Mist ex Renmark Melody, bred by Mrs M. and Miss P. Neave. Baronet not only won 12 C.C.s but became a very successful sire. He sired six show champions, one of them being Sh. Ch. Elswood Ashpenda Moonquest, winner of six C.C.s and Best in Show Leicester Championship Show, 1971; he was bred by Mrs Carol Duffield out of Sh. Ch. Iroquois Bluemoon. Owned and bred by Mr and Mrs H. Pearson out of their Ernford Zia was Sh. Ch. Monksriding Baroness. Sh. Ch. Elswood White Heatherette, bred by Mrs Johnson ex Bousae Blue Belle, was owned by Mr and Mrs D. Baldwin. Home-bred was Sh. Ch. Elswood Highlight ex Elswood Aurora. An influential daughter of Baronet's was Sh. Ch. Wistaston School Holiday, bred by Miss G. Williams out of Suntop Royal Lark of Wistaston and owned by Mrs Johnson. She was mated to Sh. Ch. Ashpenda Red Robin to produce amongst others Marus Sea Holly (see Bournehouse). Sh. Ch. Renmark Nimrod, bred and owned by Mrs M. and Miss P. Neave, was out of Renmark Hostess, who was a daughter of Baronet's litter sister Renmark Baroness.

Sadly, in May 1970 Mr Bill Foss died, greatly lamented, not only as a breeder, exhibitor, judge, and long-serving officer of the ESA, but as a person. He was in every sense a 'gentle' man. Mrs Valerie Foss has carried on this famous kennel, and in 1978 she launched into the show ring Sh. Ch.

Elswood Vagabond King. Bred by her and Miss Gilchrist, he was by Sh. Ch. Bournehouse Dancing Master out of Sh. Ch. Ashpenda Kittiwake, and owned by Mesdames V. Foss and P. Wadsworth, he went on to become the breed's record holder with 40 C.C.s He also won four gundog groups and two Championship Show Best in Show awards, a record that will surely take some beating.

Engsett, Mr and Mrs H. Wheeler

Another of the few old established kennels still currently breeding and showing. Started in the late 1940s with a son of (Sh. Ch.) Ripleygae Mallory, Shiplake Hemlington Spotlight, who was a very successful show dog, winning nine Res. C.C.s, and an influential stud dog. He produced many winners including two show champions, Sh. Ch. Engsett Elect, owned by Mr F. Wilson, who was out of the Wheeler's foundation bitch Irisit Saucy Sue, herself a winner of one C.C. and four Res. C.C.s, and Sh. Ch. Engsett Enchantress of Fiveacres, winner of 5 C.C.s, ex Engsett Evening Mist, owned by Mr and Mrs R. Harrison. Enchantress mated to Ernford Easter Parade produced Sh. Ch. Engsett Brilliance of Fiveacres, owned by Mr and Mrs Wheeler and winner of seven C.C.s. Sh. Ch. Engsett Exception (Withirlee Sheik of Frejendor ex Engsett Exotic) was Best in Show at the ESA Championship Show in 1961 before being exported to Japan. He became a Japanese Champion and sired Sh. Ch. Engsett Encounter, bred by Mrs Dunn, ex Sea Mist of Noyna, who was litter sister to Sh. Ch. Sea Fairy of Noyna. Encounter in turn sired Sh. Ch. Engsett Electrode, winner of seven C.C.s; bred by Mrs Borrowdale, he was out of Sheena of Frejendor. Electrode became a top sire, being leading stud dog in 1972, 1973 and again in 1976. He sired six show champions and one full champion. These were Sh. Ch. Segedunum Persephone, Fenman Fragrance, Upperwood Zsa Zsa, Bournehouse Enchantress, Attleford Mulberry, Upperwood Lancelot of Nethermoor and Ch. Upperwood Zoe.

Sired by the American import Am. Ch. Clariho Rough 'n' Ready and bred by Mr and Mrs Hobson ex Willowsett

The English Setter

Windrush was Sh. Ch. Willowsett Whoopsie of Engsett.

Out of the Electrode daughter Upperwood Erelle was Sh. Ch. Engsett Everready of Rohan; owned by Mr and Mrs M. Thomas, he was sired by Sh. Ch. Iroquois Whiteseal Silvermorn. Everready sired Aus. Ch. Engsett Emprey, who, mated to Bournehouse Mistlethrush of Engsett, produced Sh. Ch. Engsett Par Excellence, leading stud dog in 1985 and 1986, sire of Mr and Mrs Oxley's Sh. Ch. Slipandre Red Grouse of Raffas, Sh. Ch. Willowsett Grouse of Gunalt, bred by Mr and Mrs Hobson out of Engsett Elegant Eve and owned by Mr and Mrs Hollings, and Sh. Ch. Valsett Videostar of Wansleydale.

Winner of 12 C.C.s and also out of Bournehouse Mistlethrush of Engsett was Sh. Ch. Engsett English Charmer; she was sired by Sh. Ch. Upperwood Rainbow Warrior. Bred by Mr and Mrs Wheeler in partnership with Mr and Mrs Armstead is Sh. Ch. Extravert of Engsett at Brucelin, sired by Sh. Ch. Mindenday Music Master ex Engsett Evita; she has won six C.C.s to date and is owned by Mrs R. Davies and Mr B. Jeffery.

By Music Master's son, Sh. Ch. Much More Music of Mindenday, ex a daughter of Empery, is Sh. Ch. Engsett Noble English, winner of nine C.C.s; he is owned in partnership with Mrs Barbara Davies, who has had many successes with her dogs, so ably handled by her husband Clive.

Hurwyn, Mrs S.E. Wilkinson

This kennel was started in 1949 by Mrs Wilkinson's mother, Mrs C. Wilson, and thence was a partnership until Mrs Wilson's death. First big winner was Hurwyn Rainbow, winner of two C.C.s by (Sh. Ch.) Ripleygae Topnote out of their foundation bitch Boisdale Bluecloud. Litter sister to Rainbow, Hurwyn Shadow, mated to Hurwyn Blizzard, produced Hurwyn Bluecloud, the dam of the litter brother and sister by Int. Sh. Ch. Iroquois Casanova, Sh. Ch. Iroquois Stormcloud and Sh. Ch. Trodgers Hurwyn Heaven. Sh. Ch. Iroquois Stormcloud, mated to Hurwyn Trodgers Rika (litter sister to Sh. Ch. Trodgers Meadow Fescue), produced the outstanding orange bitch Sh. Ch. Hurwyn Morning Glory, winner of eight C.C.s Rika produced another show champion, this time by Suntop Birdsong, in Hurwyn All Glory.

This kennel over the years has consistently produced outstanding bitches, the notable exception being the orange dog Sh. Ch. Hurwyn Wigeon, by Suntop Winterbird ex Ernford Bobolink. He was a great showman, and, superbly handled by his owner Mr D. Mulholland, he was for a long time the breed record-holder, winning 28 C.C.s as well as numerous gundog groups. Sired by Suntop Birdsong ex another Ernford-bred bitch, Hurwyn Ernford Fairybird (litter sister to the famous litter brothers Sh. Ch. Monksriding Ernford Flamingo and Sh. Ch. Ernford Falcon), was Sh. Ch. Suford Hurwyn Whinchat, owned by Mrs Y. Rudin. Sh. Ch. Hurwyn Waterail of Settrenda and Sh. Ch. Settrenda Super Serenity, both owned by Mr C. Brown, were sired by Wigeon.

1975 saw the birth of not only a great show bitch but of an even greater brood. Winner of eight C.C.s and also out of Hurwyn Ernford Fairybird, sired by Birdsong's son, Hurwyn Day Boy, was Sh. Ch. Hurwyn Paper Doll, who produced (all to Hurwyn Flightmaster) Sh. Ch. Hurwyn Baby Doll and the litter sisters Sh. Ch. Hurwyn Cupie Doll and Sh. Ch. Hurwyn Paper Star.

In addition to all these outstanding bitches it should be mentioned that Hurwyn Dayboy, Hurwyn Flightmaster and more recently Hurwyn Paper Pilot have all been most influential stud dogs. Dayboy also sired the litter sisters bred by Mrs M. Jarvis, Sh. Ch. Merrysett Snowbunting and Sh. Ch. Merrysett Snow Sparkle, the trio Sh. Ch. Tattersett Eyecatcher, Sh. Ch. Tattersett Hidden Value and Sh. Ch. Tattersett Inycarra, bred by Mrs F. Grimsdell, and Miss D. Jones's Sh. Ch. Grelancot Evita, a total of seven. Hurwyn Flightmaster, who was by Int. Sh. Ch. Suntop Winter Breeze ex Dayboy's litter sister Hurwyn Dawn Chorus, was even more successful and, in addition to those previously mentioned, sired Mrs A. Morgan's Sh. Ch. Quensha Flight of Dreams of Kenidjack, Sh. Ch. Settrenda So Steady, Sh. Ch. Colverset Connoisseur, winner of six C.C.s and winner of a gundog group, and Sh. Ch. Mariglen Highlight, owned and bred by Mrs J. Dennis. This bitch is of all-Hurwyn breeding, being out of Hurwyn Chorus Girl. Flightmaster also sired Sh. Ch. Northgate Starflight of Abbonny, who was out of Northgate Woodlark and who was a daughter of Sh. Ch. Iroquois Whiteseal Silvermorn, and Mrs Morag Jarvis's Sh. Ch. Merrysett Sweet Sue, a daughter of Snowbunting.

At the time of writing, the young bitch Hurwyn Pillow Talk already has one C.C. to her credit and will surely join this illustrious band of titled ladies.

Iroquois, Mrs L.A. Allan-Scott

First English Setter purchased from Miss 'Archdale' Rumball in 1939, first litter bred in 1947 and started showing in 1952 and has since amassed over 100 C.C.s. Acquired from Mrs Broadhead what was to become the foundation bitch Iroquois Ernford Irresistible to whom all the subsequent Iroquois trace back. Mated to Sh. Ch. Prince Charming of Ketree (owned in partnership with Mr J.B. McNally) she produced in her first litter Int. Sh. Ch. Iroquois Casanova and the Continental Int.Ch. Iroquois Cinderella. A repeat mating produced Sh. Ch. Iroquois Courtesan and Sh. Ch. Pride of Noyna.

Casanova, winner of the Gundog Group, Windsor, 1960 sired five show champions, namely Sh. Ch. Littlewoodcote Carousel, the litter brother and sister Sh. Ch. Iroquois Stormcloud and Sh. Ch. Trodgers Hurwyn Heaven, who was Best of Breed at Crufts two years in succession in 1967 and 1968, and litter sisters Sh. Ch. Flying Star of Fermanar and Sh. Ch. Iroquois Cascade, who won the gundog group and was Reserve Best in Show, Three Counties, 1966.

Courtesan, who won six C.C.s, was the dam of Sh. Ch. Iroquois Bluemoon, foundation bitch of the Ashpenda Kennel, and was a winner of nine C.C.s. She was sired by Suntop Songbird. Litter sister to Sh. Ch. Littlewoodcote Carousel was Iroquois Littlewoodcote Caprice who, mated to Shiplake Shandy, produced Sh. Ch. Iroquois Cointreau, who was the dam of Iroquois Jasmine, foundation bitch

Leading Kennels

of the Bournehouse Kennel. Sh. Ch. Iroquois Stormcloud, winner of six C.C.s, was Best in Show at the ESA 1967, also winning the Stud Dog class, and was leading sire of that year. He sired Sh. Ch. Hurwyn Morning Glory, Sh. Ch. Iroquois Strathspey, Sh. Ch. Iroquois Solitaire and Sh. Ch. Iroquois Rainbow, who was Reserve Best Gundog at Crufts 1972.

Strathspey, whose dam was Cascade, sired Sh. Ch. Iroquois Mooncloud ex Solitaire (who was out of Bluemoon), Sh. Ch. Hayrick Ploughboy, Best in Show WELKS 1973, and the outstanding litter brother and sister Sh. Ch. Trodgers Scots Oat and Sh. Ch. Trodgers Bluebell. Scots Oat won the Gundog Group at Crufts 1971. Winner of 10 C.C.s and the Gundog Group WELKS 1972, also Best of Breed Crufts 1973 and 1975, was Sh. Ch. Iroquois Whiteseal Silvermorn by Sh. Ch. Lad of the Haar ex a Stormcloud daughter; he was a prolific sire and his offspring included the title holders Sh. Ch. Engsett Everready of Rohan, Sh. Ch. Kanchary Grey Ladybird of Invogue, owned by Mr and Mrs S. Henderson, and the litter brothers Sh. Ch. Iroquois Snowstorm of Sundeala and Sh. Ch. Iroquois Snowprince of Northgate.

Bred by Mrs I. Foreman, sired by Iroquois Moonstorm, was Sh. Ch. Iroquois Skylark, who was the dam of Sh. Ch. Iroquois Regalia, sired by Snowprince. Snowstorm sired Sh. Ch. Iroquois Sansovino of Sundeala. Winner of 12 C.C.s and two gundog groups, he was top-winning English Setter 1979. Snowprince and Snowstorm were out of my daughter Mrs 'Sandy' Bolton's Reserve C.C.-winning Iroquois Snowbird. Sansovino was out of Iroquois Sunstream; winning a Junior Warrant and three Reserve C.C.s, she was by Sh. Ch. Ashpenda Red Robin ex Sh. Ch. Iroquois Mooncloud. Sansovino's litter sister was the great brood bitch Iroquois Springsong, who produced the Junior Warrant winner Iroquois Sorcerer by Settrenda Super Symbol as well as the Show Champions Iroquois Concerto (by Iroquois Stormbird) and Crescendo (by Northgate Copper King). Concerto won 8 C.C.s, two gundog groups and Reserve Best in Show, Bath, 1981. He sired Mrs I. Foreman's Sh. Ch. Settrenda Serenata of Somoray and

C.C.-winning litter sister Settrenda Serenade, owned and bred by Mr C. Brown, and Mr and Mrs P. Dunk's Sh. Ch. Samelen Fanfare.

Crescendo, winner of his Junior Warrant and six C.C.s, and seven Reserve C.C.s to date, becomes the twentieth Iroquois Show Champion.

Northgate, Mr and Mrs W. Fuller

This kennel was founded in the early '60s, the first big winner being Sh. Ch. Northgate Dubonnet. Home-bred, he was by Northgate Hurricane, who was a son of Sh. Ch. Engsett Electrode ex a daughter of Sh. Ch. Oldholbans Dill.

Out of Dubonnet's litter sister Northgate Quaker Girl and by Northgate Invader, a son of Sh. Ch. Iroquois Whiteseal Silvermorn ex Hurricane's litter sister Northgate Harmony, was Sh. Ch. Northgate Blue Brocade. Further title holders were Sh. Ch. Iroquois Snowprince of Northgate, his daughter Sh. Ch. Northgate Silvermoon, whose dam was a daughter of Dubonnet, and Sh. Ch. Northgate Starflight of Abbonny (see Hurwyn). The most recent title-holder at the time of writing was Sh. Ch. Northgate Grenadier, who is by Snowprince ex Blue Brocade and is fast making his name as a successful sire.

Silbury, Mr and Mrs P. Gardiner-Swann

Another of the long-established kennels, founded in the late '40s. First big winner Silbury Jubilee Gem of Madavale, who became a great brood bitch. Breeders of the immortal Sh. Ch. Silbury Soames of Madavale, owned by Mrs A. Williams. Soames was the long-time breed record-holder with 24 C.C.s. Among his numerous successes were Best in Show at the ESA Championship Show 1962 and 1963, Birmingham National 1962, Bath 1963 as well as Reserve Best in Show WELKS and Paignton 1963. At Crufts he was Reserve Best in Show 1961 and 1963 before becoming Supreme Best in Show in 1964. He was sired by Silbury Sherper ex Silbury Springhead Serene, and his litter sister Sh. Ch. Redtops Silbury Sonya, owned by Mrs N. Treharne, also gained her title. A full brother from a later litter, Silbury Seeker, was a C.C. winner as more recently has been Yeo Blueberry of Silbury, bred by Mrs L. Sawtell.

Mrs N. Treharne also bred Sh. Ch. Redtops Rozena, owned by Mr and Mrs R. Green. She was by Sh. Ch. Kenandra Lord Helpus ex Redtops Ranastar and was Best in Show at the ESA 1983. Mrs Treharne bred the Continental Champion Redtops Rompster owned by Mrs P. Gerster.

Suntop, Miss M.D. Barnes

One of the most successful and influential kennels over the last thirty years. First title holder was Ch. Suntop Suzette of Sewerby, but all present-day Suntops trace back to Ch. Suntop Carnival Queen, through her son Suntop Songbird by Ernford Kingfisher. Songbird won his Junior Warrant and nine Reserve C.C.s and went on to become a truly great sire. He sired six show champions, namely Sh. Ch. Senglish Early Mist, Sh. Ch. Suntop Royalbird, Sh. Ch. Suntop Snowbird, Sh. Ch. Iroquois Bluemoon, Int. Sh. Ch. Noyna Rockette and Int. Sh. Ch. Suntop Seabird.

Sired by Sh. Ch. Suntop Royalbird was Sh. Ch. Royal Mark of Etherwood and the litter brothers Int. Sh. Ch. Suntop Royal Sunglint and Int. Sh. Ch. Suntop Royal Sunrise. Sunglint was the sire of Sh. Ch. Ernford Chaffinch, Sh. Ch. Ednasid Wuster, Sh. Ch. Noyna Gazelle and Sh. Ch. Fencefoot Freckles, owned and bred by Mesdames Marsden and Croft.

Int. Sh. Ch. Suntop Seabird sired Sh. Ch. Suntop Bluewings and Mrs M. Brown's Sh. Ch. Suntop Seamoss of the Haar, bred by Mrs M. Sedgley. Bluewings was the sire of Sh. Ch. Suntop Bluethrush, who was out of the Suntop Songbird daughter Suntop Songthrush, who with her litter sister Suntop Songfinch were great brood bitches.

Bluethrush was the dam of the beautiful blue dog Int. Sh. Ch. Suntop Winterbreeze sired by Suntop Winterbird. Winterbreeze himself was the sire of six show champions, the litter brothers Sh. Ch. Suntop Starling and Sh. Ch. Suntop Nightingale, the litter brothers and sisters Sh. Ch.

Suntop Dark Breeze, owned by Mrs G. Fairbairn, and Sh. Ch. Suntop True Breeze, Sh. Ch. Arnsett Alfa and Sh. Ch. Arnsett Afaya (see Arnsett).

Starling sired Sh. Ch. Suford Lucky Star of Beamans, bred by Mrs Y. Rudin, and Sh. Ch. Suntop Freckled Star, owned by Mr and Mrs D. Lewis, who also owned his son Sh. Ch. Suntop Freckled Braid of Lewkins. Nightingale sired another pair of brother-and-sister show champions in Sh. Ch. Arnsett Dark Night and Sh. Ch. Arnsett Night Daisy of Fencefoot (see Arnsett), and also sired Sh. Ch. Suntop Fair Gale, owned by Mr and Mrs S. Tait, who is the sire of Mrs L. Howarth's Sh. Ch. Moorbrook Dolly Mixture. Sh. Ch. Tragus Night Breeze, owned by Miss T. Watkins and bred by Mr and Mrs P. Upton, is a further title holder by Nightingale.

Two very influential stud dogs were Suntop Birdsong and his son, Suntop Winterbird. Birdsong sired Mrs R. Timms' home-bred Sh. Ch. Shandarrat Damask Rose and C.C.-winning litter sister Shandarrat Tiger Lily, these two being out of a daughter of Sh. Ch. Iroquois Solitaire and Sh. Ch. Hurwyn All Glory. Suntop Winterbird sired nine show champions and was one of the greatest winner producers of present times. His titled offspring were Sh. Ch. Adam Ahaseurus, owned by Mrs H. Lenzi, Sh. Ch. Carofel Whispering Romance, Sh. Ch. Hurwyn Wigeon, Sh. Ch. Oudenarde Dancing Glory, owned and bred by Mrs D. and Miss F. Hamilton, the litter brother and sister Sh. Ch. Ashpenda Red Robin and Sh. Ch. Ashpenda Kittiwake, Sh. Ch. Ashpenda Golden Eagle of Ritanor, owned by Mrs B. Wells, Sh. Ch. Wistaston School Sunshine and the aforementioned Int. Sh. Ch. Suntop Winterbreeze.

Two further title holders bred in this kennel were Mr R. Powell's Sh. Ch. Flatford Why Wonder by Suntop Wonderbird and Sh. Ch. Suntop Royal Flint, owned by Mrs C. Wiggerham.

Tattersett, Mr and Mrs A. Grimsdell

Former affix Attleford in partnership with Mrs Fran Grimsdell's mother, Mrs J. Thomas. Bred Sh. Ch. Attleford

Mulberry by Sh. Ch. Engsett Electrode, Dutch Ch. Attleford Silver Button by Sh. Ch. Iroquois Whiteseal Silvermoon and Sh. Ch. Attleford Mr Cinders by Attleford Huntsman; these three were all out of Attleford Silver Lining. Also owner-bred was Sh. Ch. Attleford Brown Betty.

Foundation bitch of the Tattersett's was Sh. Ch. Ashpenda Golden Pheasant, bred by Mrs C. Duffield, sired by Sh. Ch. Attleford Mulberry out of the great brood bitch Ashpenda Petite Etoile. Mated to Hurwyn Dayboy, Golden Pheasant produced the litter sisters, Sh. Ch. Tattersett Eyecatcher, Sh. Ch. Tattersett Hidden Value and Sh. Ch. Tattersett Inycarra. Eyecatcher's C.C. – winning son, Tattersett Star Turn, proved to be a great stud force; amongst his many winners was Sh. Ch. Tattersett Was I Right, whose son Sh. Ch. Tattersett Dutch Courage by Sh. Ch. Latest Dance of Bournehouse is the most recent title holder to date.

Tragus, Mr and Mrs P. Upton

A comparatively new but very successful kennel, founded in the mid-70s. Great foundation bitch Sh. Ch. Weatherdair Moon Breeze of Tragus, by Sh. Ch. Renmark Nimrod ex Weatherdair Lunar Lady, bred by Mrs J. Neal. In her first litter by Sh. Ch. Suntop Nightingale, she produced Sh. Ch.Tragus Night Breeze, C.C. winner Tragus Romantic Breeze, Junior Warrant and Reserve C.C. winner Tragus Nightingale's Moon, and the consistent winner Tragus Morning Breeze, owned by Mr Robert Upton. In her second and only other litter she produced Sh. Ch. Tragus Moonstorm. Romantic Breeze has produced a C.C. winner in Tragus Moon Goddess, sired by Suford Sedum, and the litter sisters by Hurwyn Paper Pilot, both of whom are Reserve C.C. winners, Tragus Romantic Moon of Carriemore and Tragus Paper Breeze of Elmwood. Moonstorm's daughter, Golden Flame of Tragus, has also won Reserve C.C.s.

By Sh. Ch. Colverset Connoisseur ex Tragus Shimmering Moon is the current Tragus title-holder at the time of writing, Sh. Ch. Tragus Shine on Harvey Moon. Nightingale's

Moon is the sire of C.C. winner Denebank Bertoloni, who in turn is the sire of Sh. Ch. Crystal Cracker of Capriole, both owned by Mrs L. Madden.

Upperwood, Mrs D. Goutorbe

Numerically speaking, there is no doubt that this is the largest kennel of English Setters since the days of the famous Shiplakes of Mrs J. English, as the Upperwood Kennel not only breeds show dogs but also breeds, trains and works field triallers. Unhappily, during the writing of this book Mr René Goutorbe died; he was very much involved in the working side and had numerous successes at field trials.

On the show side, the first big winner was Ch. Upperwood Zoe by Sh. Ch. Engsett Electrode out of the foundation bitch Withenlee Wallflower. Zoe won nine C.C.s, and attained her qualifier. This mating proved to be most successful, as a repeat produced Sh. Ch. Upperwood Lancelot of Nethermoor, winner of five C.C.s, and a further repeat mating produced Sh. Ch. Upperwood Zsa Zsa. Zoe was the dam of Mr and Mrs K. Spencer's striking orange dog Sh. Ch. Upperwood Zeno of Sorbus, and Lancelot was the sire of Mrs S. Leiper's Sh. Ch. James James from Farmacy. Winner of seven C.C.s was Mrs P. Spillane's Sh. Ch. Upperwood Rainbow Warrior, who was the sire of Sh. Ch. Engsett English Charmer.

Various other strains have been infused over the years, and two very highly successful stud dogs have emerged in Hazelbarrow Sebastian of Upperwood, by Sh. Ch. Mindenday Music Master ex a daughter of Lancelot, and Lanbar Shades of Blue from Upperwood, by a Sh. Ch. Bournehouse Dancing Master son, Upperwood Polka, ex a daughter of Sh. Ch. Iroquois Snowstorm of Sundeala.

Sebastian sired Sh. Ch. Snowstorm of Upperwood, winner of nine C.C.s and winner of a gundog group; Mr and Mrs K. Spencer's Sh. Ch. Upperwood Midnight Melody of Sorbus; Sh. Ch. Holdgrange Golden Frolic of Settella and Mrs P. Colton's Sh. Ch. Coldynne Yorkshire Relish. Midnight Melody is the dam of Sh. Ch. Sorbus Midnight Blue, her sire being Sh. Ch. Bournehouse Dancing Boy. Snowstorm is the sire of the litter brothers owned and bred by Mrs B. Hacking, Sh. Ch. Benrae Guardsman and Sh. Ch. Benrae Grenadier.

Lanbar Shades of Blue from Upperwood has sired so many winners, including the litter brother and sister Sh. Ch. Upperwood Flash Dance, who has attained his Spanish and Portuguese titles under the ownership of Mr and Mrs Requena, and Sh. Ch. Upperwood Modern Romance, owned by Mesdames S. Wallis and J. Hirst. He sired an outstanding litter, bred by Mr and Mrs N. Kelly out of Sorbus Forever Free, of which no less than five became championship show winners, the best known being the Junior Warrant winner Richecca in Blue Jeans, owned by Mrs Z. Sparkes.

Valsett, Mr and Mrs J. Watkin

This kennel really hit the headlines in the late '80s with the phenomenal success of the bitch Sh. Ch. Starlite Express of Valsett, but their successes go back much further, to the early '70s. First big winner was Weatherdair Hurricane, winner of two C.C.s, bred by Mr and Mrs F. Neal, by Suntop Wonderbird ex Suntop Royal Gleam. He was followed by his son, Aureola of Valsett, who also won two C.C.s as well as five Reserve C.C.s.

The first title-holder was Sh. Ch. Sunlight of Valsett, winner of five C.C.s, sired by Sh. Ch. Bellesett Baron of Upperwood ex a daughter of Aus. Ch. Engsett Empery. Sunlight has been a great sire and has consistently produced winners over the years, including the immortal Starlite Express, who at the time of writing has won 24 C.C.s to take the bitch breed record, 10 gundog groups (another record) and numerous Best in Show awards, including Crufts 1988.

Another lovely bitch to come from this kennel, winner of eight C.C.s, gundog groups and Best in Show at the ESA 1985 was Sh. Ch. Valsett Arominta. Home-bred, she was sired by Engsett Electrode Mark (litter brother to Sh. Ch. Engsett Par Excellence) out of Valsett Dancing Music.

Sh. Ch. Valsett Video Star of Wansleydale, owned by Mrs L. Taylor, by Sh. Ch. Engsett Par Excellence ex Valsett Spandau Ballet, also gained her title in 1988. Celestial Dreamer of Valsett (Rowmere the Dealer ex Valsett Aerobic Dancer) is also a C.C. winner.

Wistaston, Miss G. Williams

A kennel founded in the late '60s that is probably as well-known for Cocker Spaniels as English Setters, as they have produced numerous winners in both breeds. Foundation bitch of the English Setters was Suntop Royal Lark of Wistaston (Int. Sh. Ch. Suntop Royal Sunrise ex Suntop Songfinch). Mated to Sh. Ch. Elswood Renmark Baronet she produced Sh. Ch. Wistaston School Holiday, who is owned by Mrs P. Johnson and who was the dam of Marus Sea Holly, dam of the litter sisters, Sh. Ch. Bournehouse Quickstep and Sh. Ch. Bournehouse Floral Dancer, and also dam of Sh. Ch. Bournehouse Dancing Boy.

Full sister to School Holiday was Wistaston School Mystery, who was a great winner producer. To Sh. Ch. Monksriding Ernford Flamingo she produced Sh. Ch. Wistaston School Whisper of Gaewill, Sh. Ch. Wistaston School Scatterbrain, winner of 10 C.C.s, Wistaston School Summer, who was the dam of Sh. Ch. Wistaston School Snowdrift, Wistaston School Breakaway of Triora, the dam of Miss Williams's successful stud dog Wistaston School Heartbreak, his litter sister Sh. Ch. Wistaston School Sunshine, by Suntop Winterbird, and Wistaston School Report of Upperwood, the sire of Sh. Ch. Bellesett Baron of Upperwood.

Sired by Heartbreak were Sh. Ch. Wistaston School Playtime, who was out of Wistaston School Icefairy, litter sister to Snowdrift, and Wistaston School Lovebird of Holdgrange, the dam of Sh. Ch. Holdgrange Golden Frolic of Settella.

Other prominent kennels that deserve a mention, having consistently produced winning stock including title holders, are: *Brucelm* (Mrs R. Davies and Mr B. Jeffrey), *Colverset* (Mr and Mrs C. Roberts), *Grelancot* (Miss D. Jones), *Kenandra*

Leading Kennels

(Mesdames S. Wallis and J. Hirst), *Mariglen* (Mrs J. Dennis), *Mindenday* (Mr and Mrs R. Armstead), *Moorbrook* (Mr and Mrs Howarth), *Quensha* (Mrs A. Morgan), *Samelen* (Mr and Mrs P. Dunks), *Settrenda* (Mr C. Brown), *Shadowood* (Mr and Mrs M. Winch), *Soberhill* (Mr and Mrs K. Smith), *Sorbus* (Mr and Mrs K. Spencer), *Sundeala* (Mrs B. Davies), *Willowsett* (Mr and Mrs D. Hobson) and *Yeo* (Mrs L. Sawtell).

12
Ailments

It is advantageous to have some knowledge of the ailments you are likely to come up against, as many of the more minor ailments can be dealt with without taking up the time of your veterinary surgeon. If your dog shows any signs of being 'off-colour', take his temperature. The normal temperature of a healthy dog is 101.5°F (38.5°C); if the temperature rises to over 102°F or drops to under 100°F, veterinary advice should be sought. Always use a blunt-ended thermometer, which should be smeared with a little vaseline and inserted into the rectum. Should you deem it necessary to call in your veterinary surgeon, be clear and concise when informing him of the symptoms so that he will know which drugs, injections etc. to bring with him, but do remember that vets are very busy people and should not be called out except in an emergency. Most veterinary surgeons have an appointment system these days, and you should always attend the surgery if at all possible.

Anal Glands
These glands, situated either side of the anus, occasionally become blocked. Symptoms include the dog rubbing his rear along the ground or nibbling or licking under his tail. Take a fairly large piece of cotton wool and with the finger and thumb firmly squeeze each side of the anal opening which should empty the glands of any secretion that has accumulated. If the trouble persists, consult your veterinary surgeon, as an abscess may have formed.

Bites
If your dog should get bitten during a fight, wash the

Ailments

wound well with a mild solution of antiseptic. (You may need to snip the hair away from the affected area.) Dust with an antiseptic dusting powder. If the wound is severe, it may need suturing (stitching). Watch for swelling, especially if the wound is on the leg, as there may be some infection, in which case an antibiotic may be necessary.

Bloat
More correctly called gastric dilation and often resulting in torsion (twisting), this condition causes great abdominal pain. It will be noticed that the abdomen becomes very swollen and hard, and the dog may have difficulty in breathing. The causes include taking exercise too soon after feeding, and drinking after dry (complete) feeds. This is an emergency, as the gas formed must be released, and the stomach emptied very quickly. Send for your veterinary surgeon at once, or this condition might well prove fatal.

Burns (or Scalds)
Dress with acriflavin and keep the dog warm and quiet, as there is always the likelihood of shock. It is always advisable to consult your veterinary surgeon in burn cases.

Canker (Otitis)
There are many forms of this inflammation of the ear, ranging from a mild irritation which will cause the dog to scratch his ears or hold his head on one side, to otodectic mange, which is usually caused by a mite, and results in severe irritation accompanied by a dark and unpleasant smelling discharge. The interior of the ear will become red, swollen and very hot. The ear should be swabbed out gently with warm water and then dried well with cotton wool. Benzyl benzoate is very good for keeping the ears clean and free from mites. There are numerous good ear-dressings on the market, available from most pet shops. One of the best is Otodex, and an excellent ointment available from your veterinary surgeon is Panalog.

Chorea
A distressing condition which is nearly always the aftermath of distemper and leaves the dog with a violent twitch in one of its muscles, sometimes ending in total paralysis. In this case the kindest thing is humane destruction.

Conjunctivitis
Inflammation of the eye, which may be caused by a virus or bacterial infection, or a foreign body such as grit. There is often a pus-like discharge, and the membranes appear red and swollen. A certain amount of relief can be obtained by bathing the eyes with a diluted solution of sodium bicarbonate, and after drying squeeze Golden Eye Ointment in the corner of each eye. Veterinary advice should be sought, however, as antibiotic drops or ointment are almost certainly necessary.

Constipation
Almost always caused by wrong feeding. Alter the diet so that it contains laxative foods such as All Bran and dose with liquid paraffin. If the condition persists, consult your veterinary surgeon, as there may be some form of blockage.

Cough
Coughing occurs in many diseases such as distemper, hard pad, pneumonia, bronchitis and heart trouble, but by far the most common is kennel cough. This is a highly infectious condition, generally manifesting itself amongst puppies and young dogs during the summer months, although dogs of all ages can be affected. As it is made up of numerous viruses and bacteria (rather like the human common cold), dogs may catch the complaint more than once. Symptoms are a dry husky cough, retching (as if the dog had something stuck in his throat) and sometimes a discharge from the nose. Sufferers should be isolated immediately and dosed with a good cough mixture such as Benylin, but it is most important to obtain antibiotics from your veterinary surgeon as quickly as possible. *Do not take your dog to the surgery if he is coughing.* The duration of the

Sh. Ch. Starlite Express of Valsett – Crufts Supreme Champion 1988 and bitch CC record holder

Dalton

Sh. Ch. Elswood Vagabond King – breed record holder with 40 CCs and 12 Reserve CCs

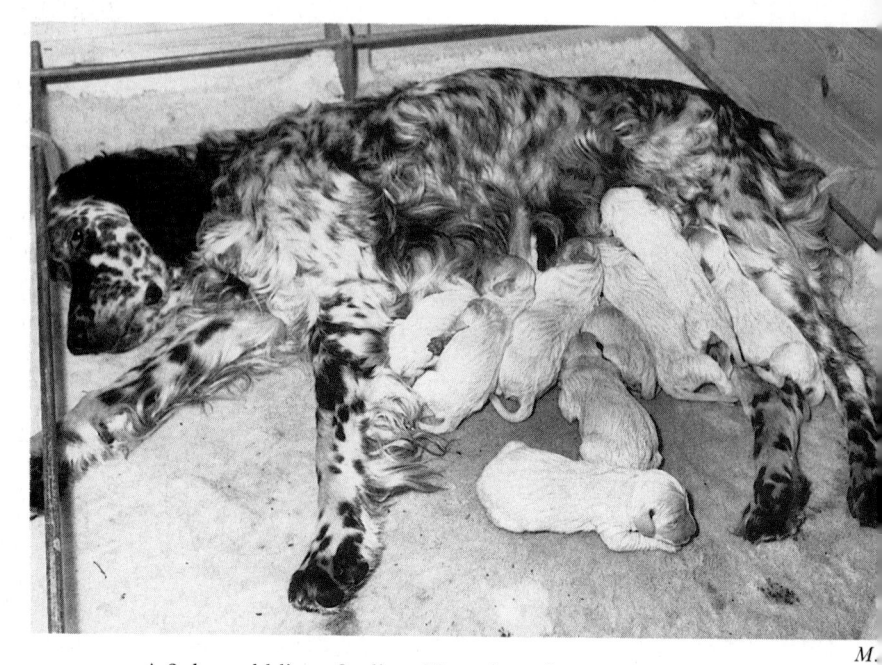

A 3 days old litter feeding. Note the rails round the whelping box

6 weeks old puppies need plenty of rest! By Sh. Ch. Upperwood Zero of Sorbus ex Bournehouse Dancing Melody

Sh. Ch. Iroquois Regalia – top winning bitch 1982

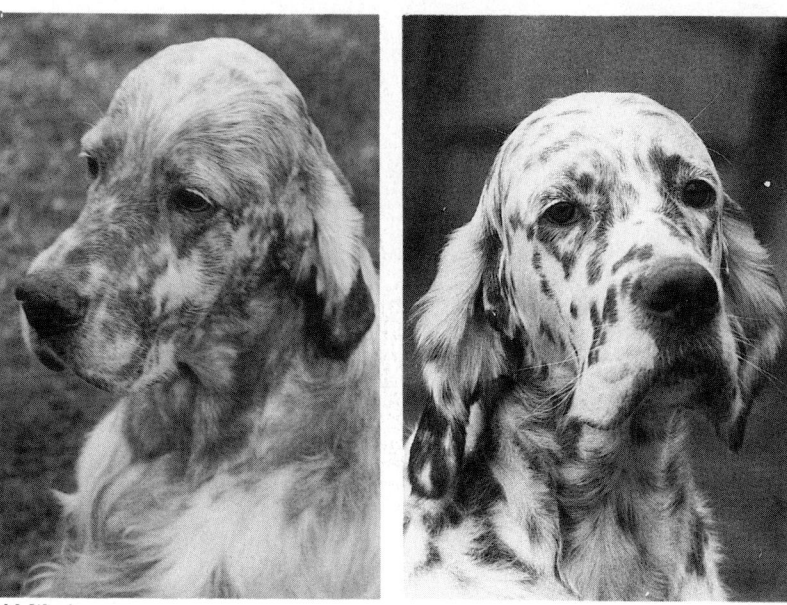

M. Winch *R. Heron*
Two head studies – Sh. Ch. Iroquois Crescendo (*left*) and Sh. Ch. Iroquois Concerto – both ex the great brood bitch Iroquois Springsong

The author with Sh. Ch. Iroquois Concerto, winner of 8 CCs and one of his puppies with the Best in Show Cup, Setter and Pointer Ch. Show

Ailments

complaint varies considerably from a few days to two or three weeks, likewise the severity. Some dogs only cough once or twice, whilst others will be quite badly affected.

Cystitis
Inflammation of the bladder usually caused by a bacterial infection. The dog may pass urine more frequently than usual, though he can sometimes appear to have trouble actually passing water, and there is often some blood present. Veterinary treatment is essential in cases of cystitis.

Diabetes
This complaint is caused by the pancreas failing to produce enough insulin, causing high sugar levels in the blood. The dog will pass an abnormal amount of urine and will drink excessively; if diabetes is suspected, consult your veterinary surgeon as the dog will need a special diet and, in severe cases, injections of insulin.

Diarrhoea
This condition is associated with many infectious diseases or may be caused by a virus or bacteria, especially if there is any blood in the motion. Consult your veterinary surgeon to administer an antibiotic. If the condition is not severe and the dog does not appear otherwise unwell, relief can often be obtained by dosing with kaolin and morphine.

Distemper
A highly infectious disease, caused by a virus. Fortunately it is much rarer these days than it used to be due to inoculation. It is essential that all puppies should be vaccinated as early as possible. Symptoms vary considerably, but most cases are accompanied by gummy eyes, runny nose, a harsh dry cough, high temperature and general listlessness. If the disease is suspected, isolate the dog immediately; keep him warm and send for the veterinary surgeon. The eyes should be kept bathed; smear vaseline or cod liver oil on the nose to prevent it becoming encrusted. The dog will probably refuse all solid food, but nutrition can be given in the form of beef broth, calf's-foot jelly or Brands Essence.

He will probably have an excessive thirst, but drinking should be restricted to a small cupful of water at a time, to which a teaspoonful of glucose should be added.

Eclampsia
A distressing condition which manifests itself in lactating bitches, caused by abnormally low calcium in the blood. Prompt veterinary treatment is essential in the form of calcium injections, but the bitch should be watched carefully as the condition may recur. The in-whelp bitch should always be given extra calcium in either liquid or tablet form during gestation, and this should be continued throughout lactation.

Eczema
There are two forms of this condition, wet and dry, the latter being the more common in English Setters. The part most generally affected is down the back, especially just above the root of the tail. It should not be confused with mange, as it is not caused by a parasite. One of the principal causes of eczema is wrong feeding. Avoid heating foods such as flaked maize or foods containing this, as do many of the 'complete feeds'. Dose with a cooling medicine such as milk of magnesia and apply benzyl benzoate to the affected parts every two or three days, then bathe with Seleen.

Fits
These can be caused by a number of things, e.g. aftermath of distemper, worms, teething in young dogs and severe abdominal pain. Indications are a sudden collapse with the limbs extended and rigid. Frequently the dog will 'paddle' his feet. The jaws will become clamped tight, and he will froth at the mouth. There is also the likelihood of involuntary passing of urine and even the emptying of bowels. A fit may only last a minute or two, and the dog may appear quite normal afterwards, but in some cases he may appear quite dazed for some hours. Sight is generally the last sense to return fully, and the dog will often walk into things. Keep the dog warm and very quiet in a darkened room

Ailments

until recovery is complete. It is not necessary to call out your veterinary surgeon as the dog will probably have recovered by the time he arrives, but the vet should be informed in order to diagnose the cause and prevent further attacks.

Fleas (see Parasites)

Gastro-Enteritis
This is a distressing complaint, a combination of gastritis and enteritis, usually starting with diarrhoea accompanied by blood in the motion. The dog may also vomit and will probably have an intense thirst. Give plenty of water to drink to prevent dehydration but feed only a light diet of white meat, fish, eggs, boiled rice. Dose with kaolin and morphine and consult your veterinary surgeon to administer antibiotics.

Growths
These can be small papillomas and warts, which should be removed by your veterinary surgeon if they show signs of rapid growth. This also applies to cysts which are generally small swellings under the skin, which may be as small as a pea, but which sometimes grow and cause discomfort. By far the most serious form of growths are tumours, the commonest being those that manifest themselves in the mammary glands of bitches. These hard lumps can sometimes stay static for some considerable time and cause no discomfort, but if they show signs of rapid growth or any sign of bursting or discharging, seek veterinary advice immediately as surgery will almost certainly be necessary.

Haematoma
A soft swelling most commonly found on the inner side of the ear flap, which is caused by a clot of blood under the skin, generally the result of the dog shaking his head. Consult your veterinary surgeon as the swelling must be opened and drained or your dog may be left with an ugly 'cauliflower' ear.

Haemorrhage

English Setters are inclined to haemorrhage after whelping; this is thought to be a form of haemophilia (an inherited defect which prevents the blood clotting). It can occur any time between three and ten days after whelping, but should not be confused with the normal dark discharge. However, if the flow becomes bright red and the loss heavy, call your veterinary surgeon at once to administer a blood coagulant. Depending on the severity, two or three injections of Vitamin K may be required. An internal haemorrhage may be caused by a road accident or by the dog swallowing some foreign body. The dog will show signs of pain and the gums and lips will be very pale. It is essential that you act quickly in cases of haemorrhage or death may result.

Hard Pad

This is a form of canine distemper, again much less common than it used to be thanks to inoculation. The symptoms are very similar to those for distemper and should be treated in the same way. The disease takes its name from the tendency of the pads to harden. It is most important to have all puppies vaccinated at eight weeks and to follow this up with a booster inoculation every year.

Harvest Mites (see Parasites)

Heart Attack

The likelihood of a heart attack is much greater in the older dog. The dog will suddenly collapse and lie as if dead. However, recovery is usually quite rapid. Keep the dog warm and quiet. A few drops of brandy can be administered, but inform your veterinary surgeon without delay, so that he may prescribe the necessary medication.

Hepatitis

This dreaded disease is a viral or bacterial infection which attacks the liver and manifests itself with alarming rapidity. The dog appears to be in great pain, accompanied by vomiting, diarrhoea and possibly convulsions. Call your

Ailments

veterinary surgeon at once if suspected, but cases are rare these days as once again we inoculate against it. The inoculation for hepatitis is given at the same time as the one for hard pad and distemper.

Hernia
Most hernias occur in the groin and require surgery. However, another common one is the umbilical hernia, or ruptured navel. This is often thought to be hereditary but can be caused by the bitch being a little too rough with a newborn puppy and biting the umbilical cord off too close to the puppy's abdomen, thus causing a small soft swelling. This can often be pushed back by gently manipulating with the fingers, or even a coin about the size of a two pence piece strapped over the lump with adhesive tape may help to push it back. If the swelling persists into adult life, it can be removed quite simply by surgery, but they generally do not cause any trouble or pain.

Hip-Dysplasia
This is a hereditary condition and is unfortunately more prevalent in English Setters than we would wish. It is a malformation of the hip joint in which the head of the femur (thigh bone) instead of fitting snugly into the acetabulem (the saucer-shaped socket) slips out and the space fills up with a calcium deposit, causing stiffness in the hind legs and difficulty in rising from a sitting or lying position. If hip-dysplasia is suspected, the dog should be X-rayed, and if severely affected, should not be bred from.

The Kennel Club runs a scheme in conjunction with the British Veterinary Association whereby X-rays submitted and scrutinized by a panel of experts are given a score from 0 to 108 (54 for each hip). The lower the score the better, and, ideally, the score should be much the same for both hips. For instance, if the score is 30, 15 left hip 15 right hip, this is far better than 25 left hip and 5 right hip. It is advisable to have all dogs and bitches intended for breeding X-rayed and scored. Do not worry too much if your dog has a high score if it is not intended for breeding purposes. I know of many dogs with scores of 50 or 60 that lead perfectly happy, healthy lives and show no trace of lameness or pain.

Leptospirosis
This disease is caused by a group of bacteria, two of which affect dogs and can be passed on to humans. The bacteria are carried by rats and are transmitted to the dog through sniffing at a dead rat or at the ground where a rat has urinated or through drinking contaminated water. Great care should be taken to keep your premises free of vermin and in the kennel all drinking bowls should be emptied and turned upside-down at night. The dog should be isolated immediately if this disease is suspected and the premises well disinfected.

1) *Leptospirosis icterohaemorrhagiae*
   This is a very serious disease. Symptoms are acute thirst, frequency of passing urine, lack of appetite, vomiting, diarrhoea containing blood and particularly evil smelling, and jaundice. Prompt veterinary attention is vital. Be sure to have your puppy vaccinated at eight weeks against this dreadful disease (the vaccine is given in conjunction with the distemper/hardpad/hepatitis vaccine). Do not neglect the annual boosters.
2) *Leptospirosis canicola*
   A milder form, showing similar symptoms with the exception of jaundice. This condition can affect the kidneys and may become critical (see Nephritis).

Lice (see Parasites)

Mange
A serious skin complaint caused by various types of mange mites which burrow into the skin, the most common being sarcoptic mange, which causes intense irritation and violent scratching. Close examination will reveal small red spots which become pustular. The most commonly affected areas are the underside of the body, under the forelegs, inside the thighs, the face and ears. This is a highly contagious condition and any dog so affected should be

Ailments

isolated, his bedding burnt and the premises treated with an insecticide. The dog should be bathed in Alugan, which is obtainable from your veterinary surgeon, and treatment should be repeated two or three times at weekly intervals.

Demodectic mange or follicular mange is much harder to cure, but fortunately much rarer and less contagious. It will manifest itself in bare patches appearing on the skin which become thickened and leathery. It is sometimes difficult to effect a complete cure of this condition.

Mastitis
This condition is an inflammation of the mammary glands and can occur if the bitch has a small litter and is producing more milk than the puppies are drawing off. It may only affect one gland, but, even so the affected gland becomes engorged with milk which becomes thick and lumpy, and the gland is hot, red, swollen and very tender to the touch. The bitch will be feverish and run a high temperature. The veterinary surgeon should be sent for at once as an abscess may have formed, and antibiotics may be necessary. However, much relief can be given by applying hot fomentations and gently drawing the milk from the affected gland.

Metritis
An infection of the uterus due to bacterial infection, usually streptococcal or staphylococcal. It occurs after whelping and may be due to a number of things, such as retained afterbirths or a dead foetus. The bitch will generally run a high temperature and may have an unpleasant smelling discharge. Veterinary attention is essential to administer antibiotics with this condition.

Nephritis
A virus infection is generally the cause of this distressing complaint which is inflammation of the kidneys. Symptoms are difficulty in passing water or passing very little, urine much darker in colour than usual, loss of weight and increased thirst. The dog should be put on a low-protein diet and given barley water to drink. There are several

brands of kidney pills on the market that will give marked relief, but contact your veterinary surgeon.

Pancreatic Deficiency
This condition is somewhat akin to diabetes, the symptoms being similar, except with this complaint the motions are very loose and an unpleasant putty colour. It is caused by a deficiency of the digestive enzymes produced by the pancreas gland. Consult your veterinary surgeon, as there are numerous tablets on the market. Generally these are made from the pancreas of some other animal such as the pig, and in effect take over the work that the deficient pancreas should be doing. I have known cases where a complete cure has been effected, but, at the worst, if the tablets are continued, the dog can enjoy a normal diet and will suffer no more discomfort. At the onset of this complaint avoid fatty foods, and keep the dog on a diet of white meat and rice until stabilized.

Pancreatitis
This is a severe condition involving inflammation of the pancreas, accompanied by severe abdominal pain, vomiting and can result in sudden death.

Parasites
These can be divided into two groups: 1) ectoparasites, which are external parasites that live in or on the skin, and 2) endoparasites, which are internal parasites that live inside the body, i.e. worms. The main external parasites encountered are:

1) *Fleas*: brown, wingless insects that run rapidly through the dog's coat, mainly along the back but can be found almost anywhere. They are easily seen and are capable of jumping on and off the dog. If the coat is combed through with a fine (flea) comb, you will find evidence of flea dirts (droppings) which resemble black grit. Fleas can cause severe irritation which makes the dog scratch and nibble, and are most common during the summer months. Treat by thoroughly dusting or

Ailments

spraying the dog's coat with a good insecticide. This treatment should be repeated at least once a week until clear. If heavily infested, bathe with a solution of Alugan. It is also necessary to spray or dust beds and bedding. Comb through the coat at least once a week to ensure the dog does not become reinfested.

2) *Lice*: these are much harder to detect, being very small and almost colourless. However, they move more slowly and their presence can be ascertained by their eggs (nits) which are usually to be found on the ears and under the armpits and resemble scurf. Lice cause intense irritation; they should be treated as fleas, and one must ensure that all nits are combed out, as they rapidly hatch into young lice. An insecticide dip is advisable.

3) *Ticks*: these parasites do not move but bury their heads into the skin. They feed by sucking the blood and become quite large when engorged. Owing to their slate-grey colour they are often mistaken for warts. They are generally to be found around the head and are usually picked up from grassland where sheep have been grazing. To remove ticks, saturate with surgical spirit, which should make the tick loosen its head; the tick can then be removed with a pair of tweezers by pulling gently. Make sure that the head has not been left behind; otherwise, the area may become infected.

4) *Harvest Mites*: as the name implies, these parasites occur around harvest time and appear as minute red clusters generally between the toes and in the crease of the ears. They cause severe irritation and should be treated with Alugan baths.

5) *Mange Mites*: a group of mites which cause mange (see Mange).

The most common internal parasites (worms) are:

1) *Roundworm*: these worms occur in dogs of all ages but are most common in pregnant bitches and young puppies. Hormones released during pregnancy activate the roundworm larvae, some of which pass to the uterus and thus infect the unborn puppy. All bitches

should be wormed two to three weeks after mating, which should prevent the puppies becoming heavily infested. The puppies themselves should be wormed at three weeks of age and thereafter at two-week intervals until they commence their vaccinations at eight weeks of age. When vaccination is completed at 16 to 18 weeks, the puppy should be wormed again and then again at six months. Always weigh the puppy or dog and make sure the dosage is correct. The worms passed (Toxocara Canis) are round, white in colour, and vary in length from two to four inches. Frequently several worms are passed at once coiled up like a spring or in a loose bunch; these should be picked up at once and burnt. The bitch should be wormed again when her puppies have finally left her, as it is more than probable she will have eaten some whilst cleaning up after the puppies.

2) *Tapeworm*: fleas are mainly responsible for this worm, as the flea larvae swallow eggs shed by dogs. These then mature into adult fleas which are often swallowed by dogs when nibbling at the irritation caused by them. The worm larvae are then released into the intestines where they will mature into adult tapeworm (Dipylidium). These worms are segmented and can measure between 20 to 30 inches in length. Dogs seldom pass the entire worm, but individual segments can often be detected around the hindquarters and under the tail and resemble grains of rice. It is essential to rid the dog of the entire worm, including the head, or it will grow again. A specific remedy for this can be obtained from your veterinary surgeon. Symptoms are a voracious appetite but failure to put on weight, dull coat, nibbling under the tail and diarrhoea.

3) *Hookworm*: a very small roundworm which lives in the small intestine and may cause diarrhoea and anaemia. Veterinary treatment is required. Never feed sheep paunch unless it is well boiled, as this nearly always is infested with hookworm. Ox tripe is quite safe to feed raw as this does not get infected with hookworm.

4) *Whipworm*: these worms are again very small and usually

Ailments

only diagnosed by testing a sample of the motions. They are not very common at the present time, but the symptoms are diarrhoea, vomiting and weight loss. Veterinary treatment is essential.

Pneumonia

Symptoms vary considerably depending on what type of pneumonia the dog has contracted, but all are accompanied by a high temperature, loss of appetite, difficulty in breathing and general lethargy. Keep the dog warm and administer small drinks of glucose and water. Send for your veterinary surgeon at once if pneumonia is suspected. This complaint is seldom fatal if treated in time.

Parvovirus

This is a killer disease and appeared in this country in 1978. It can take two forms:

1) *Myocarditis*: this affects the muscles of the heart and is generally passed on from the bitch (unvaccinated or a carrier) to her unborn puppies. This condition will manifest itself in the puppies when they start running about at four to five weeks of age, when they will suddenly collapse and die.

2) *Intestinal*: this is the much more common form and is a particularly acute form of haemorrhagic enteritis. Symptoms are severe vomiting, abdominal pain and evil-smelling diarrhoea containing blood. Speed is essential in dealing with this dreadful disease, and fluids must be administered, or dehydration will quickly result. Consult your veterinary surgeon at once; give Lectade to drink if not vomiting. All puppies should be vaccinated against this disease at 8 weeks, 12 weeks and 16 to 18 weeks, with yearly boosters. All premises in which there has been a case of parvovirus must be thoroughly scrubbed out with sodium hypochlorite (domestic bleach) and further treated with Formula H or Parvocide.

Pyometra

This is a more serious form of metritis in which there is an accumulation of pus in the uterus, most commonly occurring in bitches who have never been bred from, who have had only one litter or who have had numerous seasons stopped. Pyometra takes two forms, closed and open. The closed form is the more serious condition of the two as the womb closes, thus preventing any of the pus escaping. Symptoms are excessive drinking, loss of appetite, listlessness and a raised temperature. If this condition is suspected, prompt veterinary attention is essential, as surgical removal of the infected uterus will almost certainly be required or death may result. Open pyometra is less critical, as the pus can escape from the vulva. The pus takes the form of a reddish-brown, evil-smelling discharge. This condition usually manifests itself two to three months after a bitch has been in season or in bitches that habitually have 'phantom' (false) pregnancies. Seek veterinary advice immediately, as it may be possible to disperse this condition with antibiotics. However, surgery is frequently required, as for the closed type.

Rickets

This condition generally manifests itself in puppies and young dogs. It is mainly due to a deficiency of Vitamin D (calcium) in the diet due to poor feeding, but it can be caused by over-exercise of a very young animal. Symptoms are enlarged joints, especially the knees, weak pasterns, cow-hocks and bowed front legs. Treatment is good food with increased vitamin supplement, milk, plenty of fresh air and sunshine, restricted exercise and as much rest as possible.

Ringworm

A skin complaint and not a worm as the name implies, caused by a fungus. Symptoms are small circular patches, appearing on the body of the dog, which rapidly become devoid of hair. Isolate the dog immediately, as this condition is highly contagious to all other animals and humans. If suspected, send for your veterinary surgeon as this

Ailments

disease can be confirmed by the use of a Woods Lamp, which your veterinary surgeon will possess. If this lamp is shone over the dog's body, the affected areas will glow. These days this condition can be treated with an effective antibiotic, the old-fashioned remedy being to paint the affected area with tincture of iodine, and to apply Whitfield Ointment around the affected parts where the skin is seen to be flaking. Always make sure you wash well with disinfectant and change your clothes before going near any other dogs if you are tending ringworm cases.

Skin Trouble
Apart from mange and eczema, which have already been mentioned, many English Setters suffer from an 'itch', especially during spring and summer. The dog is usually affected on the inside of the thighs, on the stomach and legs and sometimes down the back. Careful searching reveals no cause such as parasites and all the prescribed powders and sprays appear to have no effect, the dog continuing to scratch and nibble, often causing sore, bare patches. This can be very distressing to both the dog and the owner, as there appears to be no reason for the complaint or any definite cure. I would advise dosing with a chlorpheniramine tablet such as Piriton (one tablet twice a day), freely obtainable at any chemist, and applying benzyl benzoate to any affected areas. Rub well into the affected area every three days; then on the tenth day bathe in a gentle shampoo especially for skin conditions, such as Seleen. If inflammatory skin conditions persist, you may well have to resort to drugs, but as most remedies for this condition contain cortisone they should be avoided if possible, especially if the dog is used for breeding.

Split Tail
Most English Setters are great 'tail waggers' and if housed in a comparatively small kennel, constant banging against the wall can result in the tip of the tail becoming split; it will bleed profusely. Thick sacking or soft board tacked to the inside walls of the kennel may prevent a recurrence. The wounded tip of the tail should be dressed with Savlon,

dusted with a wound powder and kept covered until healed or the dog may try to nibble at it. It is difficult to bandage the end of the tail, and still more difficult to get the bandage to stay on. I have found that a leather or kid thumbstall just fits over the end of the tail. Cover the affected tip with a light piece of gauze, the thumbstall should then be applied and firmly secured with adhesive plaster.

Worms (see *Parasites*)

APPENDIX A

GLOSSARY OF DOG TERMINOLOGY

AFFIX: The owner's kennel name, which appears before or after the dog's own name. Known more generally as the prefix or suffix. Since the Kennel Club's new ruling, the affix must appear as a prefix if the dog was bred by the owner, e.g. Suntop True Glow, and as a suffix if bred by a person other than the owner, e.g. Dancing Seaspray of Valsett.

AFTERBIRTH: The placenta attached to the puppy by the umbilical cord and expelled with the puppy at the time of birth.

ANTIBIOTIC: A substance given by injection, tablet or capsule which destroys bacteria.

BACKING: A field trial term in which one of a brace of dogs stays back and 'backs up' the more forward of the two.

BENIGN: As opposed to malignant or spreading. Usually used to describe tumours.

B.I.S.: Best in Show

B.O.B.: Best of Breed

B.O.S.: Best Opposite Sex

B.P.: Best Puppy

BONE: Good bone means firm strong legs, moderately thick. Fine bone or lack of bone denotes thin spindly legs; a fault in English Setters

BRACE: Two dogs of either sex or mixed sex, exhibited together, who should be as similar as possible.

BREECHES: The feathering or long soft hair on the thighs.

BRISKET: The bottom or the 'keel' of the rib cage between the front legs.

BUTTERFLY NOSE: One that shows flesh-coloured markings on the nostrils. A fault in an English Setter.

C.C.: Challenge Certificate, the Kennel Club award for the best of each sex at a Championship Show.

CH.: Champion; to attain the title of Champion an English Setter (as in all gundog breeds) must have won three or more Challenge Certificates under three different judges and obtained a qualifying certificate at a recognized field trial.

COARSE: A dog is said to be coarse in head if the skull is too broad or the head in general too big and lacking quality; a fault.

COUPLINGS: The body between the fore and hind legs. A dog is said to be short-coupled if he is reasonably short-backed and is well ribbed up.

COW-HOCKS: A dog is referred to as cow-hocked when the hocks turn inwards, thus throwing the hind feet outwards; a fault.

CROUP: The area of the back just forward of the root of the tail, sometimes called the rump.

CRYPTORCHID: Where neither of the testicles has descended into the scrotum; such a dog is not fertile.

DAM: A dog's female parent.

DEW CLAWS: The claws found on the inside of the front legs (and very occasionally on the hind legs), which are best removed at a few days of age.

DEWLAP: The loose pendulous skin under the throat. A dog with a pronounced dewlap is said to be throaty; a fault.

DISH FACE: When the top of the muzzle is slightly concave, a pointer type head; a fault.

DOWN FACED: The opposite of dish face, when the muzzle is convex as in a Bull Terrier; a fault.

DRIVE: The desired movement of the hocks. A dog said to lack drive in movement is one who does not use his hocks in the desired manner.

FEATHERING: The long silky hair on the chest, brisket, legs, thighs and tail.

FLAG: The tail or stern.

FOREFACE: The muzzle or part of the head in front of the eyes.

FRINGES: An alternative name for feathering or feathers.

FRONT: Generally speaking, the shoulders and forelegs. A dog is said to have a bad front if he is straight in shoulder, loose in elbow or bow-legged.

GAY TAIL: A dog who carries his tail above the level of his back, sometimes referred to as proud of his tail or flying his flag; a fault.

GESTATION: The period (63 days) for which the bitch carries her young, from the day of mating until the day of whelping.

Glossary of Dog Terminology

GOOD DOER: A dog who eats well and keeps his condition.

GOOSE RUMP: When the croup falls away to the root of the tail thus causing the tail to be low set; a fault.

HARE FEET: Long and narrow with the toes well separated as in a hare; not desirable in an English Setter.

HAW: The inner part of the lower eyelid, which shows red. An English Setter should not show the haw.

HEAT: A bitch is sometimes referred to as being 'on heat' when she is in season, the oestral period.

HEIGHT: The correct way to measure the height of a dog is from the ground to the top of the shoulders.

HERRING-GUTTED: A dog that is 'cut up' underneath like a greyhound. A fault in an English Setter.

HOCKS: The joint in the hind leg between the stifle and the pastern.

INT. CH. or INT. SH. CH. International Champion or International Show Champion. A dog who has gained his title in more than one country.

KEEL: The base of the body behind the front legs, the bottom of the rib cage, more usually referred to as the brisket.

LEATHER: The skin of the ear flap.

LEGGY: Too tall in the legs, appearing out of proportion with the body.

LIGHT EYES: Eyes of a light hazel colour; a fault.

L.K.A. Ladies Kennel Association.

LOINS: The part of the body between the last rib and the hindquarters.

MAIDEN: Generally speaking an unmated bitch. In show parlance, a dog or bitch that has not won a first prize, except in Minor Puppy or Puppy classes.

MATCH: A competition for a limited number of dogs, generally organized by breed clubs or their members.

MATRON: A brood bitch, an adult bitch that has been bred from.

MONORCHID: The term used when one or other of the two testicles has not descended into the scrotum. This condition does not render the dog infertile, but he should never be used for breeding as the condition may be hereditary.

MUZZLE: The part of the head combining the nose, lips and mouth. Also a device, usually made of leather, which fits over the nose and is fastened behind the ears to prevent a dog biting.

N.A.F.: Name applied for. A dog may be entered for a show if the application for registration has been sent to the Kennel Club. If the registration certificate has not been received at the time of entry one must insert N.A.F. after the dog's name.

OCCIPUT: The prominent bone at the top of the back of the head; this should be well defined on the English Setter.

OVERSHOT: When the teeth in the top jaw project some way over those in the bottom jaw when the mouth is closed.

PADDLE: A dog is said to paddle when he moves with a paddling action of the front legs; a fault.

PADS: The cushioned soles of the feet.

PARTURITION: Giving birth, whelping.

PASTERN: The lower part of the legs below the knee on the foreleg and below the hock on the hind leg.

PIN-TOED: When the feet turn inwards; a fault.

PLACENTA: See Afterbirth.

PREFIX: See Affix.

RESERVE: Most generally the fourth-placed exhibit in any class; however, in the Challenge it becomes the second-best exhibit of each sex, known as the RES C.C.

ROACH BACK: An arched back; a fault.

ROMAN NOSE: See Down Faced.

SEASON: See Heat.

SECOND THIGH: The muscle of the hind leg between the stifle and the hock.

SERVICE: A mating. A 'free service' is one given by courtesy of the owner of the stud dog if the bitch does not conceive from a service for which a fee has been paid. It is not obligatory.

SET ON: Where the root of the tail is set on to the hindquarters.

SH. CH.: Show Champion. A dog that has gained three or more challenge certificates under three different judges.

SIRE: A dog's male parent.

SLAB-SIDED: When the ribs are flat and lacking roundness or spring; a fault.

SNIPEY: When the muzzle lacks depth or is too long and narrow. A snipey foreface will give the head a wedged-shaped appearance; a fault.

Glossary of Dog Terminology

SPAYING: The removal of the uterus and ovaries by surgery.
SPLAY FEET: Flat feet, with the toes spread apart; a fault.
SPRING OF RIB: Well-rounded ribs.
STERN: See Flag.
STIFLE: The joint in the hind leg between the hip and the hock (corresponding to our knee). Straight in stifle means that the joint lacks the desired bend, thus giving a stilted movement; a fault.
STOP: The indenture between the eyes. A dog is said to lack stop when this indenture is not well defined.
SWAY BACK: A dipped back; a fault.
SUFFIX: See Affix.
T.A.F.: Transfer applied for. If a dog which has recently been acquired is entered for a show and the transfer from the previous owner has been applied for from the Kennel Club but the certificate of transfer is not received at the time of entry, one must insert T.A.F. after the dog's name.
TYPE: The quality essential to a dog, if he is to approach the ideal standard for the breed. A dog said to be a nice type or 'typy' embodies many of the desired features of the breed.
UNDERSHOT: When the teeth in the bottom jaw project over the teeth in the top jaw; a serious fault.
WELL-SPRUNG: Well-rounded ribs, the opposite of slab-sided.
WITHERS: The point where the neck joins the body, the top of the shoulders.

APPENDIX B

SPECIALIST BREED CLUBS IN GREAT BRITAIN

The English Setter Club (Founded 1890) (Field trials only)
Hon. Sec.: Mr C. W. Sorensen
Horsford Kennels,
Lydbury North,
Shropshire SY7 8AY
Tel: 058 88606

The Setter and Pointer Club (Founded 1924)
Hon. Sec. (Shows): Mr G. Coupe
Timadon Kennels,
Delamere Road,
Woodside, Aston,
Chester,
Cheshire CH3 8AH
Tel: 0829 51505

Sec. (Field Trials): Mrs E. Heard
Wedgewood,
Hever,
Kent TN8 7LJ
Tel: 0732 865564

The English Setter Association (Founded 1951)
Hon. Sec.: Mr J. F. Bowen
Chelmset,
Main Road, Bicknacre,
Chelmsford,
Essex CM3 4HW
Tel: 0245 320398

Specialist Breed Clubs in Great Britain

The Northern English Setter Society (Founded 1967)
Hon. Sec.: Mrs R. Davies
43 Windsor Walk,
South Aston, Nr Sheffield,
Yorks S31 7EL
Tel: 0909 567062

English Setter Society of Wales (Founded 1977)
Hon. Sec.: Mrs G. Gough
Ashville House,
Upper High Street,
Cefn-Coed, Merthyr Tydfil,
Mid Glamorgan,
Wales CF48 2HW
Tel: 0685 722279

Midland English Setter Society (Founded 1979)
Hon. Sec.: Mrs H. M. Green
Fosscot Kennels,
Street Aston, Rugby,
Warks CV23 0PL
Tel:0788 832066

English Setter Society of Scotland (Founded 1982)
Hon. Sec.: Mrs C. Normansell
Orwell, 54 James Street,
Alva, Clackmananshire,
Scotland FK12 5AJ
Tel: 0259 60866

The Southern English Setter Society (Founded 1983)
Hon. Sec.: Mrs G. Fairbairn
Middle Bourne,
Church Lane,
Holybourne,
Alton,
Hampshire GU34 4HD
Tel: 0420 87294

The English Setter Association Rescue Scheme
Mrs G. Jenkins
Quince Mead,
129 Stock Road,
Billericay,
Essex
Tel: 02774 52095

APPENDIX C

CRUFTS CHALLENGE CERTIFICATE WINNERS 1958 TO 1988

Year	Sex	Owner	Dog	Colour	Judge
1958	*D	Miss M. Jarry	SH.CH. Ripleygae Fanfare	Orange	Capt. Mears
	B	Mrs B. Enright	SH.CH. Kirket Koola	Orange	
1959	*D	Mrs J. English	SH.CH. Shiplake Swift	Tricolour	Mr A. Egglestone
	B	Mrs A. Broadhead	SH.CH. Ernford Rosy Dawn	Orange	
1960	D	Mr F. Wilson	SH.CH. Engsett Elect	Blue	Mr A.C. Crowther
	B	Mrs J. English	SH.CH. Shiplake Skyblue	Blue	
1961	*D	Mrs A. Williams	SH.CH. Silbury Soames of Madavale	Tricolour	Mr J. Braddon
	B	Mrs N. Treharne	SH.CH. Redtops Silbury Sonya	Tricolour	
1962	*D	Mrs A. Williams	SH.CH. Silbury Soames of Madavale	Tricolour	Mr L.C. James
	B	Mrs J. English	SH.CH. Shiplake Skyblue	Blue	
1963	*D	Mrs A. Williams	SH.CH. Silbury Soames of Madavale	Tricolour	Mrs Crowther
	B	Mr D. Paterson	SH.CH. Scardale Avocet	Tricolour	
1964	*D	Mrs A. Williams	SH.CH. Silbury Soames of Madavale	Tricolour	Mrs L. Daly
	B	Mr A. Jenkinson	SH.CH. Littlewoodcote Carousel	Tricolour	
1965	*D	Miss M. Barnes	SH.CH. Suntop Seabird	Blue	Mr W. Parkinson
	B	Mr and Mrs K. Bradshaw	SH.CH. Pride of Noyna	Tricolour	
1966	*D	Mrs M. Brown	SH.CH. Lad of the Haar	Tricolour	Mrs J. James
	B	Mrs A. Findlay	SH.CH. Iroquois Cointreau	Orange	
1967	D	Mr S. Boulton	SH.CH. Ednasid Wuster	Blue	Mrs D. Whitwell
	*B	Mrs A. Tate	SH.CH. Trodgers Hurwyn Heaven	Blue	
1968	D	Mesdames Marsden and Croft	SH.CH. Fencefoot Freckles	Orange	Mr W. Foss
	*B	Mrs A. Tate	SH.CH. Trodgers Hurwyn Heaven	Blue	
1969	*D	Mr G. Williams	Evening Flight of Frejendor	Tricolour	Mr W. Rasbridge
	B	Mrs H. Alkin	Tandrec Primrose	Orange	

Year		Sire / Dam	Colour	Breeder
1970	*D B	Mrs R. Burns Mrs A. Tate	SH.CH. Ernford Falcon SH.CH. Trodgers Bluebell	Orange Blue	Miss M. Barnes
1971	*D B	Mrs A. Tate Mrs A. Tate	SH.CH. Trodgers Scots Oat SH.CH. Trodgers Bluebell	Orange Blue	Mrs A. Broadhead
1972	D *B	Mr F. Kavanagh Mrs D. Bowen	Gorsebrook Barnabus SH.CH. Iroquois Rainbow	Blue Tricolour	Mrs G. Broadley
1973	*D B	Mrs L. Allan-Scott Mr G. Williams	SH.CH. Iroquois Whiteseal Silvermorn SH.CH. Bournehouse Ballerina	Tricolour Tricolour	Mrs R Furness
1974	D B	Mr H. Schofield Mr G. Williams	Thrumall Batchelor Boy SH.CH. Bournehouse Flirting Freda	Orange Tricolour	Major J. Houghton
1975	*D B	Mrs L. Allan-Scott Mr and Mrs J. Bowen	SH.CH. Iroquois Whiteseal Silvermorn SH.CH. Rebway Heron	Tricolour Tricolour	Mrs P. Gardiner-Swann
1976	D *B	Mrs B. Wells Mr and Mrs W. Parkinson	Ritandor Gorsebrook Back to Banner SH.CH. and AM.CH. Clariho Whimsey of Valley Run	Orange Orange	Mrs. V. Yates
1977	*D B	Mr G. Williams Mr A. MacAllum	SH.CH. Bournehouse Dancing Master SH.CH. Segedunum Persephone	Tricolour Blue	Mrs V. Foss
1978	D *B	Mr D. Mulholland Mrs J. Clifford	SH.CH. Hurwyn Wigeon SH.CH. Kanchary Grey Dove	Orange Blue	Mr D. McGarry
1979	D *B	Mrs S. Leiper Miss G. Williams	SH.CH. James James from Farmacy SH.CH. Wistaston School Scatterbrain	Tricolour Tricolour	Miss M. Barnes

Year	Sex	Dog	Dog	Colour	Judge
1980	*D	Mesdames Foss and Wadsworth	SH.CH. Elswood Vagabond King	Tricolour	Mrs L. Allan-Scott
	B	Mr and Mrs H. Yarnley	SH.CH. Tatterset Inycarra	Blue	
1981	*D	Mrs B. Davies	SH.CH Iroquois Sansovino of Sundeala	Blue	Mr H. Wheeler
	B	Mrs R. Davies	SH.CH. Mindenday Miss Moss	Blue	
1982	D	Mrs H. Masson	SH.CH. Sirius of Cedar	Tricolour	Mrs A. Tate
	*B	Mrs S. Wilkinson	SH.CH. Hurwyn Baby Doll	Tricolour	
1983	*D	Mr M. Tait	SH.CH. Suntop Fair Gale	Blue	Mrs S. Wilkinson
	B	Miss M. Cook	SH.CH. Merryset Snow Sparkle	Blue	
1984	*D	Mesdames Foss and Wadsworth	SH.CH. Elswood Vagabond King	Tricolour	Mrs G. Wheeler
	B	Mr and Mrs D. Hobson	Willowsett Famous Footsteps	Orange	
1985	D	Mrs R. Timms	Shandarret Hiawatha	Tricolour	Mr G. Williams
	*B	Mrs J. Dennis	SH.CH. Mariglen Highlight	Blue	
1986	*D	Mr and Mrs I. Whitehurst	SH.CH. Holdgrange Golden Frolic of Settella	Orange	Miss F. Hamilton
	B	Mr and Mrs H. Wheeler	SH.CH. Engsett English Charmer	Tricolour	
1987	*D	Mrs B. Davies and Mr and Mrs H. Wheeler	SH.CH. Engsett Noble English	Tricolour	Mr R. Harrison
	B	Mrs R. Davies and Mr B. Jeffrey	SH.CH. Extrovert of Engsett at Brucelm	Orange	
1988	D	Mrs L. Sawtell	Sh.Ch. Dancing Partner of Yeo	Blue	Mrs M. France
	*B	Mr and Mrs J. Watkin	Sh.Ch. Starlite Express of Valsett	Orange	

* Denotes Best of Breed

APPENDIX D

POST-WAR REGISTRATION FIGURES

Year	Number	Year	Number	Year	Number
1946	365				
1947	459	1961	406	1975	1217
1948	346	1962	395	1976	575*
1949	375	1963	429	1977	500
1950	372	1964	470	1978	1127**
1951	382	1965	417	1979	1638
1952	247	1966	536	1980	1706
1953	245	1967	564	1981	1246
1954	338	1968	711	1982	1013
1955	365	1969	926	1983	1248
1956	326	1970	906	1984	1205
1957	341	1971	996	1985	1166
1958	359	1972	1158	1986	1019
1959	363	1973	1254	1987	1027
1960	388	1974	1346	1988	1027

*A new system came into force this year.
**Another new system came into force.

APPENDIX E
PEDIGREES OF KEY DOGS

Pedigree of: **Sh.Ch. Silbury Soames of Madavale**
Born: 10.7.59   Breeder: Mr and Mrs P. Gardiner-Swann
Owner: Mrs A. Williams

Parents	Grandparents	Great-Grandparents	Great-Great-Grandparents
Sire Silbury Sherper	*Sire* Withinlee Bullfinch of Truslers	*Sire* Sh.Ch. Gorsebrook Berry	*Sire* Irish Ch. Banner of Crombie
			Dam Gorsebrook Cherry
		Dam Sh.Ch. Willow Wren of Truslers	*Sire* Galahad of Emeraldisle
			Dam Snowbunting of Truslers
	Dam Silbury Jubilee Gem of Madavale	*Sire* Silbury Banner of Bourne	*Sire* Sh.Ch. Rombalds Tempest
			Dam Bracken of Bourne
		Dam Golden Glory of Exevale	*Sire* Gwilliam of Emeraldisle
			Dam Golden Sorrel of Exevale
Dam Silbury Springhead Serene	*Sire* Sh.Ch. Shiplake Swift	*Sire* Sh.Ch. Rombalds Templar	*Sire* Sh.Ch. Rombalds Tempest
			Dam Rombalds Fan
		Dam Truslers Freckles of Frejendor	*Sire* Snowdrift of Truslers
			Dam Gilda of Emeraldisle
	Dam Randa of Lake	*Sire* Sh.Ch. Gayboy of Beechmount	*Sire* Beechmount Envoy of Remor
			Dam Marian of Beechmount
		Dam Lassie of Sharvogue	*Sire* Tempest of Sharvogue
			Dam Irish Ch. Flush of Beechmount

Pedigree of: **Sh.Ch. Derriford Don Giovanni**
Born: 22.1.81   Breeder: Owner   Owner: Miss J. Reed

Parents	Grandparents	Great-Grandparents	Great-Great-Grandparents
Sire Sh.Ch. Bourenhouse Dancing Master	*Sire* Sh.Ch. Monksriding Ernford Flamingo	*Sire* Sh.Ch. Oldholbans Pirate	*Sire* Hurwyn Hurricane
			Dam Hurwyn Sunset
		Dam Sh.Ch. Ernford Chaffinch	*Sire* Sh.Ch. Suntop Royal Sunglint
			Dam Sh.Ch. Ernford Rosy Dawn
	Dam Sh.Ch. Bournehouse Ballerina	*Sire* Evening Flight of Frejendor	*Sire* Highlight of Frejendor
			Dam Sheena of Frejendor
		Dam Iroquois Jasmine	*Sire* Sh.Ch. Whiteseal Ononis
			Dam Sh.Ch. Iroquois Cointreau
Dam Derriford Pavane	*Sire* Hurwyn Flightmaster	*Sire* Int.Sh.Ch. Suntop Winter Breeze	*Sire* Suntop Winterbird
			Dam Sh.Ch. Suntop Bluethrush
		Dam Hurwyn Dawn Chorus	*Sire* Suntop Birdsong
			Dam Hurwyn Dawn Glory
	Dam Derriford Coppelia	*Sire* Sh.Ch. Ashpenda Red Robin	*Sire* Suntop Winterbird
			Dam Ashpenda Petite d'Etoile
		Dam Sh.Ch. Bournehouse Solo Dancer	*Sire* Sh.Ch. Bournehouse Dancing Master
			Dam Suntop Dewberry

Pedigree of: **Sh.Ch. Elswood Vagabond King**

Born 13.5.77 Breeder: Owner Owner: Mrs V. Foss and Mrs R. Wadsworth

Parents	Grandparents	Great-Grandparents	Great-Great-Grandparents
Sire Sh.Ch. Bournehouse Dancing Master	*Sire* Sh.Ch. Monksriding Ernford Flamingo	*Sire* Sh.Ch. Oldholbans Pirate	*Sire* Hurwyn Hurricane
			Dam Hurwyn Sunset
		Dam Sh.Ch. Ernford Chaffinch	*Sire* Sh.Ch. Suntop Royal Sunglint
			Dam Sh.Ch. Ernford Rosy Dawn
	Dam Sh.Ch. Bournehouse Ballerina	*Sire* Evening Flight of Frejendor	*Sire* Highlight of Frejendor
			Dam Sheena of Frejendor
		Dam Iroquois Jasmine	*Sire* Sh.Ch. Whiteseal Ononis
			Dam Sh.Ch. Iroquois Cointreau
Dam Sh.Ch. Ashpenda Kittiwake	*Sire* Suntop Winterbird	*Sire* Suntop Birdsong	*Sire* Sh.Ch. Suntop Bluewings
			Dam Suntop Songthrush
		Dam Suntop Lucky Eve	*Sire* Suntop Lucky Bird
			Dam Suntop Eventide
	Dam Ashpenda Petite d'Etoile	*Sire* Sh.Ch. Ernford Falcon	*Sire* Sh.Ch. Oldholbans Pirate
			Dam Sh.Ch. Ernford Chaffinch
		Dam Ashpenda Silvery Moon	*Sire* Sh.Ch. Elswood Renmark Baronet
			Dam Sh.Ch. Iroquois Bluemoon

Pedigree of: **Sh.Ch. Hurwyn Wigeon**
Born: 11.11.70   Breeder: Mrs S. Wilkinson
Owner: Mr D. Mulholland

Parents	Grandparents	Great-Grandparents	Great-Great-Grandparents
Sire Suntop Winterbird	*Sire* Suntop Birdsong	*Sire* Sh.Ch. Suntop Bluewings	*Sire* Int.Sh.Ch. Suntop Seabird
			Dam Suntop Royalwings
		Dam Suntop Songthrush	*Sire* Suntop Songbird
			Dam Suntop Singsong
	Dam Suntop Lucky Eve	*Sire* Suntop Lucky Bird	*Sire* Suntop Songbird
			Dam Suntop Lady Rosa of Whiteseal
		Dam Suntop Eventide	*Sire* Suntop Songbird
			Dam Twilight of Yeo
Dam Ernford Bobolink	*Sire* Sh.Ch. Suntop Royalbird	*Sire* Suntop Songbird	*Sire* Ernford Kingfisher
			Dam Ch. Suntop Carnival Queen
		Dam Suntop Lady Rosa of Whiteseal	*Sire* Regent of Rhowood
			Dam Suntop Ladybird
	Dam Enford Dawn Of Sedgeford	*Sire* Hurwyn Blizzard	*Sire* Fairbrother of Fermanar
			Dam Hurwyn Rainbow
		Dam Ernford Rapture	*Sire* Sh.Ch. Prince Charming of Ketree
			Dam Ch. Ernford Evening Flight

Pedigree of: **Sh.Ch. Iroquois Sansvino of Sundeala**
Born: 25.2.76   Breeder: Mrs L.A. Allan-Scott
Owner: Mrs B. Davies

Parents	Grandparents	Great-Grandparents	Great-Great-Grandparents
Sire Sh.Ch. Iroquois Snowstorm of Sundeala	*Sire* Sh.Ch. Iroquois Whiteseal Silvermorn	*Sire* Sh.Ch. Lad of The Haar	*Sire* Sh.Ch. Senglish Early Mist / *Dam* Shadowlight of The Haar
		Dam Wolvershill Shadow	*Sire* Sh.Ch. Iroquois Stormcloud / *Dam* Wolvershill Silbury Sequoia
	Dam Iroquois Snowbird	*Sire* Suntop Wonderbird	*Sire* Int.Sh.Ch. Suntop Seabird / *Dam* Suntop Songfinch
		Dam Iroquois Caprice	*Sire* Sh.Ch. Iroquois Strathspey / *Dam* Iroquois Sonata
Dam Iroquois Sunstream 3 Res C.C.s J.W	*Sire* Sh.Ch. Ashpenda Red Robin	*Sire* Suntop Winterbird	*Sire* Suntop Birdsong / *Dam* Suntop Lucky Eve
		Dam Ashpenda Petite d'Etoile	*Sire* Sh.Ch. Ernford Falcon / *Dam* Ashpenda Silvery Moon
	Dam Sh.Ch. Iroquois Mooncloud	*Sire* Sh.Ch. Iroquois Strathspey	*Sire* Sh.Ch. Iroquois Stormcloud / *Dam* Sh.Ch. Iroquois Cascade
		Dam Sh.Ch. Iroquois Solitaire	*Sire* Sh.Ch. Iroquois Stormcloud / *Dam* Sh.Ch. Iroquois Bluemoon

Pedigree of: **Sh.Ch. Shiplake Swift**
Born: 1.3.53 Breeder: Mr D. Paterson
Owner: Mrs J. English

Parents	Grandparents	Great-Grandparents	Great-Great-Grandparents
Sire Sh.Ch. Rombalds Templar 20 C.C.s	*Sire* Sh.Ch. Rombalds Tempest	*Sire* Sh.Ch. Bayldone Barrister	*Sire* Bayldone Breeze
			Dam Fantail of Ardach
		Dam Bayldone Baroness	*Sire* Bayldone Breeze
			Dam Maesydd Myra
	Dam Rombalds Fan	*Sire* Rombalds Furious	*Sire* Bayldone Breeze
			Dam Rombalds Rovigo
		Dam Rombalds Rhythm	*Sire* Sh.Ch. Rombalds Tempest
			Dam Rombalds Rovigo
Dam Truslers Freckles of Frejendor	*Sire* Snowdrift of Truslers	*Sire* Archdale Corncrake of Haverbrack	*Sire* Gorse of Haverbrack
			Dam Mina of Crombie
		Dam Gaygirl of Truslers	*Sire* Pilot of Ketree
			Dam Lady Dawn of Glenavis
	Dam Gilda of Emeraldisle	*Sire* Glyn of Emeraldisle	*Sire* Llewellyn of Elsiville
			Dam Tudor of Elsiville
		Dam Emeraldisle Frolic of Chastleton	*Sire* Ivor of Elsiville
			Dam Longworth Marigold

Pedigree of: **Sh.Ch. Bournehouse Enchantress**
Born: 7.10.71   Breeder: Mr G. Williams
Owner: Mr and Mrs H. Wheeler

Parents	Grandparents	Great-Grandparents	Great-Great-Grandparents
Sire Sh.Ch. Engsett Electrode	*Sire* Sh.Ch. Engsett Encounter	*Sire* Sh.Ch. Engsett Exception	*Sire* Withinlee Sheik of Frejendor / *Dam* Engsett Exotic
		Dam Sea Mist of Noyna	*Sire* Noyna Fencefoot Farmers Lad / *Dam* Sh.Ch. Pride of Noyna
	Dam Sheena of Frejendor	*Sire* Withinlee Sheik of Frejendor	*Sire* Sultan of Frejendor / *Dam* Fernella of Frejendor
		Dam Iroquois Senglish Moonmist	*Sire* Sh.Ch. Shiplake Swift / *Dam* Senglish Suntop Moonlight
Dam Sh.Ch. Bournehouse Meadowfern	*Sire* Evening Flight of Frejendor	*Sire* Highflight of Frejendor	*Sire* Sultan of Frejendor / *Dam* Fenella of Frejendor
		Dam Sheena of Frejendor	*Sire* Withinlee Sheik of Frejendor / *Dam* Iroquois Senglish Moonmist
	Dam Iroquois Jasmine	*Sire* Sh.Ch. Whiteseal Ononis	*Sire* Sh.Ch. Tuppence of Whiteseal / *Dam* Whiteseal Sunset
		Dam Sh.Ch. Iroquois Cointreau	*Sire* Shiplake Shandy / *Dam* Iroquois Littlewoodcote Caprice

Pedigree of: **Sh.Ch. Starlite Express of Valsett**
Born: 6.2.85   Breeder: Mrs Wick
Owner: Mr and Mrs J. Watkin

Parents	Grandparents	Great-Grandparents	Great-Great-Grandparents
Sire Sh.Ch. Sunlight of Valsett	*Sire* Sh.Ch. Bellsett Baron of Upperwood	*Sire* Wistaston School Report	*Sire* Sh.Ch. Monksriding Ernford Flamingo
			Dam Wistaston School Mystery
		Dam Gillyfield Gemini	*Sire* Upperwood Jolly
			Dam Ranrou Lady Rosamund
	Dam Valsett Louisianna	*Sire* Aus.Ch. Engsett Empery	*Sire* Sh.Ch. Engsett Everready of Rohan
			Dam Ranrou Tequelah of Engsett
		Dam Valsett Sherry Dancer	*Sire* Upperwood Zebedee
			Dam Weatherdair Lucinda
Dam Origo Sea Maiden	*Sire* Bonmicmarnie Sea Shanty of Berwensett	*Sire* Sh.Ch. Upperwood Lancelot of Nethermoor	*Sire* Sh.Ch. Engsett Electrode
			Dam Withinlee Wallflower
		Dam Upperwood Masquerade of Bonmicmarnie	*Sire* Braz. Ch. Upperwood Blue Emblem
			Dam Upperwood Ballet
	Dam Moonlight Mystic Maiden of Origo	*Sire* Origo Mistral	*Sire* Int.Sh.Ch. Suntop Winterbreeze
			Dam Origo Columbine
		Dam Hazelbury June Jade	*Sire* Can.Ch. Rhoana Baron of Hazelbury
			Dam Flatford Pintail

Pedigree of: Sh.Ch. Iroquois Concerto
Born: 22.6.77 Breeder: Owner
Owner: Mrs L.A. Allan-Scott

Parents	Grandparents	Great-Grandparents	Great-Great-Grandparents
Sire Iroquois Stormbird	*Sire* Knave of The Haar	*Sire* Sh.Ch. Iroquois Whiteseal Silvermorn	*Sire* Sh.Ch. Lad of The Haar / *Dam* Wolvershill Shadow
		Dam Sh.Ch. Suntop Seamoss of the Haar	*Sire* Int.Sh.Ch. Suntop Seabird / *Dam* Sedgeford Bathsheba
	Dam Sh.Ch. Iroquois Skylark	*Sire* Iroquois Moonstorm	*Sire* Sh.Ch. Iroquois Stormcloud / *Dam* Surfside Sunset
		Dam Pirates Song	*Sire* Sh.Ch. Oldholbans Pirate / *Dam* Battle Belle
Dam Iroquois Springsong	*Sire* Sh.Ch. Iroquois Snowstorm of Sundeala	*Sire* Sh.Ch. Iroquois Whiteseal Silvermorn	*Sire* Sh.Ch. Lad of The Haar / *Dam* Wolvershill Shadow
		Dam Iroquois Snowbird	*Sire* Suntop Winterbird / *Dam* Iroquois Caprice
	Dam Iroquois Sunstream	*Sire* Sh.Ch. Ashpenda Rec Robin	*Sire* Suntop Winterbird / *Dam* Ashpenda Petite d'Etoile
		Dam Sh.Ch. Iroquois Mooncloud	*Sire* Sh.Ch. Iroquois Strathspey / *Dam* Sh.Ch. Iroquois Solitaire

Pedigree of: **Sh.Ch. Hurwyn Baby Doll,
Sh.Ch. Hurwyn Cupie Doll, Sh.Ch. Hurwyn Paper Star**
Born: 22.6.79   Breeder: Owner   Owner: Mrs S. Wilkinson
23.2.81
23.2.81

Parents	**Grandparents**	**Great-Grandparents**	**Great-Great-Grandparents**
Sire Hurwyn Flightmaster	*Sire* Sh.Ch. Suntop Winterbreeze	*Sire* Suntop Winterbird	*Sire* Suntop Birdsong
			Dam Suntop Lucky Eve
		Dam Sh.Ch. Suntop Bluethrush	*Sire* Sh.Ch. Suntop Bluewings
			Dam Suntop Songthrush
	Dam Hurwyn Dawn Chorus	*Sire* Suntop Birdsong	*Sire* Sh.Ch. Suntop Bluewings
			Dam Suntop Songthrush
		Dam Hurwyn Dawn Glory	*Sire* Suntop Winterbird
			Dam Sh.Ch. Hurwyn Morning Glory
Dam Sh.Ch. Hurwyn Paper Doll	*Sire* Hurwyn Day Boy	*Sire* Suntop Birdsong	*Sire* Sh.Ch. Suntop Bluewings
			Dam Suntop Songthrush
		Dam Hurwyn Dawn Glory	*Sire* Suntop Winterbird
			Dam Sh.Ch. Hurwyn Morning Glory
	Dam Hurwyn Ernford Fairybird	*Sire* Sh.Ch. Oldholbans Pirate	*Sire* Hurwyn Hurricane
			Dam Hurwyn Sunset
		Dam Sh.Ch. Ernford Chaffinch	*Sire* Int.Sh.Ch. Suntop Royal Sunglint
			Dam Sh.Ch. Ernford Rosy Dawn

APPENDIX F

POST-WAR CHAMPIONS AND SHOW CHAMPIONS

Name of Champion	Sex	Sire	Dam	Owner	Breeder	Date of Birth
Ch. Shiplake Shining Light (Tricolour)	B	Rombalds Punchinello	Diana of Canfield	Mr W. Bennetto	Mrs J. English	30.9.43
Ch. Shiplake Symphony of Swo (Tricolour)	B	Archdale Corncrake of Haverbrack	Srolta of Swo	Mrs J. English	Mrs K. Oliver	21.7.45
Ch. Drumgannon Daybreak (Tricolour)	D	Rombalds Tempest	Dolly Daydream	Mrs L. Daly	Mrs Marsh	23.8.43
Ch. Hurricane of Craiglands (Tricolour)	D	Marker of Crombie	Spindrift of Portavogie	Messrs J. Braddon and N. Gaukroger	Mr S. Adair	3.6.43
Ch. Shiplake Stonechat of Truslers (Tricolour)	D	Archdale Corncrake of Haverbrack	Gay Girl of Truslers	Mrs J. English	Miss H. Allen	16.1.47
Ch. Silverlining of Ide (Tricolour)	B	Ch. Hurricane of Craiglands	Ch. Shiplake Shining Light	Mrs J. English	Mr J. Braddon	8.10.47
Ch. Boisdale Buttercup (Orange)	B	Boisdale Bellman	Shiplake Snowhite	Mrs M. Darling	Mrs J. English	7.5.45
Ch. Suntop Suzette of Sewerby (Tricolour)	B	Kirket Mariner of Haverbrack	Grace of Gorsehill	Miss M. Barnes	Mrs Smith	27.1.49
Ch. Shiplake Dean of Crombie (Blue)	D	Sh.Ch. Ripleygae Mallory	Crombie Sally of Sharvogue	Mrs J. English	Mr G. Crawford	8.1.52
Ch. Ernford Evening Flight (Orange)	B	Ernford Easter Parade	Teal of Yareside	Mrs A. Broadhead	Mr A. Webb	14.9.51

212

Name of Champion	Sex	Sire	Dam	Owner	Breeder	Date of Birth
Sh.Ch. Rombalds Flack	D	Rombalds Furious	Rombalds Rhythm	Mrs M. Crowther	Mrs M. Crowther	22.6.45
Sh.Ch. Nelle of Archdale (Blue)	B	Raider of Templehurst	Sallyann of Swo	Miss E. Archdale Rumball	Mrs K. Oliver	6.2.45
Sh.Ch. Ripleygae Mallory (Tricolour)	D	Archdale Corncrake of Haverbrack	Heaterdrake Diane	Miss M. Jarry	Miss E. Clarke	15.4.46
Sh.Ch. Gorsebrook Berry (Tricolour)	D	Irish Ch. Banner of Crombie	Gorsebrook Cherry	Mr and Mrs C. Upton	Mr and Mrs C. Upton	5.6.47
Sh.Ch. Parmina of Ketree (Blue)	B	Longrove Gayboy	Boisdale Beryl	Mrs E. Foss	Mrs K. Pearce	25.12.43
Sh.Ch. Rombalds Foxup Flamingo (Lemon)	D	Rombalds Faust	Marceline of Lightwood	Mrs M. Crowther	Mrs Barrell	31.7.48
Sh.Ch. Raycroft Jewel (Tricolour)	B	Marker of Crombie	Spindrift of Portavogie	Miss R. Lamb	Mr S. Adair	20.8.45
Sh.Ch. Archdale Sapphire (Tricolour)	B	Archdale Corncrake of Haverbrack	Heatherdrake Dianne	Miss E. Archdale Rumball	Miss E. Clarke	15.4.46
Sh.Ch. Shiplake Sheila of Sharvogue (Blue)	B	Beechmount Envoy of Remor	Irish Ch. Flush of Beechmount	Mrs J. English	Mr W. Currie	4.9.47
Sh.Ch. Rombalds Sentinel (Tricolour)	D	Gorse of Haverbrack	Rombalds Rhythm	Mr J. Chapman	Mrs M. Crowther	-.12.45
Sh.Ch. Rombalds Templar (Tricolour)	D	Rombalds Tempest	Rombalds Fan	Mrs M. Crowther	Mrs M. Crowther	16.3.49
Sh.Ch. Ripleygae Top Note (Blue)	D	Sh.Ch. Ripleygae Mallory	Ripleygae Music	Miss M. Jarry	Miss M. Jarry	10.4.49

Name of Champion	Sex	Sire	Dam	Owner	Breeder	Date of Birth
Sh.Ch. Shiplake Shining Change (Tricolour)	B	Ch. Hurricane of Craiglands	Ch. Shiplake Shining Light	Mrs J. English	Mrs J. English	8.10.47
Sh.Ch. Ripleygae Gorsebrook Bramble (Tricolour)	B	Irish Ch. Banner of Crombie	Gorsebrook Cherry	Miss M. Jarry	Mr and Mrs C. Upton	5.6.47
Sh.Ch. Delores of Elsiville (Tricolour)	B	Ch. Drumgannon Daybreak	Jenifer of Elsiville	Mr S. Christopher	Mrs E. Ford	15.9.46
Sh.Ch. Gayboy of Beechmount (Lemon)	D	Beechmount Envoy of Remor	Marian of Beechmount	Capt. S. Kendall	Miss E. Kirkland	19.12.47
Sh.Ch. Elswood Blue Lady (Blue)	B	Rombalds Tempest	Blue Dawn	Mr and Mrs W. Foss	Miss E. Thompson	18.5.46
Sh.Ch. Rombalds Lochranza Salome (Lemon)	B	Wincey Silverstar of Ide	Rombalds Fairy	Mrs M. Cowther	Miss J. Macmillan	13.3.49
Sh.Ch. Elswood Dotterel (Tricolour)	D	Sh.Ch. Gorsebrook Berry	Sh.Ch. Elswood Blue Lady	Mr and Mrs W. Foss	Mr and Mrs W. Foss	10.10.49
Sh.Ch. Ernford Cill Dara Yvonne (Tricolour)	B	Raycroft Orange Boy	Sh.Ch. Raycroft Jewel	Mr and Mrs L.C. James	Miss Kelly	16.3.52
Sh.Ch. Kirket Marinette (Tricolour)	B	Kirket Mariner of Haverbrack	Shiplake Sunrise	Mrs D. Enright	Mrs D. Enright	9.5.50
Sh.Ch. Shiplake Shot Silk (Tricolour)	B	Ch. Shiplake Stonechat of Truslers	Sh.Ch. Shiplake Sheila of Sharvogue	Mrs J. English	Mrs J. English	-.7.51

Name of Champion	Sex	Sire	Dam	Owner	Breeder	Date of Birth
Sh.Ch. Typhoon of Frejendor (Tricolour)	D	Ch. Hurricane Craiglands	Emeraldisle Frolic of Chastleton	Mrs D. Borrodale	Mrs D. Borrodale	21.1.49
Sh.Ch. Dawn of Crombie (Blue)	B	Sh.Ch. Ripleygae Mallory	Crombie Sally of Sharrogue	Mr G. Crawford	Mr G. Crawford	8.1.52
Sh.Ch. Postmaster of Ketree (Blue)	D	Tallahson Major	Proud Lady of Ketree	Mr S. Christopher	Mrs Pearce and Mr Murray	30.7.50
Ch. Mawdsley Lisette of Langlea (Blue)	B	Sh.Ch. Ripleygae Mallory	Langley Molly of Beechmount	Mr T. Watkinson	Miss E. Kirkland	16.5.52
Ch. Shiplake Daystar of Crombie (Tricolour)	B	Sh.Ch. Ripleygae Mallory	Crombie Sally of Sharvogue	Mrs J. English	Mr G. Crawford	8.1.52
Ch. Ernford Cill Dara Felicity (Tricolour)	B	Grouse of Capard	Minx of Medehamstede	Mrs A. Broadhead	Mrs A. Broadhead	16.5.50
Ch. Suntop Carnival Queen (Tricolour)	B	Ernford Easter Parade	Raycroft Scilla	Miss M. Barnes	Capt. S. Kendall	28.10.53
Ch. Breeze of Bowbridge (Tricolour)	D	Sh.Ch. Rombalds Templar	Sonia of Frejendor	Mrs M. Pears	Mrs M. Pears	6.4.56
Ch. Scardale Avocet (Tricolour)	B	Ch. Breeze of Bowbridge	Kestrel of Scardale	Mr D. Paterson	Mr D. Paterson	25.1.58
Sh.Ch. Shiplake Swift (Blue)	D	Sh.Ch. Rombalds Templar	Truslers Freckles of Frejendor	Mrs J. English	Mr D. Paterson	1.3.53
Sh.Ch. Willow Wren of Truslers (Orange)	B	Rothina Galahad of Emeraldisle	Snowbunting of Truslers	Miss H. Allen	Miss H. Allen	27.9.49
Sh.Ch. Marilyn of Crombie (Blue)	B	Crombie Lawrence of Langlea	Mitzi of Crombie	Mr G. Crawford	Mr G. Crawford	2.10.52

Name of Champion	Sex	Sire	Dam	Owner	Breeder	Date of Birth
Sh.Ch. Irisit Spion Kop (Blue)	D	Sh.Ch. Rombalds Templar	Rombalds Audine	Mrs K. Duncan	Mrs K. Duncan	8.5.52
Sh.Ch. Ripleygae Fanfare (Orange)	D	Sh.Ch. Ripleygae Mallory	Ripleygae Music	Miss M. Jarry	Miss M. Jarry	14.7.52
Int.Sh.Ch. Ernford Highflier (Orange)	D	Ernford Apollo	Teal of Yareside	Mrs A. Broadhead	Mrs A. Broadhead	19.12.54
Sh.Ch. Shiplake Ernford Cowslip (Orange)	B	Ernford Easter Parade	Teal of Yarside	Mrs J. English	Mrs A. Broadhead	13.5.54
Sh.Ch. Langlea Ernford Genista (Orange)	B	Ernford Easter Parade	Withinlee Willow Wren	Mr G. Crawford	Mrs A. Broadhead	6.9.54
Sh.Ch. Kirket Koola (Orange)	B	Ernford Easter Parade	Sh.Ch. Kirket Marinette	Mrs D. Enright	Mrs D. Enright	10.12.54
Sh.Ch. Kirket Karen (Tricolour)	B	Sh.Ch. Ripleygae Mallory	Kirket Karmina	Mrs E. Perkins	Mrs D. Enright	26.6.53
Sh.Ch. Engsett Enchantress of Fiveacres (Orange)	B	Shiplake Hemlington Spotlight	Engsett Evening Mist	Mr and Mrs R. Harrison	Mr and Mrs H. Wheeler	4.4.55
Sh.Ch. Tuppence of Whiteseal (Tricolour)	D	Sh.Ch. Ripleygae Mallory	Ripleygae Penelope	Mr and Mrs W. Jackson	Mr and Mrs W. Jackson	14.4.51
Sh.Ch. Prince Charming of Ketree (Blue)	D	Boisdale Dragonfly	Princess of Ketree	Mr B. McNally and Mrs L. Allan	Mr Murray and Mrs Pearce	27.6.55
Sh.Ch. Whiteseal Ononis (Tricolour)	D	Sh.Ch. Tuppence of Whiteseal	Whiteseal Sunset	Mr and Mrs W. Jackson	Mr and Mrs W. Jackson	2.8.56
Sh.Ch. Wiseman of Truslers (Blue)	D	Ch. Shiplake Dean of Crombie	Sh.Ch. Willow Wren	Miss P. Barlass of Truslers	Miss H. Allen	14.11.54

Name of Champion	Sex	Sire	Dam	Owner	Breeder	Date of Birth
Sh.Ch. Engsett Elect (Blue)	D	Shiplake Hemlington Spotlight	Irisit Saucy Sue	Mr F. Wilson	Mr and Mrs H. Wheeler	24.8.56
Sh.Ch. Shiplake Skyblue (Blue)	B	Sh.Ch. Shiplake Swift	Shiplake Somone	Mrs J. English	Mrs J. English	5.2.57
Sh.Ch. Regalia of Littlewoodcote (Blue)	B	Suntop Highlight	Raytone Fantasy	Mr and Mrs A. Jenkinson	Mr and Mrs A. Jenkinson	21.4.55
Sh.Ch. Shiplake Sweet Briar (Tricolour)	B	Ch. Shiplake Dean of Crombie	Sh.Ch. Shiplake Shot Silk	Mrs J. English	Mrs J. English	12.8.55
Sh.Ch. Ernford Rosy Dawn (Orange)	B	Sh.Ch. Prince Charming of Ketree	Ch. Ernford Evening Flight	Mrs A. Broadhead	Mrs A. Broadhead	5.12.57
Int.Sh.Ch. Iroquois Casanova (Orange)	D	Sh.Ch. Prince Charming of Ketree	Iroquois Ernford Irresistible	Mrs L. Allan-Scott	Mr and Mrs I. Allan	8.6.57
Sh.Ch. Silbury Soames of Madavale (Tricolour)	D	Silbury Sherper	Silbury Springhead Serene	Mrs A.Williams	Mr and Mrs P. Gardiner-Swann	10.7.59
Int.Sh.Ch. Engsett Exception (Tricolour)	D	Withinlee Sheik of Frejendor	Engsett Exotic	Mr and Mrs H. Wheeler	Mr and Mrs H. Wheeler	26.11.58
Sh.Ch. Shiplake Silverflash (Blue)	B	Sh.Ch. Shiplake Swift	Randa of Lake	Mrs J.English	Mrs J. Guarella	21.6.56
Sh.Ch. Littlewoodcote Temptress (Tricolour)	B	Regent of Littlewoodcote	Pandora of Whiteseal	Mr and Mrs A. Jenkinson	Mr and Mrs J. Pragnell	18.7.57
Sh.Ch. Littlewoodcote Carousel (Tricolour)	B	Int.Sh.Ch. Iroquois Casanova	Sh.Ch. Littlewoodcote Trickster	Mr and Mrs A. Jenkinson	Mr and Mrs A. Jenkinson	11.12.59
Sh.Ch. Pride of Noyna (Tricolour)	B	Sh.Ch. Prince Charming of Ketree	Iroquois Ernford Irresistible	Mr and Mrs K. Bradshaw	Mr C. Bowhill	12.10.59

Name of Champion	Sex	Sire	Dam	Owner	Breeder	Date of Birth
Sh.Ch. Iroquois Stormcloud (Blue)	D	Int.Sh.Ch. Iroquois Casanova	Hurwyn Bluecloud	Mrs L. Allan-Scott	Mesdames Wilson and Wilkinson	29.12.61
Int.Sh.Ch. Suntop Royal Sunglint (Orange)	D	Sh.Ch. Suntop Royalbird	Suntop Eventide	Miss M.Barnes	Miss M. Barnes	21.6.62
Sh.Ch. Littlewoodcote Trickster (Tricolour)	B	Regent of Littlewoodcote	Pandora of Whiteseal	Mr and Mrs A. Jenkinson	Mr and Mrs J. Pragnell	18.7.57
Sh.Ch. Suntop Snowbird (Blue)	D	Suntop Songbird	Suntop Quickstep	Miss M. Barnes	Miss M. Barnes	3.2.61
Sh.Ch. Sea Fairy of Noyna (Blue)	B	Noyna Fencefoot Farmers Lad	Sh.Ch. Pride of Noyna	Mr and Mrs K. Bradshaw	Mr and Mrs K. Bradshaw	27.10.60
Sh.Ch. Flying Star of Fermanar (Orange)	B	Int.Sh.Ch. Iroquois Casanova	Fairystar of Fermanar	Miss K. Lewis	Col C. Broome	29.9.61
Sh.Ch. Redtops Silbury Sonya (Tricolour)	B	Silbury Sherper	Silbury Springhead Serene	Mrs N. Treharne	Mr and Mrs P. Gardiner-Swann	10.7.59
Sh.Ch. Mawdsley Ladybird of Barningham (Blue)	B	Ernford Kingfisher	Ch. Suntop Carnival Queen	Mr T. Watkinson	Capt S. Kendall	27.7.57
Sh.Ch. Waxwing (Tricolour)	D	Sh.Ch. Tuppence of Whiteseal	Engsett Wild Honey	Mr W. Wilson	Mr W. Wilson	16.6.60
Sh.Ch. Sunstar of Crombie (Tricolour)	D	Steadfast of Crombie	Shiplake Alma of Crombie	Mr G. Crawford	Mr G. Crawford	28.10.61
Sh.Ch. Engsett Encounter (Orange)	D	Int.Sh.Ch. Engsett Exception	Sea Mist of Noyna	Mr and Mrs H. Wheeler	Mrs E. Dunn	5.4.62
Sh.Ch. Oldholbans Pirate (Tricolour)	D	Hurwyn Hurricane	Hurwyn Sunset	Mrs A. Findlay	Mrs A.Findlay	12.2.61

Name of Champion	Sex	Sire	Dam	Owner	Breeder	Date of Birth
Sh.Ch. Jewell of Thrumall (Blue)	B	Mawdsley Thrumall Talent	Mawdsley Bella	Mr H. Schofield	Mr T. Watkinson	23.11.62
Sh.Ch. Engsett Brilliance of Fiveacres (Orange)	B	Ernford Easter Parade	Sh.Ch. Engsett Enchantress of Fiveacres	Mr and Mrs H. Wheeler	Mr and Mrs R. Harrison	27.7.59
Sh.Ch. Senglish Early Mist (Tricolour)	D	Suntop Songbird	Senglish Evening Star	Mrs D. Kay	Mrs D. Kay	9.10.58
Sh.Ch. Iroquois Courtesan (Orange)	B	Sh.Ch. Prince Charming of Ketree	Iroquois Ernford Irresistible	Mrs L. Allan-Scott	Mr C. Bowhill	12.10.59
Sh.Ch. Suntop Royalbird (Tricolour)	D	Suntop Songbird	Suntop Lady Rosa of Whiteseal	Miss M. Barnes	Group-Capt. A. Sutton	17.6.60
Sh.Ch. Ernford Chaffinch (Orange)	B	Int.Sh.Ch. Suntop Royal Sunglint	Sh.Ch. Ernford Rosy Dawn	Mrs A. Broadhead	Mrs A. Broadhead	19.1.64
Sh.Ch. Iroquois Bluemoon (Orange)	B	Suntop Songbird	Sh.Ch. Iroquois Courtesan	Mrs C. Duffield	Mrs L. Allan-Scott	22.10.62
Sh.Ch. Iroquois Cointreau (Orange)	B	Shiplake Shandy	Iroquois Littlewoodcote Caprice	Mrs A. Findlay	Mrs L. Allan-Scott	28.5.61
Int.Sh.Ch. Suntop Royal Sunrise (Orange)	D	Sh.Ch. Suntop Royalbird	Suntop Eventide	Miss M. Barnes	Miss M. Barnes	21.6.62
Sh.Ch. Trodgers Meadow Fescue (Tricolour)	B	Ch. Boisdale Puffin	Trodgers Red Clover	Mrs A. Tate	Mrs A. Tate	30.8.63

Name of Champion	Sex	Sire	Dam	Owner	Breeder	Date of Birth
Sh.Ch. Hepton Saucy Sue (Orange)	B	Hepton Jaffa	Mawdsley Misty Maiden	Mr J. Taylor	Mr J. Taylor	19.7.65
Sh.Ch. Ednasid Wuster (Blue)	D	Int.Sh.Ch. Suntop Royal Sunglint	Ednasid Senglish Whisper	Mr S. Boulton	Mr S. Boulton	5.10.64
Sh.Ch. Trodgers Hurwyn Heaven (Blue)	B	Int.Sh.Ch. Iroquois Casanova	Hurwyn Bluecloud	Mrs A. Tate	Mesdames Wilson and Wilkinson	29.12.61
Sh.Ch. Suntop Royal Mark of Etherwood (Blue)	D	Sh.Ch. Suntop Royalbird	Mawdsley Magnolia Blossom	Mr and Mrs S. Crane	Mr T. Watkinson	9.8.63
Sh.Ch. Fencefoot Freckles (Orange)	D	Int.Sh.Ch. Suntop Royal Sunglint	Fencefoot Fast Miss	Mrs M.Marsden	Mrs M. Marsden	16.10.64
Int.Sh.Ch. Suntop Seabird	D	Suntop Songbird	Vassals Frolic	Miss M.Barnes	Mrs H. Baker	6.4.63
Sh.Ch. Noyna Rockette (Blue)	B	Suntop Songbird	Sh.Ch. Sea Fairy of Noyna	Mr and Mrs K. Bradshaw	Mr and Mrs K. Bradshaw	30.1.63
Sh.Ch. Iroquois Cascade (Orange)	B	Int.Sh.Ch. Iroquois Casanova	Fairystar of Fermanar	Mrs L. Allan-Scott	Col C. Broome	29.9.61
Sh.Ch. Elswood Renmark Baronet (Blue)	D	Sh.Ch. Senglish Early Mist	Renmark Melody	Mr and Mrs W. Foss	Mrs M. and Miss P. Neave	19.12.63
Ch. Boisdale Puffin (Tricolour)	D	Boisdale Kestor	Boisdale Butterpuff	Mrs M. Darling	Mrs M. Darling	22.3.60
Ch. Scardale Teal (Tricolour)	D	Sh.Ch. Senglish Early Mist	Ch. Scardale Avocet	Mr D. Paterson	Mr D. Paterson	17.6.63

Name of Champion	Sex	Sire	Dam	Owner	Breeder	Date of Birth
Sh.Ch. Lad of the Haar (Tricolour)	D	Sh.Ch. Senglish Early Mist	Shadowlight of the Haar	Mrs M. Brown	Mrs M. Brown	23.7.63
Sh.Ch. Noyna Gazelle (Orange)	B	Int.Sh.Ch. Suntop Royal Sunglint	Sh.Ch. Pride of Noyna	Mr and Mrs K. Bradshaw	Mr and Mrs K. Bradshaw	17.6.65
Sh.Ch. Kherim Bey of Sudenalla (Tricolour)	D	Mawdsley Woodcock	Silver Jasmine of Healey	Mr D. Clegg	Mr D. Clegg	25.6.65
Sh.Ch. Monksriding Ernford Flamingo (Orange)	D	Sh.Ch. Oldholbans Pirate	Sh.Ch. Ernford Chaffinch	Mr and Mrs H. Pearson	Mrs A. Broadhead	27.7.66
Sh.Ch. Hurwyn Morning Glory (Orange)	B	Sh.Ch. Iroquois Stormcloud	Hurwyn Trodgers Rika	Mrs S. Wilkinson	Mrs S. Wilkinson	27.4.66
Sh.Ch. Flatford Why Wonder (Orange)	B	Suntop Wonderbird	Suntop Footstep	Mr R. Powell	Miss M. Barnes	23.6.66
Sh.Ch. Ernford Falcon (Orange)	D	Sh.Ch. Oldholbans Pirate	Sh.Ch. Ernford Chaffinch	Mr and Mrs R. Burns	Mrs A. Broadhead	27.7.66
Sh.Ch. Suntop Seamoss of the Haar (Orange)	B	Int.Sh.Ch. Suntop Seabird	Sedgford Bathsheba of Beclands	Mrs M. Brown	Mrs Sedgley	5.3.66
Sh.Ch. Trodgers Impala (Blue)	D	Trodgers Oregon	Trodgers Red Clover	Mrs J. Furneaux	Mrs A. Tate	16.5.67
Sh.Ch. Hepton Jaffas Girl (Orange)	B	Hepton Jaffa	Oldholbans Black Princess	Mr J. Taylor	Mr Bell	3.9.66
Sh.Ch. Trodgers Bluebell (Blue)	B	Sh.Ch. Iroquois Guy Fawkes	Sh.Ch. Trodgers of Neighbours	Mrs A. Tate	Mrs A. Tate	9.12.67

Name of Champion	Sex	Sire	Dam	Owner	Breeder	Date of Birth
Sh.Ch. Iroquois Solitaire (Blue)	B	Sh.Ch. Iroquois Stormcloud	Sh.Ch. Iroquois Bluemoon	Mrs L. Allan-Scot	Mrs C. Duffield	15.2.66
Sh.Ch. Trodgers Scots Oat (Orange)	D	Sh.Ch. Iroquois Strathspey	Sh.Ch. Trodgers Meadow Fescue	Mrs A. Tate	Mrs A. Tate	9.12.67
Sh.Ch. Yankee of Neighbours (Blue)	D	Shiplake Skidbys Guy Fawkes	Silbury Satin Neighbours	Mrs C. Ercolani	Mrs C. Ercolani	14.11.64
Sh.Ch. Iroquois Rainbow (Tricolour)	B	Sh.Ch. Iroquois Stormcloud	A'Dale Redwing	Mrs D. Bowen	Mrs C. Allan	15.5.65
Sh.Ch. Noyna Sunfairy (Orange)	B	Noyna Suntop Royal Wizard	Noyna Cassandra	Mrs L. Sawtell	Mr and Mrs K. Bradshaw	16.8.68
Sh.Ch. Elswood Ashpenda Moonquest (Blue)	D	Sh.Ch. Elswood Renmark Baronet	Sh.Ch. Iroquois Bluemoon	Mr and Mrs W. Foss	Mrs C.Duffield	23.8.67
Sh.Ch. Suntop Bluethrush (Blue)	B	Sh.Ch. Suntop Bluewings	Suntop Songthrush	Mr R. Powell	Miss M. Barnes	19.9.66
Sh.Ch. Suntop Bluewings (Blue)	D	Int.Sh.Ch. Suntop Seabird	Suntop Royalwings	Mr and Mrs A. MacCallum	Miss M. Barnes	15.5.65
Sh.Ch. Bournehouse Ballerina (Tricolour)	B	Evening Flight of Frejendor	Iroquois Jasmine	Mr G. Williams	Mr G. Williams	28.9.68
Sh.Ch. Iroquois Whiteseal Silvermorn (Tricolour)	D	Sh.Ch. Lad of the Haar	Wolvershill Shadow	Mrs L. Allan-Scott	Mrs V. Neill	24.9.68
Sh.Ch. Oldholbans Dill (Tricolour)	D	Hepton Orangeman	Oldholbans Patience	Mrs G. Bond	Mrs A. Findlay	3.3.68

Name of Champion	Sex	Sire	Dam	Owner	Breeder	Date of Birth
Ch. Upperwood Zoe (Orange)	B	Sh.Ch. Engsett Electrode	Withinlee Wallflower	Mr R. Goutorbe	Mr R. Goutorbe	11.6.69
Sh.Ch. Bournehouse Meadowfern (Tricolour)	B	Evening Flight of Frejendor	Iroquois Jasmine	Mr G. Williams	Mr G. Williams	9.9.66
Sh.Ch. Iroquois Strathspey (Orange)	D	Sh.Ch. Iroquois Stormcloud	Sh.Ch. Iroquois Cascade	Mrs L. Allan-Scott	Mrs L. Allan-Scott	7.8.66
Sh.Ch. Engsett Electrode (Tricolour)	D	Sh.Ch. Engsett Encounter	Sheena of Frejendor	Mr and Mrs H. Wheeler	Mrs D. Borrodale	9.8.66
Sh.Ch. Monksriding Baroness (Blue)	B	Sh.Ch. Elswood Renmark Baronet	Ernford Zia	Mr and Mrs H. Pearson	Mr and Mrs H. Pearson	27.5.68
Sh.Ch. Hepton Maudsley Aloysius (Blue)	D	Mawdsley Nickodemus	Mawdsley Harvest Moon	Mr J. Taylor	Mr T. Watkinson	3.12.69
Sh.Ch. Elswood White Heatherette (Blue)	B	Sh.Ch. Elswood Renmark Baronet	Bousave Blue Belle	Mr and Mrs D. Baldwin	Mrs Johnson	15.6.66
Sh.Ch. Fenman Fragrance (Orange)	B	Sh.Ch. Engsett Electrode	Oldholbans Jay	Mr and Mrs H. Wheeler	Mrs Truman	9.9.70
Sh.Ch. Iroquois Mooncloud (Blue)	B	Sh.Ch. Iroquois Strathspey	Sh.Ch. Iroquois Solitaire	Mrs L. Allan-Scott	Mrs C. Appleton	25.11.69
Sh.Ch. Ednasid Merrell Blue Baron (Tricolour)	D	Sh.Ch. Ednasid Wuster	Gorsebrook Blonden	Mr and Mrs S. Boulton	Mrs A. Kenneally	7.7.69
Sh.Ch. Hurwyn All Glory (Tricolour)	B	Suntop Birdsong	Hurwyn Trodgers Rika	Mrs S. Wilkinson	Mrs S. Wilkinson	19.3.69

Name of Champion	Sex	Sire	Dam	Owner	Breeder	Date of Birth
Sh.Ch. Upperwood Lancelot of Nethermoor (Orange)	D	Sh.Ch. Engsett Electrode	Withinlee Wallflower	Mr J. Brunt	Mr R. Goutorbe	30.12.70
Sh.Ch. Rebway Heron (Tricolour)	B	Renmark Edgar	Mursett Azure Ann	Mr J. Bowen	M. Johnson and B. Lewis	15.2.69
Sh.Ch. Elswood Highlight (Blue)	B	Sh.Ch. Elswood Renmark Baronet	Elswood Aurora	Mrs V. Foss	Mr and Mrs W. Foss	7.7.69
Sh.Ch. Carofel Sunshine (Orange)	D	Sh.Ch. Ednasid Merrell Blue Baron	Carofel Firefly	Mrs D. Walker	Mrs D. Walker	12.11.71
Sh.Ch. Hayrick Ploughboy (Blue)	D	Sh.Ch. Iroquois Strathspey	Hayrick Trodgers Goosegrass	Mrs J. Martin	Mrs C. Maclean	10.9.70
Sh.Ch. Bournehouse Figaro (Tricolour)	D	Sh.Ch. Monksriding Ernford Flamingo	Bournehouse Blue Moon	Mr T. Rooney and Mrs J. Knowles	Mr G. Williams	26.2.73
Sh.Ch. Attleford Mr Cinders (Tricolour)	D	Attleford Huntsman	Attleford Silver	Mrs M. Thomas	Mrs M. Thomas	8.9.69
Sh.Ch. Hurwyn Wigeon (Orange)	D	Suntop Winterbird	Ernford Bobolink	Mr D .Mullholland	Mrs S. Wilkinson	11.11.70
Sh.Ch. and Am.Ch. Clariho Whimsey of Valley Run (Orange)	B	Am.Ch. Clariho Rough Rider	Am.Ch. Pinney Paige of Valley Run	Mr and Mrs W. Parkinson	Mr and Mrs Wright	12.3.71
Sh.Ch. Ashpenda Red Robin (Orange)	D	Suntop Winterbird	Ashpenda Petite Etoile	Mrs C. Duffield	Mrs C. Duffield	27.6.71
Sh.Ch. Suford Hurwyn Whinchat (Blue)	B	Suntop Birdsong	Hurwyn Ernford Fairybird	Mrs Y. Rudin	Mrs Wilkinson	29.1.71

Name of Champion	Sex	Sire	Dam	Owner	Breeder	Date of Birth
Sh.Ch. Barranco Bournehouse Diorama (Orange)	D	Sh.Ch. Suntop Royal Mark of Etherwood	Bournehouse Honeydew	Mr and Mrs V. Haynes	Mr G. Williams	24.8.70
Sh.Ch. Oudenarde Dancing Glory (Orange)	B	Suntop Winterbird	Oudenarde Merry Dancer	Mrs D. Hamilton and Miss Hamilton	Mrs D. Hamilton and Miss Hamilton	18.6.71
Sh.Ch. Adam Ahasuerus (Orange)	D	Suntop Winterbird	Oldholbans Caraway	Mrs H. Lenzi	Mrs Scott	7.3.70
Sh.Ch. Briaghculan Saucy Sue (Orange)	B	Trodgers Bryony	Farmacy Althoea	Mr and Mrs G. Burton	Mrs P. McClelland	10.10.68
Sh.Ch. Attleford Brown Betty (Orange)	B	Factor of Fermanar	Dash of Whiteseal	Mrs M. Thomas	Mrs M. Thomas	11.5.68
Sh.Ch. Bournehouse Enchantress (Orange)	B	Sh.Ch. Engsett Electrode	Sh.Ch. Bournehouse Meadowfern	Mr and Mrs H. Wheeler	Mr G. Williams	7.10.71
Sh.Ch. Carofel Whispering Romance (Tricolour)	B	Suntop Winterbird	Carofel Gay Whisper	Mrs D. Walker	Mrs D. Walker	8.8.70
Sh.Ch. Renmark Nimrod (Blue)	D	Sh.Ch. Elswood Renmark Baronet	Renmark Hostess	Mrs M. and Miss P. Neave	Mrs M. and Miss P. Neave	20.2.72
Sh.Ch. Ashpenda Kittiwake (Tricolour)	B	Suntop Winterbird	Aspenda Petite Etoile	Mrs C. Duffield	Mrs C. Duffield	27.6.71
Int.Sh.Ch. Suntop Winter Breeze (Blue)	D	Suntop Winterbird	Sh.Ch. Suntop Bluethrush	Miss M. Barnes	Miss M. Barnes	30.8.72

Name of Champion	Sex	Sire	Dam	Owner	Breeder	Date of Birth
Sh.Ch. Shandarret Damask Rose (Blue)	B	Suntop Birdsong	Iroquois Kismet	Mrs R. Timms	Mrs R. Timms	9.10.70
Sh.Ch. Wistaston School Holiday (Blue)	B	Sh.Ch. Elswood Renmark Baronet	Suntop Royal Lark of Wistaston	Mr and Mrs R. Johnson	Miss G. Williams	29.7.71
Sh.Ch. Gorsebrook Patsy Tuesday (Orange)	B	Sh.Ch. Ednasid Merrell Blue Baron	Gorsebrook Tawny Silk	Mrs P. Harewood	Mr and Mrs C. Upton	27.6.72
Sh.Ch. Upperwood Zsa Zsa (Orange)	B	Sh.Ch. Engsett Electrode	Withinlee Wallflower	Mr and Mrs R. Goutorbe	Mr and Mrs R. Goutorbe	1.7.72
Sh.Ch. Ritanor Gorsebrook Back to Banner (Ornage)	D	Ritanor Monarch of Coolderry	Gorebrook Lisette of Starcroft	Mrs B. Wells	Mr and Mrs C. Upton	23.7.71
Sh.Ch. Hurwyn Waterail of Settrenda (Blue)	B	Sh.Ch. Hurwyn Wigeon	Hurwyn Blue Sky	Mr C. Brown	Mrs S. Wilkinson	28.10.73
Sh.Ch. Engsett Everready of Rohan (Tricolour)	D	Sh.Ch. Iroquois Whiteseal Silvermorn	Upperwood Erelle	Mr and Mrs D. Thomas	Mr and Mrs H. Wheeler	1.12.74
Sh.Ch. Segedunum Persephone (Blue)	B	Sh.Ch. Engsett Electrode	Segedunum Junos Joy	Mr A. MacCallum	Mr A. MacCallum	12.3.73
Sh.Ch. Bournehouse Dancing Master (Tricolour)	D	Sh.Ch. Monksriding Ernford Flamingo	Sh.Ch. Bournehouse Ballerina	Mr G. Williams	Mr G. Williams	2.4.73
Sh.Ch. Wistaston School Scattabrain (Tricolour)	B	Sh.Ch. Monksriding Ernford Flamingo	Wistaston School Mystery	Miss G. Williams	Miss G. Williams	28.5.75

Name of Champion	Sex	Sire	Dam	Owner	Breeder	Date of Birth
Sh.Ch. Shandarret Damask Rose (Blue)	B	Suntop Birdsong	Iroquois Kismet	Mrs R. Timms	Mrs R. Timms	9.10.70
Sh.Ch. Wistaston School Holiday (Blue)	B	Sh.Ch. Elswood Renmark Baronet	Suntop Royal Lark of Wistaston	Mr and Mrs R. Johnson	Miss G. Williams	29.7.71
Sh.Ch. Gorsebrook Patsy Tuesday (Orange)	B	Sh.Ch. Ednasid Merrell Blue Baron	Gorsebrook Tawny Silk	Mrs P. Harewood	Mr and Mrs C. Upton	27.6.72
Sh.Ch. Upperwood Zsa Zsa (Orange)	B	Sh.Ch. Engsett Electrode	Withinlee Wallflower	Mr and Mrs R. Goutorbe	Mr and Mrs R. Goutorbe	1.7.72
Sh.Ch. Ritanor Gorsebrook Back to Banner (Ornage)	D	Ritanor Monarch of Coolderry	Gorebrook Lisette of Starcroft	Mrs B. Wells	Mr and Mrs C. Upton	23.7.71
Sh.Ch. Hurwyn Waterail of Settrenda (Blue)	B	Sh.Ch. Hurwyn Wigeon	Hurwyn Blue Sky	Mr C. Brown	Mrs S. Wilkinson	28.10.73
Sh.Ch. Engsett Everready of Rohan (Tricolour)	D	Sh.Ch. Iroquois Whiteseal Silvermorn	Upperwood Erelle	Mr and Mrs D. Thomas	Mr and Mrs H. Wheeler	1.12.74
Sh.Ch. Segedunum Persephone (Blue)	B	Sh.Ch. Engsett Electrode	Segedunum Junos Joy	Mr A. MacCallum	Mr A. MacCallum	12.3.73
Sh.Ch. Bournehouse Dancing Master (Tricolour)	D	Sh.Ch. Monksriding Ernford Flamingo	Sh.Ch.Bournehouse Ballerina	Mr G. Williams	Mr G. Williams	2.4.73
Sh.Ch. Wistaston School Scattabrain (Tricolour)	B	Sh.Ch. Monksriding Ernford Flamingo	Wistaston School Mystery	Miss G. Williams	Miss G. Williams	28.5.75

Name of Champion	Sex	Sire	Dam	Owner	Breeder	Date of Birth
Sh.Ch. Hurwyn Paper Doll (Orange)	B	Hurwyn Dayboy	Hurwyn Ernford Fairybird	Mrs S. Wilkinson	Mrs S. Wilkinson	19.6.75
Sh.Ch. Amber Starlight (Orange)	D	Sh.Ch. Ednasid Merrell Blue Baron	Northland Dollybird	Mr and Mrs F. Vallender	Mrs J. Dubber	15.2.74
Int.Sh.Ch. Suntop Nightingale (Blue)	D	Int.Sh.Ch. Suntop Winter Breeze	Wonderstar of Suntop	Miss M. Barnes	Mr and Mrs Harris	17.4.75
Sh.Ch. Dundabhean Gaiety Girl (Tricolour)	B	Sh.Ch. Hepton Mawdsley Aloysius	Hepton Heritage	Mrs M. Younge	Mrs M. Younge	2.12.72
Sh.Ch. Iroquois Snowstorm of Sundeala (Blue)	D	Sh.Ch. Iroquois Whiteseal Silvermorn	Iroquois Snowbird	Mrs B. Davies	Mrs A. Bolton	8.9.74
Sh.Ch. Bournehouse Solo Dancer (Tricolour)	B	Sh.Ch. Bournehouse Dancing Master	Suntop Dewberry	Miss B. Reed	Mr G. Williams	29.8.74
Sh.Ch. Mindenday Music Master (Tricolour)	D	Sh.Ch. Bournehouse Dancing Master	Mindenday Minuet	Mr and Mrs R. Armstead	Mr and Mrs R. Armstead	29.7.75
Sh.Ch. Bournehouse Flirting Freda (Tricolour)	B	Sh.Ch. Monksriding Ernford Flamingo	Bournehouse Blue Moon	Mr G. Williams	Mr G. Williams	26.2.72
Sh.Ch. Iroquois Skylark (Orange)	B	Iroquois Moonstorm	Pirates Song	Mrs L. Allan-Scott	Mrs I. Foreman	26.5.71
Sh.Ch. Suntop True Breeze (Blue)	B	Int.Sh.Ch. Suntop Winter Breeze	Suntop Regal Thrush	Miss M. Barnes	Miss M. Barnes	27.3.76

Name of Champion	Sex	Sire	Dam	Owner	Breeder	Date of Birth
Sh.Ch. Ashpenda Golden Pheasant (Orange)	B	Sh.Ch. Attleford Mulberry	Ashpenda Petite Etoile	Mrs F. Grimsdell	Mrs Duffield	5.10.73
Sh.Ch. Attleford Mulberry (Blue)	D	Sh.Ch. Engsett Electrode	Attleford Silver Lining	Mrs P. Malins	Mrs M. Thomas	29.3.71
Sh.Ch. Wistaston School Whisper of Gaewill (Blue)	B	Sh.Ch. Monksriding Ernford Flamingo	Wistaston School Mystery	Mrs G. Williams	Miss G. Williams	1.5.73
Sh.Ch. Northgate Dubonnet (Tricolour)	D	Northgate Hurricane	Jucridor Evening Mist of Northgate	Mr and Mrs W. Fuller	Mr and Mrs W. Fuller	5.10.73
Sh.Ch. Suntop Starling (Blue)	D	Int.Sh.Ch. Suntop Winter Breeze	Wonderstar of Suntop	Miss M. Barnes	Mr and Mrs Harris	17.4.75
Sh.Ch. Segedunum Re Vera (Tricolour)	D	Segedunum Indica	Segedunum Octavia	Mr A. MacCallum	Mr A. MacCallum	21.5.74
Sh.Ch. James James from Farmacy (Tricolour)	D	Sh.Ch. Upperwood Lancelot of Nethermoor	Farmacy Festival Queen	Mrs S. Leiper	Mr Murray	22.5.75
Sh.Ch. Penderlew Pearly King of Whitcroft	D	Sh.Ch. Bournehouse Figaro	Fair Claire of Stamford	Mr and Mrs S. Jackson	S. Penrith	21.4.76
Sh.Ch. Iroquois Sansovino of Sundeala (Blue)	D	Sh.Ch.Iroquois Snowstorm of Sundeala	Iroquois Sunstream	Mrs B. Davies	Mrs L. Allan-Scott	25.2.76
Sh.Ch. Suntop Dark Breeze (Blue)	D	Int.Sh.Ch. Suntop Winter Breeze	Suntop Regal Thrush	Mrs G. Fairbairn	Miss M. Barnes	27.3.76

Name of Champion	Sex	Sire	Dam	Owner	Breeder	Date of Birth
Sh.Ch. Monksriding in Blue of Foscott (Blue)	B	Sh.Ch. Monksriding Ernford Flamingo	Sh.Ch. Monksriding Baroness	Mr and Mrs P. Green	Mrs H. Pearson	23.1.74
Sh.Ch. Jetsett Canopus of Oldfield (Blue)	B	Thrumall Advocate	Thrumall Brandysnap	Mr C. Bexon	Mr and Mrs D. Christie	9.11.73
Sh.Ch. Bournehouse Quickstep (Orange)	B	Sh.Ch. Bournehouse Dancing Master	Marus Sea Holly	Mr G. Williams	Mr G. Williams	10.11.77
Sh.Ch. Elswood Vagabond King (Tricolour)	D	Sh.Ch. Bournehouse Dancing Master	Sh.Ch. Ashpenda Kittiwake	Mesdames V. Foss and P. Wadsworth	Mrs V. Foss and Miss M. Gilchrist	13.5.77
Sh.Ch. Arnsett Afaya (Tricolour)	B	Int.Sh.Ch. Suntop Winter Breeze	Suntop Summer Belle	Mrs A. Child	Mrs A. Child	15.8.76
Sh.Ch. Limestone Liberty (Tricolour)	B	Suntop Daystar	Gorsebrook Pennyweight	Mrs P. Williams	Mr N. Healy	12.11.74
Sh.Ch. Tattersett Inycarra (Blue)	B	Hurwyn Dayboy	Sh.Ch. Ashpenda Golden Pheasant	Mr and Mrs M. Yarnley	Mr and Mrs A. Grimsdell	2.4.77
Sh.Ch. Merrysett Snowbunting (Orange)	B	Hurwyn Dayboy	Ellisland Highland Delight	Mrs M. Jarvis	Mrs M. Jarvis	17.12.77
Sh.Ch. Misty Pendragon At Stiperden (Blue)	D	Thrumall Batchelor Boy	Ballacraine Double Knocker	Mr and Mrs C. Roberts	Mr J. Buck	6.1.74
Sh.Ch. Kanchary Grey Dove (Blue)	B	Sh.Ch. Renmark Nimrod	Northgate Heaven of Kanchary	Mrs J. Clifford and Miss S. Marsden	Mrs J. Clifford	10.7.74
Sh.Ch. Bellesett Baron of Upperwood (Tricolour)	D	Wistaston School Report of Upperwood	Gilleyfield Gemini	Messrs F. and P. Clews	Mr and Mrs A. Farmer	7.8.74

Name of Champion	Sex	Sire	Dam	Owner	Breeder	Date of Birth
Sh.Ch. Wistaston School Sunshine (Orange)	B	Suntop Winterbird	Wistaston School Breakaway of Triora	Miss G. Williams	Miss G. Williams	25.6.77
Sh.Ch. Mindenday Miss Moss (Blue)	B	Sh.Ch. Mindenday Music Master	Mindenday Mornings Bright	Mrs R. Davies and Mr B. Jeffrey	Mr and Mrs R. Armstead	13.12.76
Sh.Ch. Kenandra Lord Helpus (Tricolour)	D	Willowsett Warbeck of Upperwood	Engsett Elusive	Mesdames S. Wallis and J. Hirst	Mesdames S. Wallis and J. Hirst	19.3.76
Sh.Ch. Tattersett Eyecatcher (Orange)	B	Hurwyn Dayboy	Sh.Ch. Ashpenda Golden Pheasant	Mr and Mrs A. Grimsdell	Mr and Mrs A. Grimsdell	2.4.77
Sh.Ch. Derriford Ondone (Tricolour)	B	Sh.Ch. Ashpenda Red Robin	Sh.Ch. Bournehouse Solo Dancer	Miss B.J. Reed	Miss B.J. Reed	3.10.76
Sh.Ch. Willowsett Whoopsie of Engsett (Orange)	B	Am.Ch. Clariho Rough 'n' Ready	Willowsett Windrush	Mr and Mrs H. Wheeler	Mr and Mrs D. Hobson	22.10.76
Sh.Ch. Weatherdair Moon Breeze of Tragus (Blue)	B	Sh.Ch. Renmark Nimrod	Weatherdair Lunar Lady	Mr and Mrs P. Upton	Mr F. Neal	24.2.75
Sh.Ch. Bluedoyenne Ballerina (Orange)	B	Sh.Ch. Amber Starlight	Bluedoyenne Simona	Mr and Mrs F. Vallender	Mr H. Smith	22.12.77
Sh.Ch. Iroquois Concerto (Blue)	D	Iroquois Stormbird	Iroquois Springsong	Mrs L. Allan-Scott	Mrs L. Allan-Scott	22.6.77
Sh.Ch. Ashpenda Golden Eagle of Ritanor (Orange)	D	Suntop Winterbird	Ashpenda Petite Etoile	Mrs B. Wells	Mrs C. Duffield	19.7.75
Sh.Ch. Mr Macawber of Foscott (Orange)	D	Reveddam Drambuie	Bruclem Jay	Mr and Mrs M. Grassby	Mrs A. Redfern	26.5.75

Name of Champion	Sex	Sire	Dam	Owner	Breeder	Date of Birth
Sh.Ch. Kanchary Grey Ladybird of Invogue (Blue)	B	Sh.Ch. Iroquois Whiteseal Silvermorn	Northgate Heaven of Kanchary	Mr and Mrs S. Henderson	Mrs J. Clifford	18.10.75
Sh.Ch. Northgate Blue Brocade (Blue)	B	Northgate Invader	Northgate Quaker Girl	Mr and Mrs W. Fuller	Mr and Mrs W. Fuller	14.6.79
Sh.Ch. Settrenda Super Serenity (Orange)	B	Sh.Ch. Hurwyn Wigeon	Ashpenda Super Honey of Settrenda	Mr C. Brown	Mr C. Brown	10.2.77
Sh.Ch. Iroquois Snowprince of Northgate (Blue)	D	Sh.Ch. Iroquois Whiteseal Silvermorn	Iroquois Snowbird	Mr and Mrs W. Fuller	Mrs A. Bolton	8.9.74
Sh.Ch. Hurwyn Baby Doll (Tricolour)	B	Hurwyn Flightmaster	Sh.Ch. Hurwyn Paper Doll	Mrs S. Wilkinson	Mrs S. Wilkinson	24.6.79
Sh.Ch. Sirius of Cedar (Tricolour)	D	Hurwyn Corunna Bay	Aultmore Superblend from Kyleglen	Mr and Mrs D. Masson	Mr A. Belton	25.12.76
Sh.Ch. Upperwood Zeno of Sorbus (Orange)	D	Carofel Gilt Edge of Upperwood	Ch. Upperwood Zoe	Mr and Mrs K. Spencer	Mr and Mrs R. Goutorbe	2.6.77
Sh.Ch. Suntop Freckled Star (Blue)	D	Sh.Ch. Suntop Starling	Suntop Winterfinch	Mr and Mrs D. Lewis	Miss M. Barnes	22.6.78
Sh.Ch. Tattersett Hidden Value (Blue)	B	Hurwyn Dayboy	Sh.Ch. Ashpenda Golden Pheasant	Mr and Mrs A. Grimsdell	Mr and Mrs A. Grimsdell	2.4.77
Sh.Ch. Upperwood Midnight Melody of Sorbus (Tricolour)	B	Hazelbarrow Sebastian of Upperwood	Upperwood Reflection	Mrs and Mrs K. Spencer	Mr and Mrs R. Goutorbe	14.6.79

Name of Champion	Sex	Sire	Dam	Owner	Breeder	Date of Birth
Sh.Ch. Monksriding Amazing Grace of Scratchwood (Orange)	B	Sh.Ch. Monksriding Ernford Flamingo	Sh.Ch. Monksriding Baroness	Mr and Mrs M. Grassby	Mrs M. Pearson	20.8.75
Sh.Ch. Penmartan Opal (Tricolour)	B	Penmartan Logic	Penmartin Limestone	Mrs P. Williams	Mrs P. Williams	25.8.78
Sh.Ch. Upperwood Rainbow Warrior (Orange)	D	Upperwood Zebedee	Upperwood Golden Coral	Mrs P. Spillane	Mr and Mrs R. Goutorbe	22.8.78
Sh.Ch. Northgate Silver Moon (Blue)	B	Sh.Ch. Iroquois Snowprince of Northgate	Harvest Moon of Northgate	Mr and Mrs W. Fuller	Mr and Mrs W. Fuller	21.8.77
Sh.Ch. Iroquois Regalia (Blue)	B	Sh.Ch. Iroquois Snowprince of Northgate	Sh.Ch. Iroquois Skylark	Mrs L.Allan-Scott	Mrs L. Allan-Scott	12.8.78
Sh.Ch. Kenandra Spring Fashion (Orange)	B	Sh.Ch. Bellesett Baron of Upperwood	Torwood Sally	Mesdames S. Wallis and J. Hirst	Mesdames S. Wallis and J. Hirst	9.2.76
Sh.Ch. Suntop Fair Gale (Blue)	D	Int.Sh.Ch. Suntop Nightingale	Suntop Winterfinch	Mr and Mrs S. Tait	Miss M. Barnes	26.9.77
Sh.Ch. Merrysett Snow Sparkle (Blue)	B	Hurwyn Dayboy	Ellisland Highland Delight	Mrs M. Cook	Mrs M. Jarvis	17.12.77
Sh.Ch. Bournehouse the Waltz King (Tricolour)	D	Sh.Ch. Bournehouse Dancing Master	Suntop Dewberry	Mrs B. Davies	Mr G. Williams	12.11.76
Sh.Ch. Arnsett Alfa (Blue)	D	Int.Sh.Ch. Suntop Winter Breeze	Suntop Summer Belle	Mrs A. Child	Mrs A. Child	15.8.76

Name of Champion	Sex	Sire	Dam	Owner	Breeder	Date of Birth
Sh.Ch. Redtops Rozena (Orange)	B	Sh.Ch. Kendandra Lord Helpus	Redtops Ranastar	Mr and Mrs R. Green	Mrs N. Treharne	14.6.79
Sh.Ch. Much More Music of Mindenday (Orange)	D	Sh.Ch. Mindenday Music Master	Bella Signorina	Mr and Mrs R. Armstead	Mr L. Richards	15.7.80
Sh.Ch. Bournehouse Floral Dancer (Orange)	B	Sh.Ch. Bournehouse Dancing Master	Marus Sea Holly	Mr G. Williams	Mr G. Williams	20.11.77
Sh.Ch. Grelancot Evita (Orange)	B	Hurwyn Dayboy	Grelancot Perchance to Dream	Miss D. Jones	Miss D. Jones	19.11.78
Sh.Ch. Valsett Arrominta (Orange)	B	Engsett Electrode Mark	Valsett Dancing Breeze	Mr and Mrs J. Watkin	Mr and Mrs J. Watkin	18.8.80
Sh.Ch. Bournehouse Dancing Boy (Blue)	D	Sh.Ch. Bournehouse Dancing Master	Marus Sea Holly	Mr G. Williams	Mr G. Williams	14.8.79
Sh.Ch. Hurwyn Cupie Doll (Tricolour)	B	Hurwyn Flightmaster	Sh.Ch. Hurwyn Paper Doll	Mrs S. Wilkinson	Mrs S. Wilkinson	23.2.81
Sh.Ch. Arnsett Night Daisy of Fencefoot (Tricolour)	B	Int.Sh.Ch. Suntop Nightingale	Suntop Summer Belle	Mesdames Marsden and Croft	Mrs A. Child	30.3.79
Sh.Ch. Engsett Par Excellence (Tricolour)	D	Aus.Ch. Engsett Empery	Bournehouse Mistlethrush of Engsett	Mr and Mrs H. Wheeler	Mr and Mrs H. Wheeler	5.8.78
Sh.Ch. Snowstorm of Upperwood (Tricolour)	D	Hazelbarrow Sebastian of Upperwood	Millcot Morning Glow	Mr and Mrs R. Goutorbe	Mr and Mrs P. Castle	9.4.80

Name of Champion	Sex	Sire	Dam	Owner	Breeder	Date of Birth
Sh.Ch. Engsett English Charmer (Tricolour)	B	Sh.Ch. Upperwood Rainbow Warrior	Bournehouse Mistlethrush of Engsett	Mr and Mrs H. Wheeler	Mr and Mrs H. Wheeler	26.5.81
Sh.Ch. Wistaston School Scallywag of Triora (Blue)	B	Sh.Ch. Bournehouse Dancing Master	Wistaston School Mystery	Mr and Mrs J. Naylor	Miss G. Williams	21.5.77
Sh.Ch. Wistaston School Snowdrift (Tricolour)	B	Sh.Ch. Bournehouse Dancing Master	Wistaston School Summer	Mrs P. Downes	Miss G. Williams	16.3.79
Sh.Ch. Sunlight of Valsett (Orange)	D	Sh.Ch. Bellesett Baron of Upperwood	Valsett Louisiana of Adversane	Mr and Mrs J. Watkin	Mrs S. Barnard	2.7.79
Sh.Ch. Hurwyn Paper Star (Orange)	B	Hurwyn Flightmaster	Sh.Ch. Hurwyn Paper Doll	Mrs S. Wilkinson	Mrs S. Wilkinson	25.2.81
Sh.Ch. Northgate Starflight of Abbonny (Blue)	B	Hurwyn Flightmaster	Northgate Woodlark	Mr and Mrs G. Morroll	Mr and Mrs W. Fuller	11.1.78
Sh.Ch. Settrenda So Steady (Orange)	D	Hurwyn Flightmaster	Settrenda Super Sequin	Miss L. Mercer	Mr C. Brown	17.1.80
Sh.Ch. Soberhill Sundancer (Orange)	D	Fencefoot Front Bencher	Upperwood Special Request	Mr and Mrs K. Smith	Mr and Mrs K. Smith	4.11.80
Sh.Ch. Scratchwood Tattycoram (Tricolour)	B	Sh.Ch. Bournehouse Dancing Master	Sh.Ch. Monksriding Amazing Grace of Scratchwood	Mr and Mrs M. Grassby	Mr and Mrs M. Grassby	23.2.80
Sh.Ch. Holdgrange Golden Frolic of Settella (Orange)	D	Hazelbarrow Sebastian of Upperwood	Wistaston School Lovebird of Holdgrange	Mr and Mrs I. Whitehurst	Mr and Mrs J. Grainger	4.9.81

Name of Champion	Sex	Sire	Dam	Owner	Breeder	Date of Birth
Sh.Ch. Colverset Connoisseur (Orange)	D	Hurwyn Flightmaster	Kenidjack Mirage of Colverset	Mr and Mrs C. Roberts	Mr and Mrs C. Roberts	24.10.80
Sh.Ch. Latest Dance at Bournehouse (Tricolour)	D	Sh.Ch. Bournehouse Dancing Master	Sh.Ch. Limestone Liberty	Mr G. Williams	Mrs P. Williams	4.4.83
Sh.Ch. Settrenda Serenata at Somoray (Orange)	B	Sh.Ch. Iroquois Concerto	Sh.Ch. Settrenda Super Serenity	Mrs I. Foreman	Mr C. Brown	2.2.82
Sh.Ch. Earldoms Jubilee Queen at Ownways (Orange)	B	Ownways Jubilee Event	Earldoms Snow Queen	Mrs J. Parsons	Mrs V. Cole	3.8.81
Sh.Ch. Silpandre Red Grouse of Raffas (Orange)	D	Sh.Ch. Engsett Par Excellence	Silpandre Ptarmigan	Mr and Mrs G. Oxley	Mr and Mrs G. Oxley	4.2.80
Sh.Ch. Upperwood Modern Romance (Orange)	B	Lanbar Shades of Blue from Upperwood	Upperwood Maid Marion	Mesdames S. Wallis and J. Hirst	Mr and Mrs R. Goutorbe	6.4.83
Sh.Ch. Upperwood Flash Dance (Orange)	D	Lanbar Shades of Blue from Upperwood	Upperwood Maid Marion	Mr and Mrs R. Goutorbe	Mr and Mrs R. Goutorbe	6.4.83
Sh.Ch. Mariglen Highlight (Blue)	B	Hurwyn Flightmaster	Hurwyn Chorus Girl	Mrs J. Dennis	Mrs J. Dennis	10.11.81
Sh.Ch. Moorbrook Summer Night (Blue)	B	Hillbeck Claudius	Hockley Winter Flower	Mrs L. Howarth	Mrs L. Howarth	19.7.80

236

Name of Champion	Sex	Sire	Dam	Owner	Breeder	Date of Birth
Sh.Ch. Derrifod Don Giovanni (Orange)	D	Sh.Ch. Bournehouse Dancing Master	Derriford Pavane	Miss B.J. Reed	Miss B.J. Reed	22.1.81
Sh.Ch. Tragus Moonstorm (Tricolour)	D	Suntop Shining Breeze	Sh.Ch. Weatherdair Moon Breeze of Tragus	Mr and Mrs P. Upton	Mr and Mrs P. Upton	9.11.81
Sh.Ch. Starlite Express of Valsett (Orange)	B	Sh.Ch. Sunlight of Valsett	Origo Sea Maiden at Northpoint	Mr and Mrs J. Watkin	Mrs A. Wick	6.2.85
Sh.Ch. Saffander Sylvester (Orange)	D	Arnsett Fays Fable	Annapurna Starlet of Saffander	Mrs and Mrs W. Anderson	Mr and Mrs W. Anderson	27.7.83
Sh.Ch. Quensha Flight of Dreams at Kenidjack (Orange)	B	Hurwyn Flightmaster	Tangerine Dream of Quensha	Mrs A. Morgan	Mrs A. Morgan	11.4.82
Sh.Ch. Suford Lucky Star at Beamans (Tricolour)	D	Sh.Ch. Suntop Starling	Suford Evening Flight	Mrs J. Chilvers	Mrs Y. Rudin	19.3.82
Sh.Ch. Arnsett Dark Night (Tricolour)	D	Int.Sh.Ch. Suntop Nightingale	Suntop Summer Belle	Mrs A. Child	Mrs A. Child	30.3.79
Sh.Ch. Tattersett Was I Right (Orange)	B	Tattersett Star Turn	Bournehouse Norfolk Dancer	Mr and Mrs A. Grimsdell	Mr and Mrs A. Grimsdell	28.10.82

Name of Champion	Sex	Sire	Dam	Owner	Breeder	Date of Birth
Sh.Ch. Benrae Guardsman (Orange)	D	Sh.Ch. Snowstorm of Upperwood	Sheldsett Sesame	Mrs B. Hacking	Mrs B. Hacking	3.11.82
Sh.Ch. Merrysett Sweet Sue (Orange)	B	Hurwyn Flightmaster	Sh.Ch. Merrysett Snowbunting	Mrs M. Jarvis	Mrs M. Jarvis	25.5.82
Sh.Ch. Willowsett Grouse of Gunalt (Blue)	B	Sh.Ch. Engsett Par Excellence	Engsett Elegant Eve	Mr and Mrs S. Holling	Mr and Mr sD. Hobson	4.7.80
Sh.Ch. Engsett Noble English (Tricolour)	D	Sh.Ch. Much More Music of Mindenday	Novims Lady Fantasy	Mr and Mrs H. Wheeler and Mrs C. Davies	Mr and Mrs H. Wheeler	28.11.83
Sh.Ch. Extrovert of Engsett at Brucelm (Orange)	B	Sh.Ch. Mindenday Music Master	Engsett Evita	Mrs R. Davis and Mr B. Jeffrey	Mr and Mrs R. Armstead and Mr and Mrs H. Wheeler	20.9.82
Sh.Ch. Iroquois Crescendo (Orange)	D	Northgate Copper King	Iroquois Springsong	Mrs L. Allan-Scott	Mrs L. Allan-Scott	25.5.83
Sh.Ch. Suntop Freckled Braid at Lewkins (Blue)	D	Sh.Ch. Suntop Freckled Star	Suntop True Silk	Mr and Mrs D. Lewis	Miss M. Barnes	18.9.81
Sh.Ch. Wistaston School Playtime (Orange)	B	Wistaston School Heartbreak	Wistaston School Icefairy	Miss G. Williams	Miss G. Williams	31.5.82
Sh.Ch. Oldholbans Bertram (Tricolour)	D	Furore of Fermanar	Oldholbans Wicked Woman	Mr and Mrs R. Whewell	Mrs A. Findlay	13.6.79
Sh.Ch. Invogue Headliner (Blue)	D	Sh.Ch. Bournehouse Dancing Master	Sh.Ch. Kanchary Grey Ladybird of Invogue	Miss S. Marsden	Mr and Mrs S. Henderson	28.3.80

Name of Champion	Sex	Sire	Dam	Owner	Breeder	Date of Birth
Sh.Ch. Shadowood Blue Moon of Chelmset (Blue)	B	Invogue Minstrel Boy	Bournehouse Dancing Melody	Mr and Mrs J. Bowen	Mr and Mrs M. Winch	27.11.81
Sh.Ch. Hawthorn Lady Grace (Orange)	B	Sh.Ch. Bournehouse Dancing Master	Kenandra Romantic Style	Mr and Mrs R.Hales and Mrs P. Williams	Mr and Mrs R. Hales	24.3.84
Sh.Ch. Samelen Fanfare (Orange)	D	Sh.Ch. Iroquois Concerto	Samelen Duchess	Mr and Mrs P. Dunks	Mr and Mrs P. Dunks	22.9.82
Sh.Ch. Bournehouse Dark Prize (Blue)	B	Sh.Ch. Dancing Partner of Yeo	Sh.Ch. Bournehouse Floral Dancer	Mrs P. Williams	Mr G. Williams	14.10.84
Sh.Ch. Moorbrook Dolly Mixture (Blue)	B	Sh.Ch. Suntop Fair Gale	Tattersett Tip Toe	Mrs L. Howarth	Mrs L. Howarth	12.8.85
Sh.Ch. Sorbus Midnight Blue (Blue)	B	Sh.Ch. Bournehouse Dancing Boy	Sh.Ch. Upperwood Midnight Melody of Sorbus	Mr and Mrs D. Otty	Mr and Mrs K. Spencer	15.1.83
Sh.Ch. Mariglen Silent Prayer (Blue)	B	Keningale Adonis Blue	Sh.Ch. Mariglen Highlight	Mrs J. Dennis	Mrs J. Dennis	18.8.83
Sh.Ch. Suntop Royal Flint (Blue)	D	Suntop Royal Thrush	Suntop Sunbeam	Mrs C. Wiggerham	Miss M. Barnes	22.4.81
Sh.Ch. Tragus Night Breeze ()Blue)	D	Int.Sh.Ch. Suntop Nightingale	Sh.Ch. Weatherdair Moon Breeze of Tragus	Miss T. Watkins	Mr and Mrs P. Upton	16.3.79
Sh.Ch. Benrae Grenadier (Orange)	D	Sh.Ch. Snowstorm Upperwood	Sheldsett Sesame	Mrs B. Hacking	Mrs B. Hacking	3.11.82
Sh.Ch. Dancing Partner of Yeo (Blue)	D	Sh.Ch. Bournehouse Dancing Master	Barrowdowns Moonbeam of Yeo	Mrs L. Sawtell	Mrs L. Sawtell	18.7.80

Name of Champion	Sex	Sire	Dam	Owner	Breeder	Date of Birth
Sh.Ch. Northgate Grenadier (Blue)	D	Sh.Ch. Iroquois Snowprince of Northgate	Sh.Ch. Northgate Blue Brocade	Mr and Mrs W. Fuller	Mr and Mrs W. Fuller	11.3.83
Sh.Ch. Hurwyn Swing High (Orange)	B	Brenholm Only Boy	Sh.Ch. Hurwyn Cupie Doll	Mr K. Craddock	Mrs S. Wilkinson	31.1.84
Sh.Ch. Coldynne Yorkshire Relish (Orange)	D	Hazelbarrow Sebastian of Upperwood	Upperwood Spring Song of Coldynne	Mrs P. Colton	Mrs P. Colton	18.3.82
Sh.Ch. Tattersett Dutch Courage (Orange)	D	Sh.Ch. Latest Dance at Bournehouse	Sh.Ch. Tattersett Was I Right	Mr and Mrs A. Grimsdell	Mr and Mrs A. Grimsdell	3.8.85
Sh.Ch. Valsett Video Star of Wansleydale (Tricolour)	B	Sh.Ch. Engsett Par Excellence	Valsett Spandau Ballet	Mrs L. Taylor	Mr and Mrs J. Watkin	17.11.83
Sh.Ch. Koiya The Highflier from Bournehouse (Orange)	D	Sh.Ch. Latest Dance at Bournehouse	Sh.Ch. Hawthorn Lady Grace	Mr. G. Williams	Mr and Mrs R. Hales	2.6.86
Sh.Ch. Caleydene Gilded Gale (Orange)	D	Sh.Ch. Suntop Fair Gale	Suntop Redwing at Caleydene	Mrs A. Tait	Mrs A. Tait	13.7.83
Sh.Ch. Fencefoot Floss (Blue)	B	Sh.Ch. Arnsett Alfa	Fencefoot Fortunes Choice	Mr and Mrs H. Buchanan	Mesdames Marsden and Croft	5.10.80
Sh.Ch. Crystal Cracker of Capriole	B	Denebank Bertoloni	Roistine Rumba	Miss L. Madden	Mrs L. Smetham	30.3.84

APPENDIX G

POST-WAR FIELD TRIAL CHAMPIONS

Name of Champion	Sex	Sire	Dam	Owner	Breeder	Date of Birth
F.T.Ch. Adare Nima (Liver/White)	D	Bade Bondhu	Smuts of Adare	Dr. J. Maurice	Corbett	1945
F.T.Ch. Yankee Bondhu (Liver/White)	D	Hartleys Hydius	Kitty Windem	Mr W. Humphrey	R.F. Chapman	1942
F.T.Ch. Cannon Bondhu (Liver/White)	D	F.T.Ch. Yankee Bondhu	Horsford Dashing Destine	Mr W. Humphrey	Mr W. Humphrey	1948
F.T.Ch. Sharnberry Whitestone (Black/White/Tan)	D	F.T.Ch. Yankee Bondhu	Strife Bondhu	Capt. W. Parlour	E.C. Scott	1950
F.T.Ch. Downsman Tufter (Lemon)	D	F.T.Ch. Adare Nima	F.T.Ch. Tidy Windem	Dr. J. Maurice	Dr. J. Maurice	1956
F.T.Ch. Sharnberry Kandy (Black/White)	D	Dashing Spot	F.T.Ch. Waygood	Capt. W. Parlour	Capt. W. Parlour	1959
F.T.Ch. Cambusmore Roderick (Black/White/Tan)	D	Wade Windem	Cambusmore Brun	Maj. E. Robinson	Maj. E. Robinson	1959
F.T.Ch. Sharnberry Ormond Jet (Black/White/Tan)	D	Irish F.T. Ch. Ferdia of Nenagh	Grouse of Emlough	Capt. W. Parlour	J. Mahoney	1963

Name of Champion	Sex	Sire	Dam	Owner	Breeder	Date of Birth
F.T. Ch. Cream of the Barley (White)	D	Irish F.T. Ch. Dashing Stubble Bondhu	Kerry Barley	Mr N. Buggy	Mr N. Buggy	1966
F.T. Ch. Sharnberry Gordon (Black/White/Tan)	D	F.T. Ch. Sharnberry Ormond Jet	Sharnberry Gay	Capt. W. Parlour	Capt. W. Parlour	1966
F.T. Ch. Sharnberry Pat (Black/White)	D	Irish F.T. Ch. Dashing Stubble Bondhu	Dashing Pearl	Capt. W. Parlour	C. Hickey	1966
F.T. Ch. Sharnberry Redbracken (Black/White/Tan)	D	F.T. Ch. Sharnberry Kandy	F.T. Ch. Sharnberry Glayva	Capt. W. Parlour	Capt. W. Parlour	1966
F.T. Ch. Sharnberry Mattahroo (Orange/White)	D	Irish F.T. Ch. Moka De La Salle Vert	Lemoni	Capt. W. Parlour	T. McCarthy	1970
F.T. Ch. Sharnberry Glenahroo (Orange/White)	D	Irish F.T. Ch. Moka De La Salle Vert	Lemoni	Capt. W. Parlour	T. McCarthy	1970
F.T. Ch. Dirk Ile (Black/White)	D	Jinker of Ile	Crathes Isla	Dr J. Maurice	Lord Margadale	1971
F.T. Ch. Langbourne Well of Redwood (Black/White/Tan)	B	Dashing Llewellin Ben Winden of Killculliheen	Dashing Lady of Killculliheen	Mr W. Humphrey	R. Chapman	1943
F.T. Ch. The Jolly Beggar (Liver/White)	B	F.T. Ch. Adare Nima	Jet of Langwall	Dr J. Maurice	H. Debenham	1946

Name of Champion	Sex	Sire	Dam	Owner	Breeder	Date of Birth
F.T. Ch. Coolcorran Jess (Black/White)	B	Irish F.T. Ch. Flash of the Glebe	Stylish Stocksize	Mr & Mrs G. Llewellyn	J. Blake	1945
F.T. Ch. Coolcorran Sandy (Liver/White)	B	Irish F.T. Ch. Flash of the Glebe	Stylish Stocksize	Maj. E. Staines	J. Blake	1947
F.T. Ch. Baroness Windem (Black/White)	B	Yankee Windem	Marie Windem	Mr W. Humphrey	Mr W. Humphrey	1949
F.T. Ch. Glorious Windem (Orange)	B	Toney Windem	Yank Windem	Mr W. Humphrey	Mr W. Humphrey	1949
F.T. Ch. Segonitium Blackear (Black/White/Tan)	B	Irish F.T. Ch. Flash of the Glebe	Pride of Gaby	Col A. Balding	Rev. G. Perdue	1950
F.T. Ch. Tidy Windem (Lemon)	B	Toppers Tony	Fly Windem	Dr J. Maurice	Mr W. Humphrey	1952
F.T. Ch. Sharnberry Nita (Lemon)	B	F.T. Ch. Sharnberry Whitestone	Need Windem	Capt. W. Parlour	Capt. W. Parlour	1952
F.T. Ch. Downsman Bracken (Lemon)	B	Illiana Wind Wraith	Adare Lady Beatrice	Dr J. Maurice	Mrs P. Maurice	1952
F.T. Ch. Flashaway Eve (Black/White/Tan)	B	F.T. Ch. Sharnberry Whitestone	F.T. Ch. Segonitum Blackear	Col A. Balding	Col A. Balding	1954
F.T. Ch. Waygood Fiona (Black/White/Tan)	B	F.T. Ch. Sharnberry Whitestone	Downsmans Revel	Capt. W. Parlour	Mrs P. Maurice	1955

Name of Champion	Sex	Sire	Dam	Owner	Breeder	Date of Birth
F.T. Ch. Sharnberry Glayva (Black/White/Tan)	B	F.T. Ch. Sharnberry Whitestone	Assynt Faith	Capt. W. Parlour	R. Vesty	1955
F.T. Ch. Downsman Tansy (Liver/White)	B	F.T. Ch. Adare Nima	F.T. Ch. Tidy Windem	Dr J. Maurice	Dr J. Maurice	1956
F.T. Ch. Sharnberry Freda (Black/White/Tan)	B	Sharnberry Waygood David	F.T. Ch. Waygood Fiona	Capt. W. Parlour	Capt. W. Parlour	1957
Irish F.T. Ch & F.T. Ch. Babe Windem (Black/White)	B	Brag Windem	Dashing Storm Bondhu	Rev. F. Bannon	Mr W. Humphrey	1957
F.T. Ch. Dashing Sun Bondhu (Black/White)	B	Dashing Game	Dashing Dora Bondhu	Mr W. Humphrey	Mr W. Humphrey	1960
F.T. Ch Sharnberry Flash (Black/White/Tan)	B	Sharnberry Gleam	F.T. Ch. Sharnberry Freda	Capt. W. Parlour	Capt. W. Parlour	1962
F.T. Ch. Dashing Grand Bondhu (Black/White)	B	Dashing Splash Bondhu	Dashing Giddy Bondhu	Rev. F. Bannon	Mr. W. Humphrey	1961
F.T. Ch. Downsmans Tormentil (Liver/White)	B	Downsman Devils Rendezvous	Downsmans Thrift	Dr J. Maurice	Dr J. Maurice	1965
F.T. Ch. Betty of Bonavalley (Liver/White)	B	Irish F.T. Ch. Moka De La Salle Vert	Dame Gillian	Mr J. Black	Mr J. Black	1966

Name of Champion	Sex	Sire	Dam	Owner	Breeder	Date of Birth
F.T. Ch. Sharnberry Fleur (Black/White)	B	F.T. Ch. Sharnberry Red Bracken	Sharnberry Grouse	Capt. W. Parlour	Capt. W. Parlour	1968
F.T. Ch. Sharnberry Lilly (Black/White/Tan)	B	F.T. Ch. Sharnberry Ormond Jet	F.T. Ch. Sharnberry Flash	Mr L. Abbot	Capt. W. Parlour	1969
F.T. Ch. Sharnberry Ling (Black/White/Tan)	B	F.T. Ch. Sharnberry Ormond Jet	F.T. Ch. Sharnberry Flash	Mr A. Longworth	Capt. W. Parlour	1969
F.T. Ch. Sharnberry Little Do-Di (Liver/White)	B	Irish F.T. Ch. Moka De La Salle Vert	Lemoni	Capt. W. Parlour	T. McCarthy	1970
F.T. Ch. Cloncurragh Betsy (Black/White)	B	F.T. Ch. Scinn Amach Grouse	F.T. Ch. Babe Windem	Rev. J. Bannon	Rev. J. Bannon	1965
F.T. Ch. Neighbours Noblesse (Lemon/White)	D	F.T. Ch. Sharnberry Glenarhoo	Neighbours Sybilla	Mrs H. Alkin	Mrs C. Ercolani	1972
F.T. Ch. Bringwood Caprice (Black/White/Tan)	D	F.T. Ch. Sharnberry Red Bracken	Bringwood Briar	Mr H. Embrey	D. Longworth	1972
F.T. Ch. Sharnberry Dougal (Black/White/Tan)	D	Wassetfell Jem of Sharnberry	F.T. Ch. Little Do-Di of Sharnberry	Capt. W.P arlour	Capt. W. Parlour	1973
F.T. Ch. Migdale Beanwagh (Black/White/Tan)	D	F.T. Ch. Stylish Ranger the Second	F.T. Ch. Moymore Nada	Mr D. Maclean	Mr D. Maclean	1974

Name of Champion	Sex	Sire	Dam	Owner	Breeder	Date of Birth
F.T. Ch. Boy Blue of Naron (Black/White/Tan)	D	Ike Llew	Ruby Valley	R. McElinney	J. Barrat	1974
F.T. Ch. Sharnberry Duke (Black/White/Tan)	D	Wassetfell Jem of Sharnberry	F.T. Ch. Little Do-Di of Sharnberry	Capt. W. Parlour	Capt. W. Parlour	1974
F.T. Ch. Ryvoan Smoker (Black/White)	D	Semendria Deucalion	Cambusmore Rena	Dr G. Clark	Dr G. Clark	1976
F.T. Ch. Sharnberry Breeze (Black/White)	D	Bringwood Caprice	F.T. Ch. Little Do-Di of Sharnberry	Exors of Late Capt. W. Parlour	Exors of Late Capt. W. Parlour	1977
F.T. Ch. Sharnberry Donald (Black/White)	D	Bringwood Caprice	F.T. Ch. Little Do-Di	Mrs E. Town	Exors of Late Capt. W. Parlour	1977
F.T. Ch. Sharnberry Brock (Black/White/Tan)	D	F.T. Ch. Sharnberry Duke	F.T. Ch. Sharnberry Breeze	Exors of Late Capt. W. Parlour	1977 Capt. W. Parlour	
F.T. Ch. Mawingo of Auchintoul (Lemon/White)	D	F.T. Ch. Sharnberry Duke	Pondarha Rozanne	Mr R. Wylie	W.J. Hogg	1978
F.T. Ch. Moymore Nada	B	unable to trace	unable to trace	Mr D. Maclean	unable to trace	—
F.T. Ch. Stylish Ranger the Second	D	unable to trace	unable to trace	Mr D. Maclean	unable to trace	—

Name of Champion	Sex	Sire	Dam	Owner	Breeder	Date of Birth
F.T. Ch. Silverview Patricia		------------no other details available------------P.J. Peoples			unable to trace	
F.T. Ch. Bringwood Fen of Ryoan (Liver/White)	B	Assynt Broom	Bringwood Cress	Dr G. Clarke	D. Longworth	1976

APPENDIX H

BIBLIOGRAPHY

The English Setter, Lesley Allan–Scott. Published by K&R Books Ltd (now out of print).
The English Setter, Valerie Foss. Published by W & G Foyle Ltd.
The English Setter Handbook, Clifford L.B. Hubbard. Published by Nicholson & Watson (now out of print).
English Setters, No author listed. Published by T.F.H. Publications Ltd.
English Setter (How to Raise and Train), Susan S. Maire. Published by T.F.H Publications Ltd.
Illustrated Guide to Gundog Breeds, James Johnson. Published by Kelso Graphics.
Know Your Setters and Pointers, William F. Brown. Published by Pet Library Ltd.
English Setter: The New Complete (revised Elsworth Howell), Davis Tuck. Published by Howell Book House.
Dog Steps: Illustrated Gait at a Glance, Rachel P. Elliot. Published by Howell Book House.
Gundogs: Training and Field Trials, P.R.A. Moxon. Published by Popular Dogs.
The Setter, Edward Laverack. Published by Longmans Green & Co.
English Setter: Ancient & Modern, Margaret D. Barnes. Published by Muffin Books (available only from the author).
The Dog Encyclopaedia. Published by Hutchinson (now out of print).
The Doglopaedia: A Complete Guide to Dog Care, J.M. Evans and Kay White. Published by Henston Ltd.
The English Setter Association Year Books (available from the Secretary).
English Setter Champions and Show Champions 1947–1987, compiled by Kaye Bliss.

INDEX

ailments, 174–190
   (see also under names of ailments)
Allan-Scott, Mrs L.A., 164, 209, 213, 246
Allen, Miss M., 27
American Kennel Club Standard, 153–156
anal glands, 174
Archdale Kennel, 23
Armstead, Mr and Mrs R., 158, 162, 173
Arnsett Kennel, 157
Ashpenda Kennel, 35, 133, 159
Attleford Kennel, 168, 169

Barnes, Miss M.D., 30, 35, 146, 167, 168, 249
Bayldone Kennel, 23, 138
Bilton, Mrs M., 22
Birket, Mr M., 21
bitch:
   gestation table, 87
   in season, 82
   in whelp, care of, 86, 88, 89
   mating of, 84, 85
   misalliance, 83
   nursing bitch, care of, 93
   whelping, 90, 91, 92
   whelping bed, 88
bites, 174
Blenmar (Davium) Kennel, 34
Boisdale Kennel, 23, 131
bloat, 175
Borrowdale, Mrs D., 30
Bournehouse Kennel, 30, 143, 145, 158, 159, 211
Boulton, Mr and Mrs S., 34

Bowen, Mr J., 159, 196
Bradshaw, Mr and Mrs K., 32
breed Clubs of America, 153
breeding, 73
Broadhead, Mrs A., 28, 29, 76, 138
Brown, Mrs M., 34
Brown, Mr C., 165, 166
burns, 175

Canadian Kennel Club Standard, 119–124
canker, 175
Carofel Kennel, 34
Chelmset Kennel, 159
Child, Mrs L.A., 157
Child, Mr B., 27
chorea, 176
Christopher, Mr S., 33
Cockerton, Mr J., 21
Collins, Mr A., 27
Colverset Kennel, 169
conjunctivitis, 176
constipation, 176
controls of Australia, 115, 116
cough, 176
Crane, Mr S., 26
Crawford, Mr G., 22, 29
Crombie Kennel, 22, 27, 112, 113, 136
Crowther, Mr and Mrs A., 23, 25, 27
Crufts C.C. Winners, 199–201
cystitis, 177

Darling, Mrs M., 23, 28

Davies, Mr and Mrs C., 158, 162, 173
Davies, Mrs R. and Jeffrey, Mr B., 162, 172
Derriford Kennel, 159, 160, 206
diabetes, 177
diarrhoea, 177
distemper, 177
Duffield, Mrs C., 35, 159

Eadington, Mrs M., 22
Early Dog Shows, 20, 21
eclampsia, 178
eczema, 178
Ednasid Kennel, 34
Eggleston, Mr A., 23
Elswood Kennel, 25, 160, 207
English, Mrs J., 22, 25, 27, 29, 30, 131, 210
English Setter:
  body, 44
  books on, 249
  character, 36, 37, 41
  colour, 48, 78
  conformation, 37
  ears, 42
  establishing a line, 73
  eyes, 41
  faults, 49
  feet, 46, 47
  forequarters, 43, 44, 45
  head and skull, 40, 41
  history of, 15–18
  mouth, 42–43
  movement, 47, 48
  neck, 44
  outstanding post-war dogs and bitches, 25–35
  outstanding pre-war dogs and bitches, 21–24
  overseas, 112–156
  size and weight, 49
  tail, 48
  temperament, 41
Engsett Kennel, 138, 140, 143, 158, 161, 162, 170, 171
Enright, Mrs B., 27

Ernford Kennel, 28, 138, 151
Ercolani, Mrs C., 31

Fencefoot Kennel, 157, 167, 168
Fermanar Kennel, 23, 130, 138
field trials, 110, 111
Findlay, Mrs A., 32, 137
fits, 178
fleas, 184
Foreman, Mrs I., 165
Foss, Mrs V., 35, 160, 207, 249
Foss, Mr and Mrs W., 25, 160
France, Mrs M., 158
Frejendor Kennel, 30
Fuller, Mr and Mrs W., 166
Furness, Mrs R., 25

Gardiner-Swann, Mr and Mrs P., 166, 205
gastro-enteritis, 179
Gorsebrook Kennel, 30
Goutorbe, Mrs D., 170
Goutorbe, Mr R., 170
Grimsdell, Mr and Mrs A., 168
growths, 179
gun-training, 108, 109

Haar Kennel, 34
haematoma, 179
haemorrhage, 93, 180
hardpad, 180
heart attack, 180
hepatitis, 180
Hepton Kennel, 26, 31
hip dysplasia, 181
hernia, 181
Hurwyn Kennel, 115, 134, 144, 146, 147, 162, 163, 168, 208, 214

Iroquois Kennel, 33, 114, 133, 160, 162, 164, 165, 166, 209, 213

Jackson, Mr and Mrs W.A., 31
Jarry, Miss M., 26, 31, 137
Jenkinson, Mr A., 33

Index

Kay, Mrs D., 34
Kendall, Capt., 26
Kennel Club Standard, 37
Kennel Club titles, 100, 101
Ketree Kennel, 33
Kingstree Kennel, 130, 142, 143
Kirket Kennel, 27

Laverack, Edward, 16, 17, 18, 21, 249
leptospirosis, 182
Lewis, Miss, K., 23
lice, 185
line breeding, 74, 75, 76
Littlewoodcote Kennel, 33
Llewellin, Purcell, 16, 18, 21
Lort, William, 16
Lovat, Lord, 16
Maesydd Kennel, 21
Mallwyd Kennel, 21
mange, 182
Marsden and Croft, Mesdames, 157, 167
mastitis, 183
Mawdsley Kennel, 25
McNally, Mr B., 33, 164
metritis, 183
Mindenday Kennel, 158, 162, 170, 173
Murray, Mr and Pearce, Mrs, 33

Neave, Mrs M. and Miss P., 35, 160
Neighbours Kennel, 31
nephritis, 183
Northgate Kennel, 164, 166
Noyna Kennel, 32, 113, 132

Oldholbans Kennel, 31, 137
Ossulton, Lord, 16

pancreatic deficiency, 184
pancreatitis, 184
parasites, 184–187
Parkinson, Mr and Mrs W., 34
Paterson, Mr D., 30, 31, 210

parvovirus, 187
Pearson, Ms and Mrs H., 29
Pennine Kennel, 23
Perkins, Mr N., 27
pneumonia, 187
post-war Champions, 215, 216
post-war Field Trial Champions, 243–248
post-war Show Champions, 216–242
post-war registration figures, 203
puppy:
  accommodation, 69
  bathing, 65
  car training, 60
  drying, 66
  exercise, 62
  faults, 52
  feeding, 54–58, 95
  general care, 64
  good points, 52
  grooming, 63
  house training, 58, 59
  inoculations, 55
  kennels, 69, 70
  lead training, 60
  rearing, 94
  runs, 70, 71, 72
  selecting, 51
  selling, 53, 54, 97
  teething, 56
  trimming, 66, 67, 68
  weaning, 95
pyometra, 188

Raycroft Kennel, 25, 136
Redtops Kennel, 132, 167
Reed, Miss J., 158, 159, 206
Renmark Kennel, 143, 160
Rhodes, Mr and Mrs A., 23
rickets, 188
ringworm, 188, 189
Ripleygae Kennel, 26
Roberts, Mr and Mrs C., 172
Rombalds Kennel, 23, 25, 27, 113, 138
Rumball, Miss E., 13, 23, 26

Sawtell, Mrs L., 32, 125, 173
Scofield, Mr H., 26
Seafield, Earl of, 16
Senglish Kennel, 34
Settrenda Kennel, 165, 166
Shiplake Kennel, 113, 131, 132, 136, 138, 210
shows, 98–100
  entering for, 102
  equipment for, 105, 106
  judging of, 106, 107
  preparation for, 102–104
  showing, 103–106
  trimming for, 104
Silbury Kennel, 30, 166, 205
skin trouble, 189
Sorbus Kennel, 170, 171, 173
Southesk, Earl of, 16
Spencer, Mr and Mrs K., 170, 173
split tail, 189
Steadman, David, 21, 22, 23
Steadman, Thomas, 21, 22, 130
stud dog, 73
successful Kennels, 157–173
Sundeala Kennel, 165, 173
Suntop Kennel, 34, 115, 132, 144, 146, 147, 151, 163, 167, 168

tabulated pedigrees, 205–214
Tate, Mrs A., 32
Taylor, Mr J., 26, 31
Tattersett Kennel, 163, 168, 169

terminology, dog, 191–195
titles in Germany, 127–128
Tragus Kennel, 134, 169
Treharne, Mrs N., 132, 167
Trodgers Kennel, 32, 113, 162
Truslers Kennel, 27
Turton-Price, Prof., 22

Upperwood Kennel, 145, 161, 162, 170
Upton, Mr and Mrs C., 30
Upton, Mr and Mrs P., 169

Valsett Kennel, 134, 158, 171, 172, 212
Verbaan, Mr D., 130, 142, 143

Walker, Mrs D., 34
Watkin, Mr and Mrs J., 11, 212
Watkinson, Mr T., 25
Webster, Mrs F., 26
Wheeler, Mr and Mrs H., 138, 158, 161, 211
Whiteseal Kennel, 31
Wilkinson, Mrs S.E., 125, 146, 162, 208, 214
Williams, Miss G., 159, 172
Williams, Mr and Mrs G., 30, 35, 211
Wistaston Kennel, 159, 172
Wolfe, Mrs P., 27
worms, 185, 186

Yeo Kennel, 125, 173